IMAGES
of America

WILLIAMSPORT'S BASEBALL HERITAGE

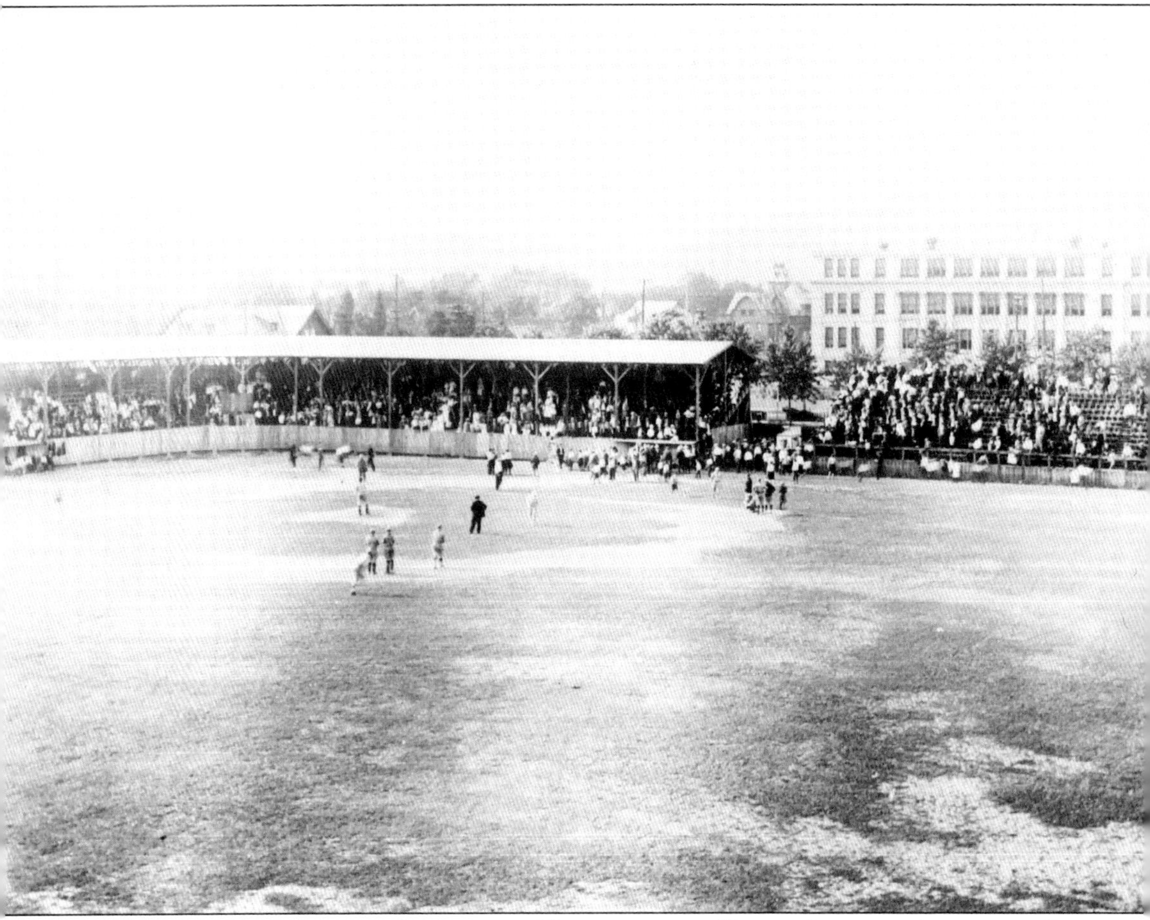

WILLIAMSPORT GRAYS' GAME AT WILLIAMSPORT HIGH SCHOOL ATHLETIC FIELD (1924). (DVS-LCHS.)

IMAGES
of America

WILLIAMSPORT'S BASEBALL HERITAGE

James P. Quigel Jr. and Louis Hunsinger Jr.

ARCADIA
PUBLISHING

ISBN 978-0-7385-8574-1

Published by Arcadia Publishing
Charleston, South Carolina

Printed in the United States of America

Library of Congress Catalog Card Number: 98-89447

For all general information contact Arcadia Publishing at:
Telephone 843-853-2070
Fax 843-853-0044
E-Mail sales@arcadiapublishing.com
For customer service and orders:
Toll-Free 1-888-313-2665

Visit us on the Internet at www.arcadiapublishing.com

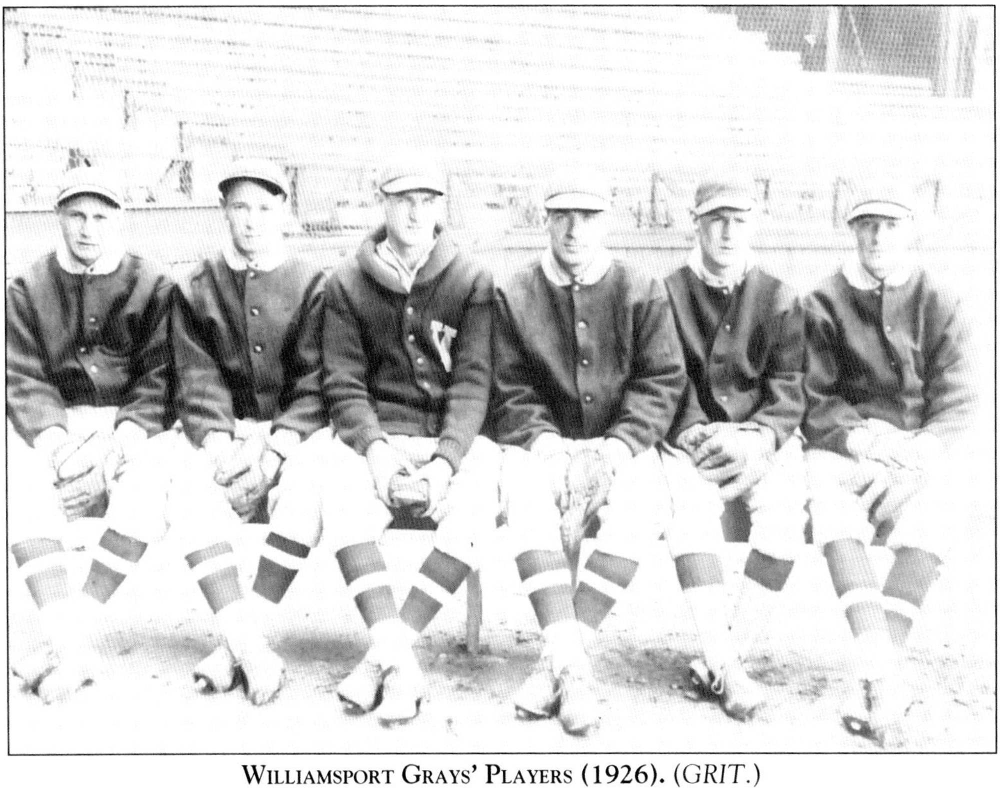

WILLIAMSPORT GRAYS' PLAYERS (1926). (*GRIT.*)

Contents

Acknowledgments

The publication of any pictorial history is truly a collective endeavor. It is even more so when an entire community shares a passion for the subject at hand. We would like to extend our thanks to all the individuals, institutions, and organizations in Williamsport responsible for bringing our project to fruition. We are especially indebted to John Brockway and Michael Rafferty—formerly of *The Grit* newspaper and publishing company—who intervened on our behalf to salvage several rare baseball photograph files in danger of being lost to posterity. Through their efforts, the Grit Baseball Photograph Collection [*GRIT*] was donated to the James V. Brown Library [JVB] and subsequently inventoried, organized, and cataloged. The staff of the Brown Library allowed us unfettered access to the collection and kindly granted permission to produce prints from original images of the collection.

Sandra Rife (Director) and Jack Buckle (Photograph Collections Curator) of the Lycoming County Historical Society and Museum [LCHS] navigated our way through the D. Vincent Smith [DVS-LCHS] and Putsee Vannucci [PV-LCHS] photograph collections, identified other baseball-related images relevant to our project, and made arrangements for processing prints from the museum's valuable photographic holdings. Jim Carpenter and Leon Pollom of the *Williamsport Sun-Gazette* [*WS-G*] assisted in our search of the newspaper's photograph archive and identified several rare images used for this publication. Private donors contributed as well. A. Rankin Johnson Jr. allowed us the use of several images from his personal photo albums chronicling his professional baseball career. Pat Thorne Jr. kindly granted us permission to photograph a Williamsport Municipal Athletic Field Stock Certificate in his possession. Several rare images from the Tommy Richardson Photograph Collection [TR] were loaned by co-author Louis Hunsinger Jr. for use in this publication. Special thanks are also owed to Evan R. Rosser Jr., who helped us identify significant figures associated with Williamsport's baseball past.

Finally, we extend our thanks to Wayne Palmer of Palmer Multimedia Imaging, Williamsport, Pennsylvania. He prepared the bulk of the photographic prints for publication, did masterful restoration work on several images, and provided valuable technical assistance in the layout of our book.

James P. Quigel Jr.
New Brunswick, NJ
October 1998

Louis Hunsinger Jr.
Williamsport, PA
October 1998

INTRODUCTION

Williamsport, Pennsylvania, has always been a baseball town. Renowned as the "Birthplace of Little League Baseball" and host of the annual Little League World Series, the city has also been heir to a rich minor-league legacy that few communities of comparable size possess. Professional baseball has been an integral part of Williamsport's civic identity and social fabric during the past century—spanning the independent professional Tri-State League of the early 1900s to the current Williamsport franchise of the Class A New York-Penn League. Between 1904 and 1976 the city hosted some of the best minor-league baseball played anywhere in America and served as a gateway to the Major Leagues.

Hundreds of pro ballplayers donned the uniforms and caps of the various Williamsport teams (the Grays, Tigers, Mets, Tomahawks, Astros, Billsox, Bills, and Cubs) before advancing to the Majors. Williamsport's historic Bowman Field—built in 1926, and presently the second-oldest operating minor-league ballpark in the country—served as a backdrop to the budding careers of Hall of Famers Jim Bunning and Nolan Ryan, countless barnstorming Major and Negro League teams, and famous baseball personalities such as Connie Mack, Branch Rickey, and Casey Stengel. Area fans at the uptown ballpark cheered and supported local sandlot stars—Don Manno, Dick Welteroth, Ed Ott, and Mike Mussina—on their rise to the big leagues.

Williamsport's Baseball Heritage provides an authoritative and comprehensive photographic essay chronicling the city's halcyon professional baseball era. This publication chiefly documents Williamsport's affiliation with the Class AA Eastern League from 1923 to 1976, and to a lesser extent, the city's experience with the independent Tri-State League (1904–1910), the semi-professional Pennsylvania Railroad League (1920–1921), and the short-season New York-Penn League (1968–1972). Drawing upon the *GRIT* newspaper's extensive baseball photograph collection (deposited at the James V. Brown Library), selected images culled from the D. Vincent Smith and Putsee Vannucci photographic collections (among other holdings) of the Lycoming County Historical Society and Museum, and prints from private donors, our book attempts to recapture a by-gone era when the game of baseball loomed larger in the lives of local residents and served as a rallying point for community pride.

Our publication is divided into three main chapters: Diamonds; Players, Managers, and Teams; and Boosters, Promotions, and Events. The first section offers a visual chronicle of Williamsport's distinctive ballparks that provided the venue for minor-league play down through the years, particularly historic Bowman Field. Images of notable players, managers, and teams that represented the city in league play and defined its baseball history make up the bulk of our publication. Finally, the heart and soul of sustaining professional baseball in Williamsport rested with its citizens. The third section is a visual testament to the efforts of those whose love of baseball was only exceeded by their sense of civic responsibility to nurture the game for posterity. Whether a club director, team financier, or local merchant sponsoring a night at the ballpark, their hard work made possible many special memories associated with Bowman Field and Williamsport baseball.

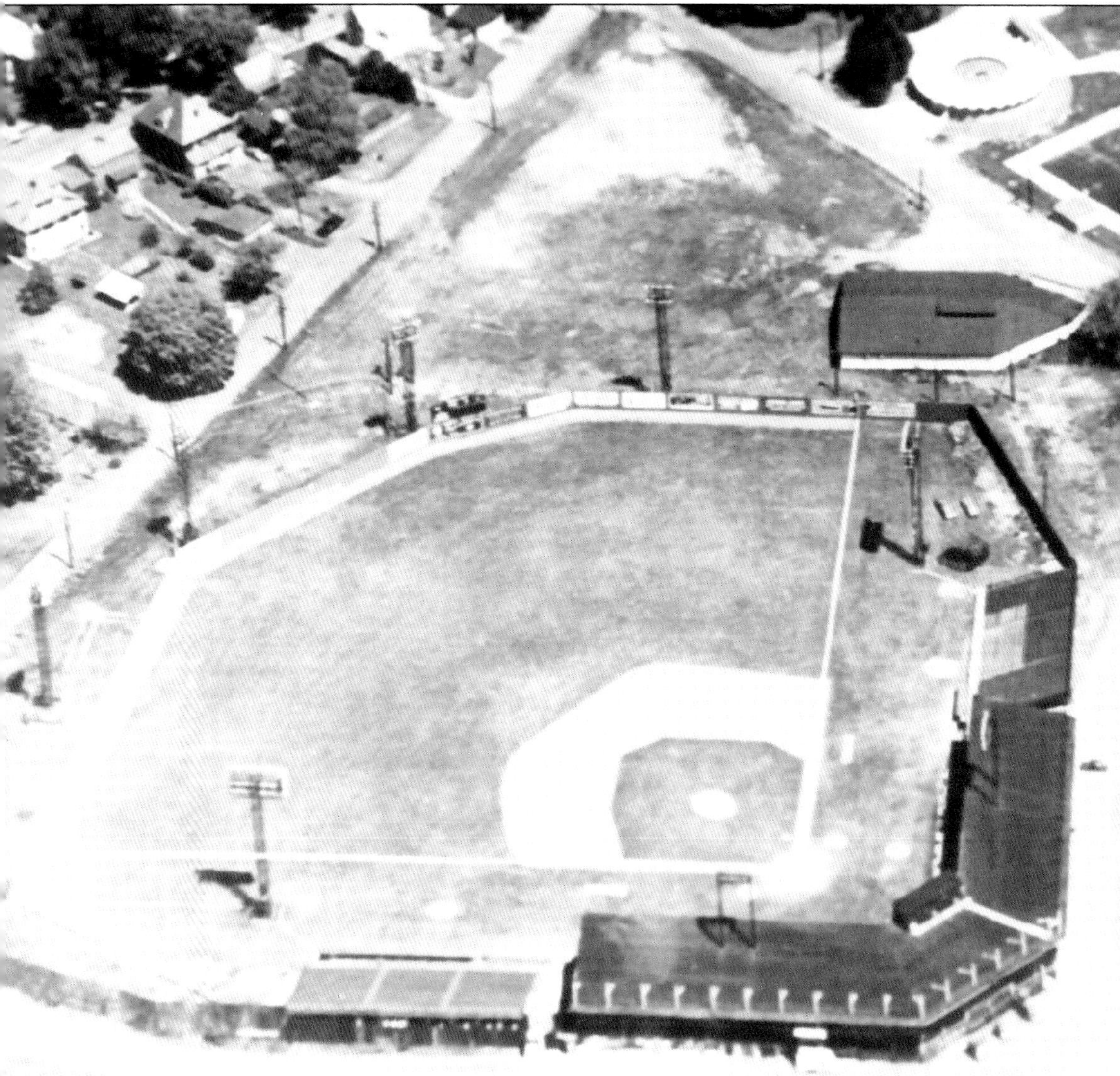

Aerial View of Bowman Field (1967). (*GRIT.*)

One

Diamonds

On July 29, 1865, the first recorded game of organized baseball in Williamsport took place along a green expanse situated below Academy Street and bordering the north bank of the Susquehanna River. Upon the city's "pleasant greens," the Williamsport Athletic [Baseball] Club played the Philadelphia and Erie Railroad team to a 27-27 tie before a boisterous crowd cheering on the hometown nine. Since this inaugural game, baseball diamonds have been an indelible feature of the Williamsport cityscape.

The city's earliest amateur baseball clubs scheduled game matches on the city's common grounds and sandlot fields without much concern for fan amenities. By the 1870s encroaching professionalism had supplanted the genteel amateur game; baseball became a business. Club investors and local lumber barons envisioned larger ballparks with grandstand seating to accommodate paying crowds. The local baseball scene shifted to the inner concourse of the Old Oak (Herdic) Park race track where fans flocked to witness some of the best baseball played in the north-central tier of Pennsylvania. Williamsport's rivalry with its upriver neighbor, Lock Haven, drew thousands of leather-lunged fans to the ballpark throughout the decade.

During the 1880s the city's entry into professional league play demanded a new venue for baseball. R.H. Crum, president and manager of the Williamsport club, enlisted city investors to construct a new enclosed field along Packer Street, opposite the old city fairgrounds. Playing as an independent professional team, and later as a member of the Pennsylvania State Association, Williamsport hosted several major-league teams in exhibition games at the Packer Field. The Union Park Fairgrounds became the main site for city and corporate-sponsored baseball leagues when the professional game waned during the 1890s.

Athletic Park, built in 1902, served as the venue for Williamsport's professional Tri-State League games from 1904 to 1910. The park became a focal point for community pride following the Williamsport Millionaires' championship seasons of 1905 and 1907–1908. Thousands of fans attended parades and celebrations at the park to honor their local baseball heroes. When Williamsport disbanded its professional team in 1910, semi-professional city trolley league and industrial league games flourished. Williamsport's best teams, including the city's Pennsylvania Railroad League entry, played at the new Williamsport High School Athletic Field, built in 1916. This field served as the first home for the Williamsport Grays of the New York-Pennsylvania League from 1923 to 1925. With the construction of Memorial (Bowman) Field in 1926, Williamsport entered the modern era of professional minor-league baseball.

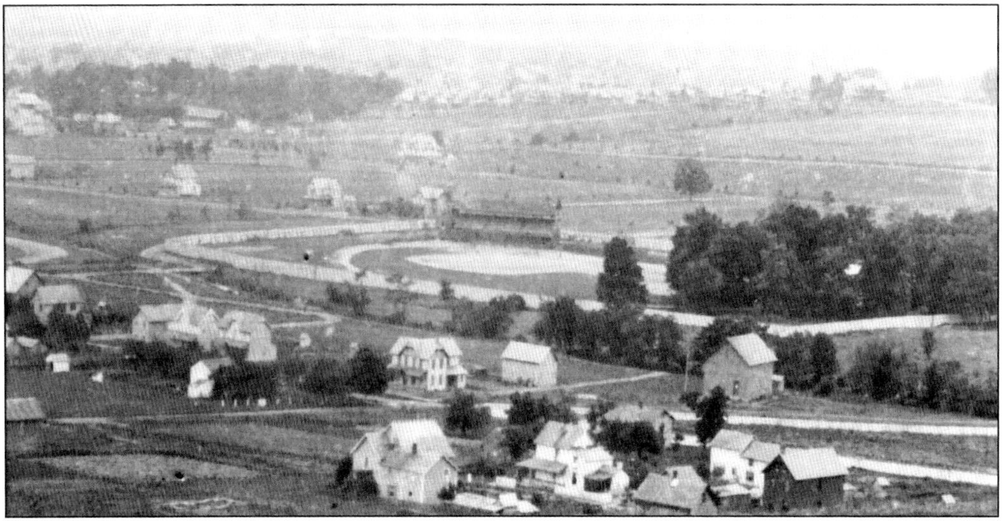

UNION PARK, SOUTHEAST VIEW FROM GRAMPIAN HILL (1890s). Located on the site of the present-day Penn Street Armory Field, the Union Park complex contained a grandstand, race track, and ball field. The ball diamond was a venue for the city's best semi-professional teams during the 1890s. Teams such as the Demorests (Demorest Sewing Machine Company), Brandons, Lycoming Rubber Works, the Keystones, and Joe Ottenmiller's Brewery Colts played here. (DVS-LCHS.)

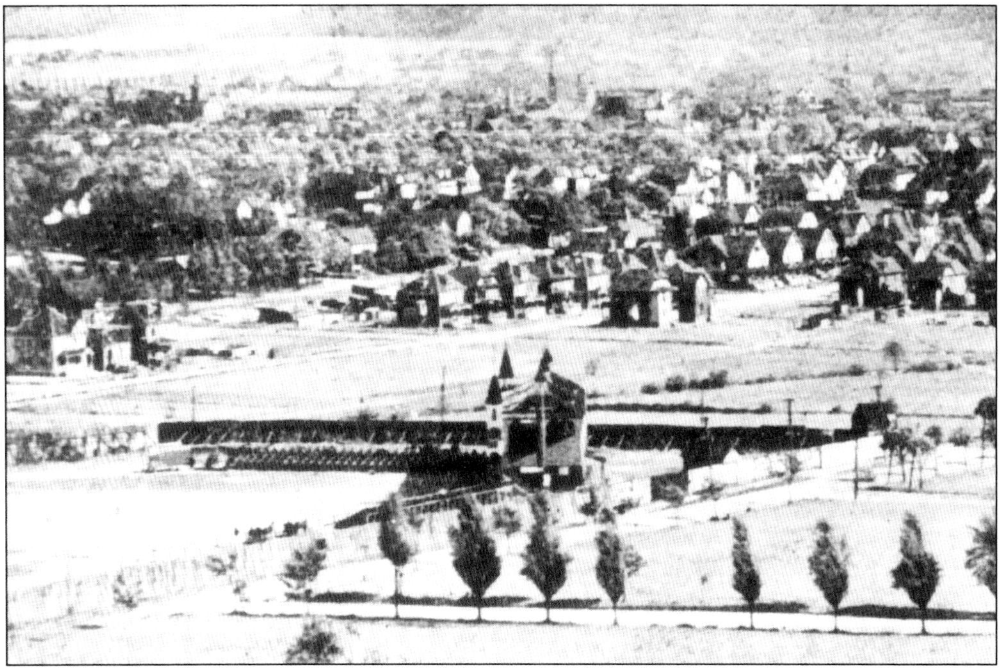

ATHLETIC PARK GRANDSTAND (1901–1902). Athletic Park's distinctive steepled grandstand is visible in this vista looking southeast from Vallamont Park. Constructed just after the turn of the century, Athletic Park served as the site for Williamsport's Pennsylvania State League games (1902), and later, home of the Tri-State League Williamsport Millionaires (1904–1910). William Abbot Whitman, president of the State League, surveyed the new field in 1902 and declared it "one of the finest baseball grounds in the state." (DVS-LCHS.)

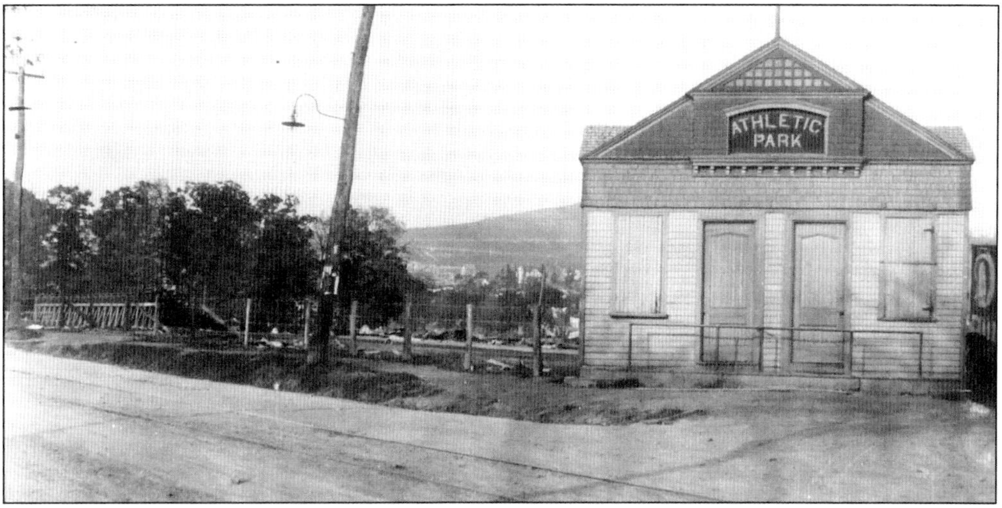

ENTRANCE TO ATHLETIC PARK (1903). The old wooden A-framed portal to Athletic Park was a familiar landmark to thousands of local fans attending Williamsport Millionaires' baseball games, area college football games, and special civic events. Athletic Park occupied the site of the present-day Cochran Elementary School and its adjoining recreation field bordering Cherry Street. (LCHS.)

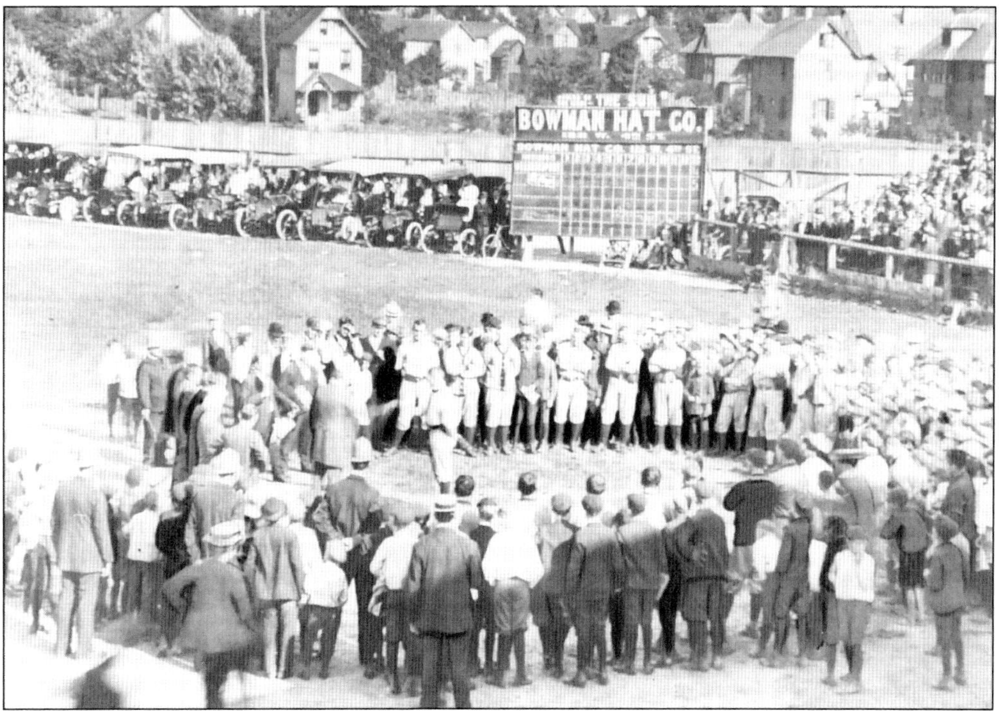

1907 CHAMPIONSHIP CELEBRATION, HOME PLATE AREA, ATHLETIC PARK. Encircled by Williamsport baseball club directors, players, city and Tri-State League officials, and local constabulary, Williamsport Millionaires' manager Harry Wolverton, accepts a diamond ring as part of the celebration marking another pennant-winning team. Six thousand jubilant fans attended the event on September 14, 1907, following Williamsport's victory over Lancaster on the last day of the season. (*GRIT.*)

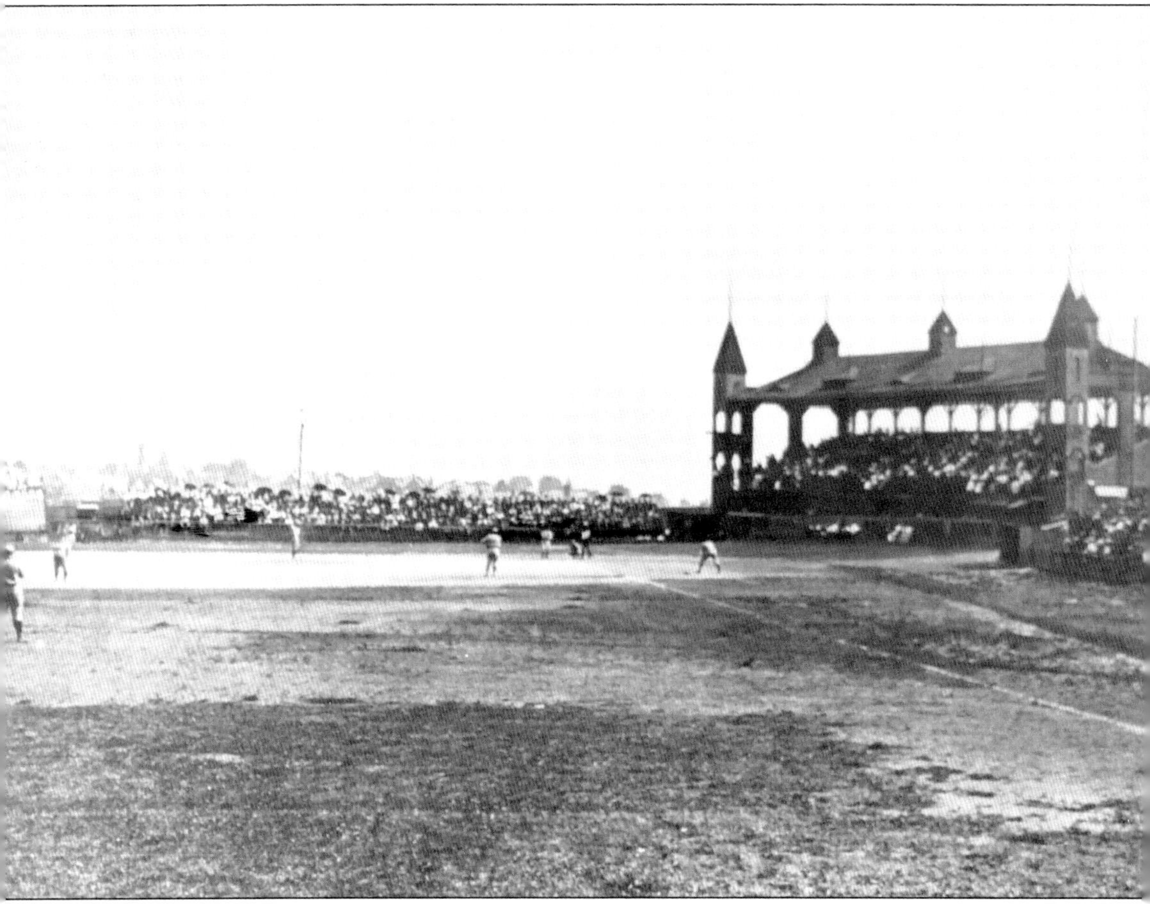

TRI-STATE LEAGUE GAME, ATHLETIC PARK (1905). Here is a left field view of a Williamsport Millionaires' baseball game in progress with Athletic Park's steepled grandstand as a backdrop. Branded an "outlaw" league because it lay outside the National Association of Professional Baseball Leagues, the Tri-State played big league ball and paid large salaries. The league competed with the Majors and minor leagues in signing high-priced baseball talent, and Williamsport's lumber barons spared no expense in securing proven major-league players. When Williamsport outspent Harrisburg and Altoona, the sporting press of these rival communities pinned the derisive moniker of "Millionaires" on the Williamsport club. In 1905 Williamsport successfully landed such established major-league players as Jimmy Sebring (Cincinnati Reds) and Fred "Snitz" Applegate (Philadelphia A's). Both contributed to Williamsport's first Tri-State League championship in 1905. (LCHS.)

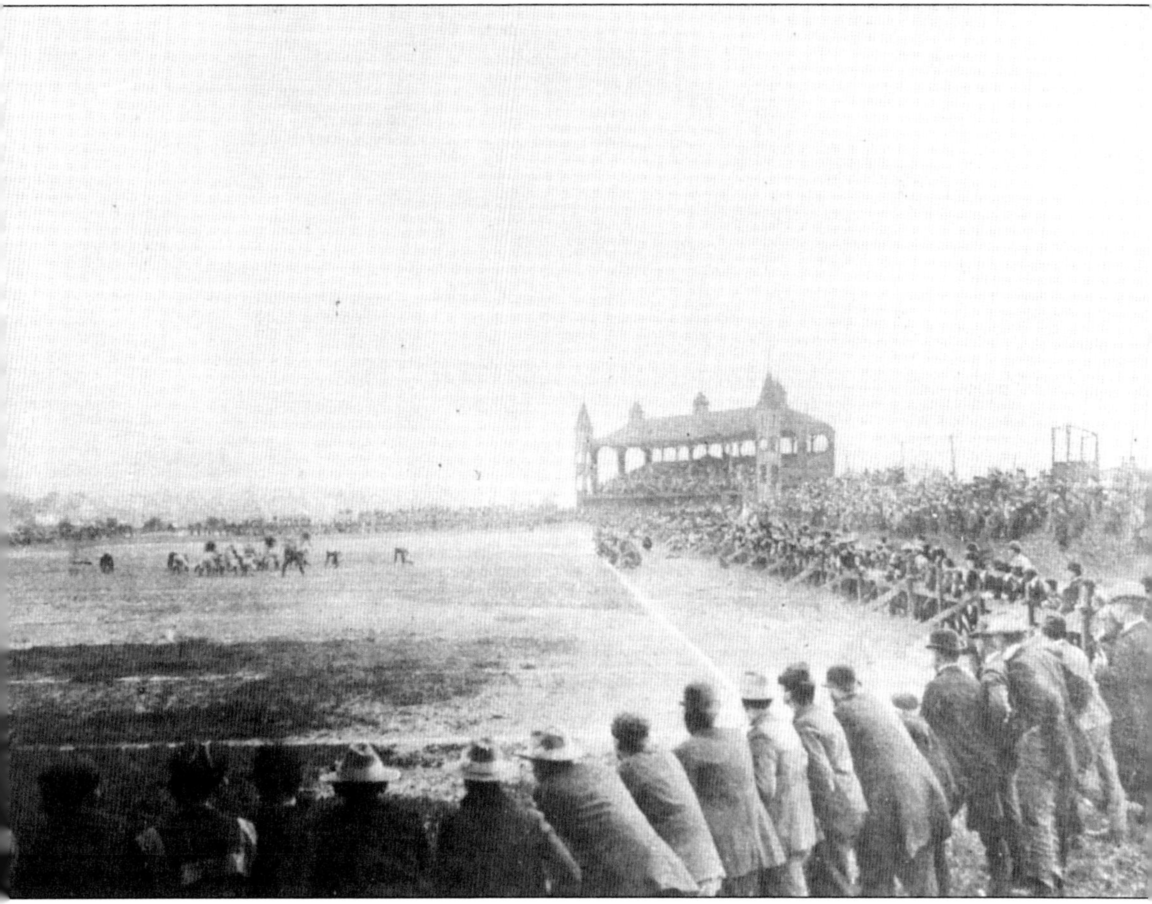

FOOTBALL GAME, ATHLETIC PARK (EARLY 1900S). This mirror image opposite the previous page shows Athletic Park reconfigured for football. Several area colleges—Bucknell, the Pennsylvania State College (Penn State), and Dickinson Seminary (Lycoming College)— used Athletic Field as a football venue to accommodate games of regional significance and to attract larger crowds. Nearly 10,000 gridiron fans encircled the park to watch this historic pigskin match-up between Penn State and Carlisle Indian College, led by the legendary All-American running back Jim Thorpe and Coach Glen "Pop" Warner. Note the formal attire worn by spectators to the game. (JVB.)

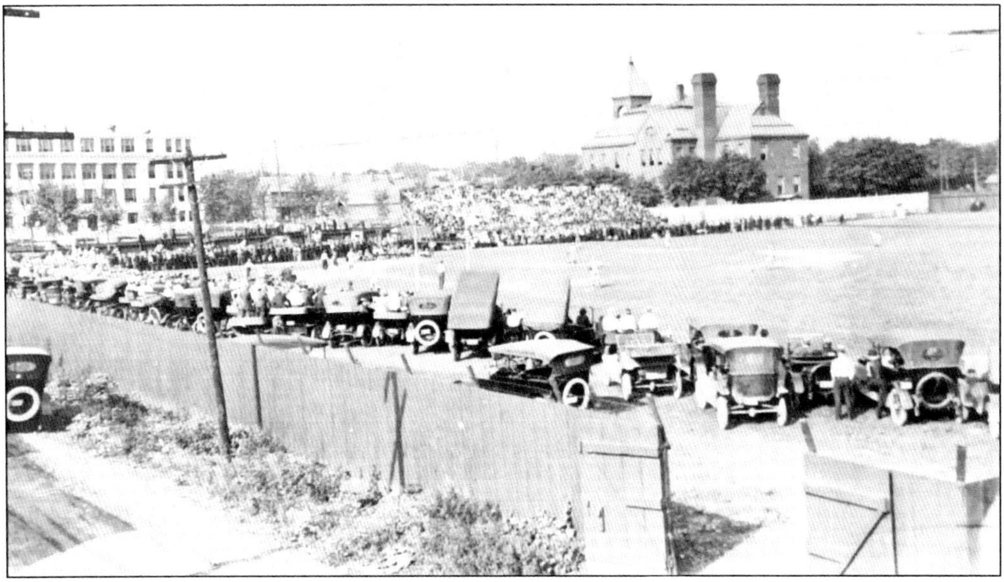

WILLIAMSPORT HIGH SCHOOL ATHLETIC FIELD, WEST THIRD AND SUSQUEHANNA STREET (1920). Built in 1916, the old high school field hosted City Industrial League, Pennsylvania Railroad League, and New York-Pennsylvania League baseball games. On October 5, 1920, more than 9,000 fans witnessed Williamsport's dramatic 1-0 triumph over Pitcarin to capture the Pennsylvania Railroad's Grand Division championship. A few spectators at this railroad league ballgame enjoyed the action from the vantage point of their automobiles, conveniently parked along the perimeter of the field. (DVS-LCHS.)

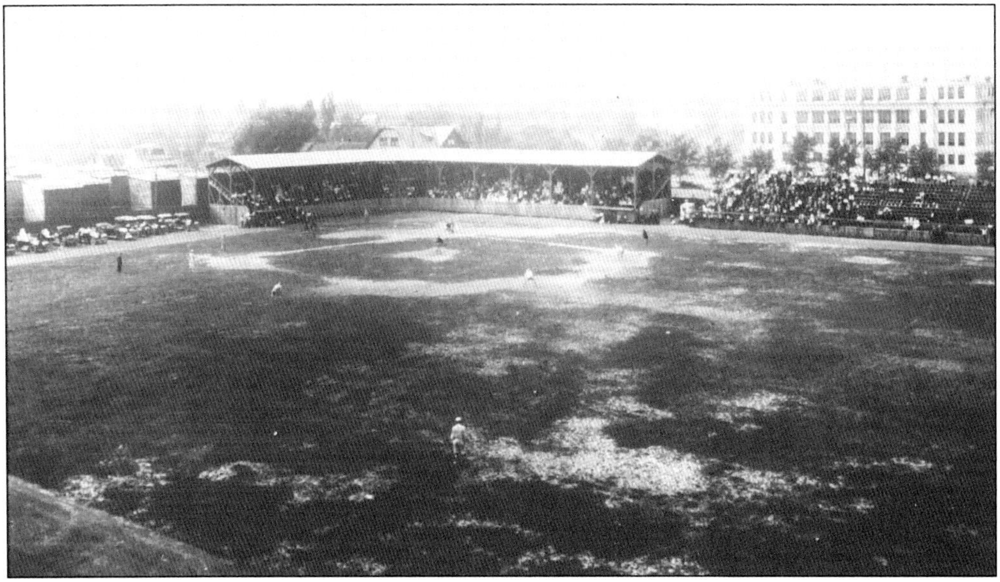

NEW YORK-PENNSYLVANIA LEAGUE GAME, WILLIAMSPORT HIGH SCHOOL ATHLETIC FIELD (1924). This bird's-eye view, taken from the roof of the Culler Furniture Factory beyond the center field fence, captures a New York-Pennsylvania League game in progress. The year before, Babe Ruth's Traveling All-Stars defeated the Williamsport club in an exhibition game played at the field. Ruth is reputed to have hit a ball 450 feet over the giant rocking chair perched atop the factory roof near the vantage point that this photograph was taken. (DVS-LCHS.)

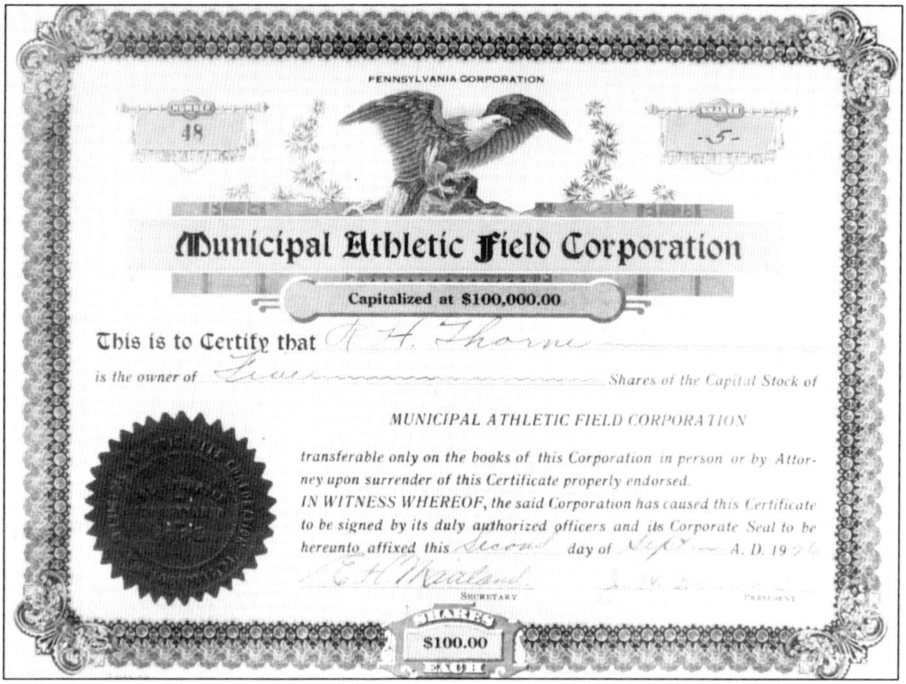

PENNSYLVANIA CORPORATION

48 -5-

Municipal Athletic Field Corporation

Capitalized at $100,000.00

This is to Certify that R. H. Thorne

is the owner of Five *Shares of the Capital Stock of*

MUNICIPAL ATHLETIC FIELD CORPORATION

transferable only on the books of this Corporation in person or by Attorney upon surrender of this Certificate properly endorsed.

IN WITNESS WHEREOF, the said Corporation has caused this Certificate to be signed by its duly authorized officers and its Corporate Seal to be hereunto affixed this Second *day of* Sept *A. D. 19*26

E. H. Maitland

SECRETARY PRESIDENT

SHARES $100.00 EACH

MUNICIPAL ATHLETIC FIELD CORPORATION STOCK CERTIFICATE (1926). Pictured is one of the original stock certificates issued to investors in the new Memorial Field enterprise. This particular certificate was issued to Ralph "Pat" Thorne and bears the signatures of Williamsport Grays Club President J. Walton Bowman and Club Secretary Edgar Maitland. Other prominent backers of the $75,000 venture included James and Irvin Gleason, Max Jaffe, Joseph Mosser, J. Roman Way, the Reese-Sherriff Lumber Company, and Harder's Sporting Goods. (Certificate courtesy of Ralph "Pat" Thorne Jr.)

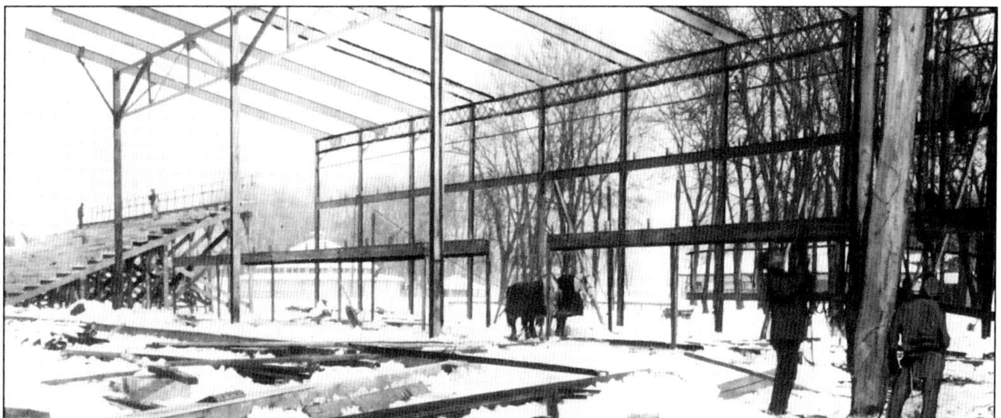

CONCRETE AND STEEL FOUNDATION, MEMORIAL FIELD (1925–1926). Investors and city officials chose the northwest corner of Memorial Park (land originally owned by the Williamsport Water Company) as the site of the new ballpark, Memorial Field. Ground was broken in October 1925 and construction proceeded through the winter months of 1926. The James V. Bennett Construction Company of Williamsport, the Drennen Brothers Construction Co. of Philadelphia, and the J.C. Dressler Construction Co. of Cleveland completed the stadium in May 1926, in time for the opening of the new baseball season. (*WS-G.*)

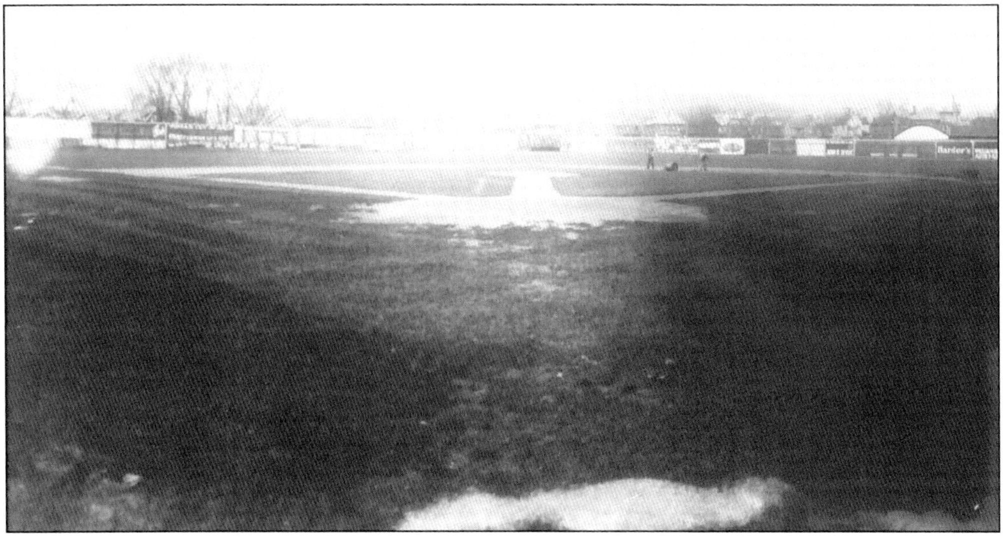

MEMORIAL FIELD, GROUND LEVEL (1926). This image offers an interesting visual perspective of Memorial Field's new diamond taking shape. Like many ballparks of its era, Memorial Field's outfield fence was adorned with billboard advertising. The field also had a "catcher's walk," or dirt path, between home plate and the pitcher's mound. The path was ultimately removed during the 1950s—a disappointment to many old-timers. (*GRIT.*)

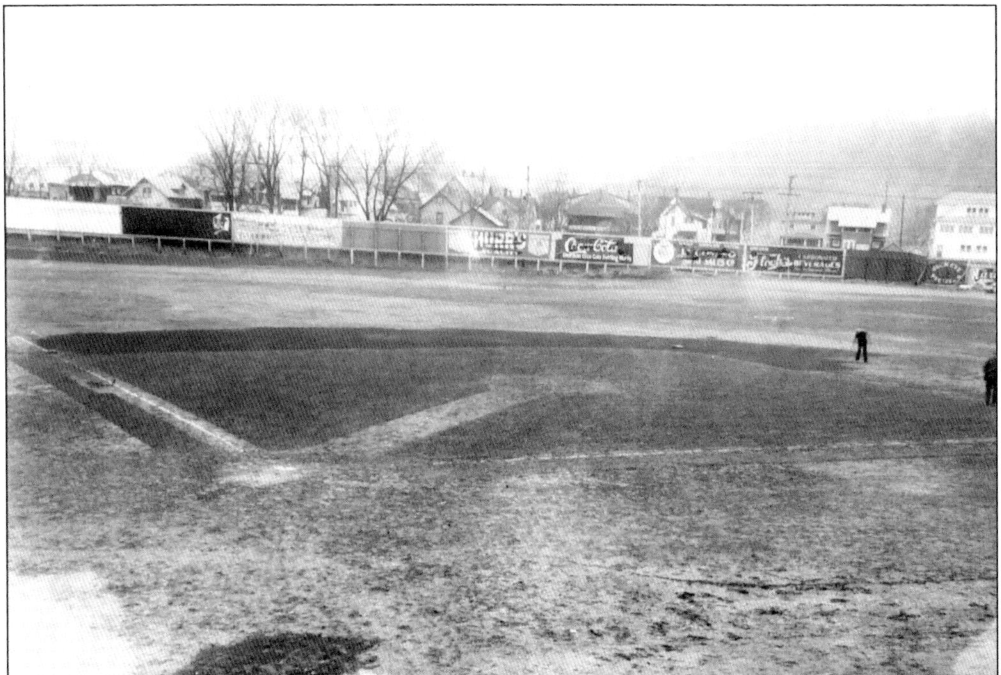

MEMORIAL FIELD, VIEW OF LEFT-CENTER FIELD FROM THE GRANDSTAND (1926). The outer configuration of Memorial Field also began to take shape in mid-March of 1926. Completion of the base of the outfield fence and the painting of billboard advertisements were all that remained to be done. The ballpark's distinctive left field terrace is also visible in this photograph. (*GRIT.*)

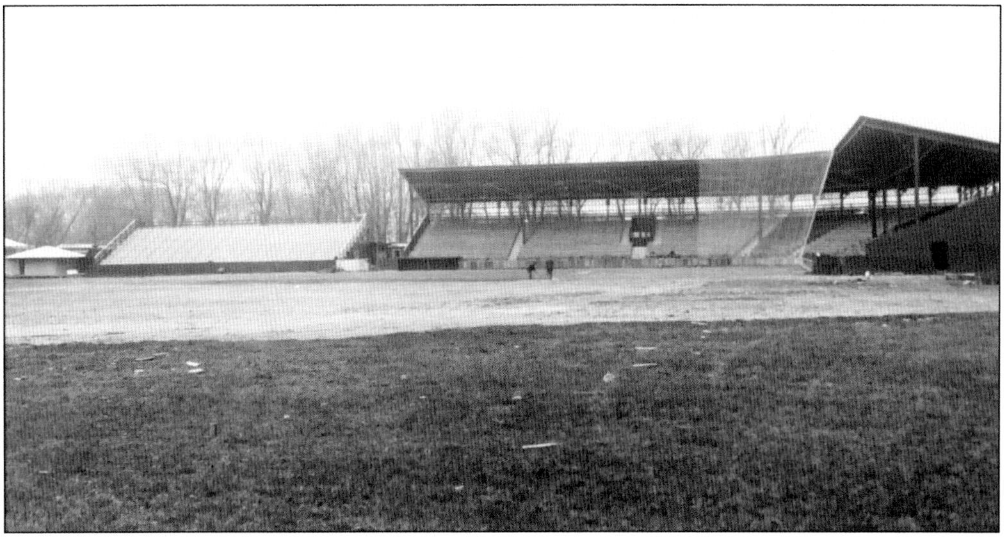

MEMORIAL FIELD, BEFORE OPENING DAY (1926). This view of Memorial Field, looking toward the infield and grandstand, was captured before the opening of the ballpark in May 1926, most likely early to mid-March, as portions of the playing field had not yet been sodded. At this early date the ballpark did not have left field bleachers. (*GRIT*.)

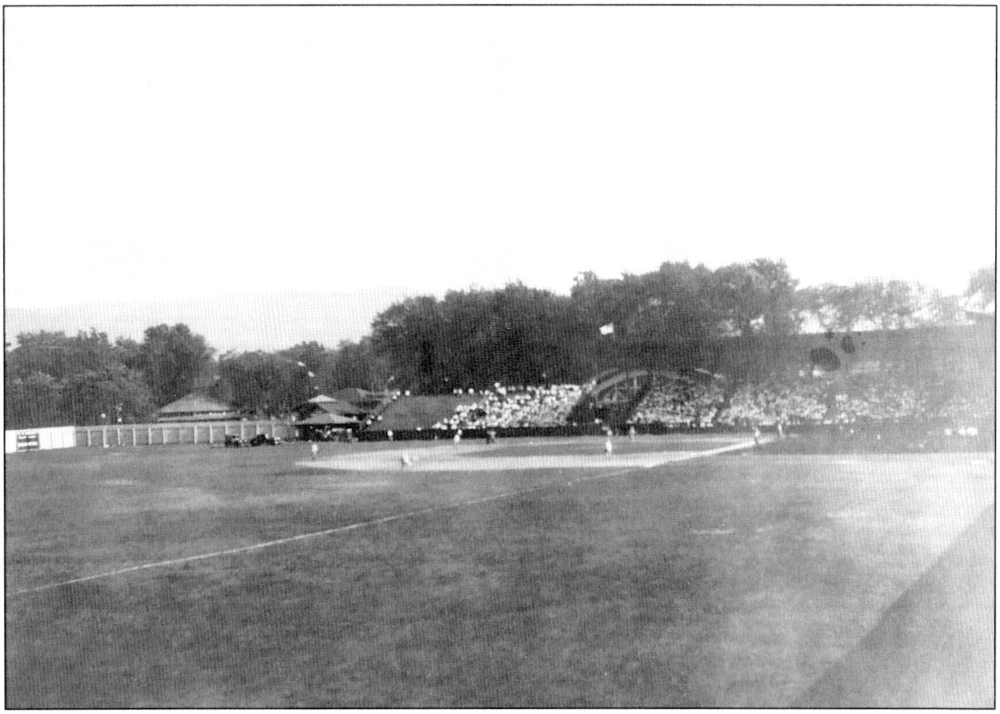

BOWMAN FIELD, LEFT FIELD PERSPECTIVE (1930). Memorial Field's original dimensions—400 feet to left field, 450 feet to center, and 367 feet to right field—were cavernous compared to the current measurements of Bowman Field. From 1926 to 1933 (the last year before the outfield dimensions were reduced) only ten home runs were hit out of Memorial Field. The previous year Memorial Field had been rededicated as "Bowman Field" in honor of longtime baseball benefactor J. Walton Bowman. (DVS-LCHS.)

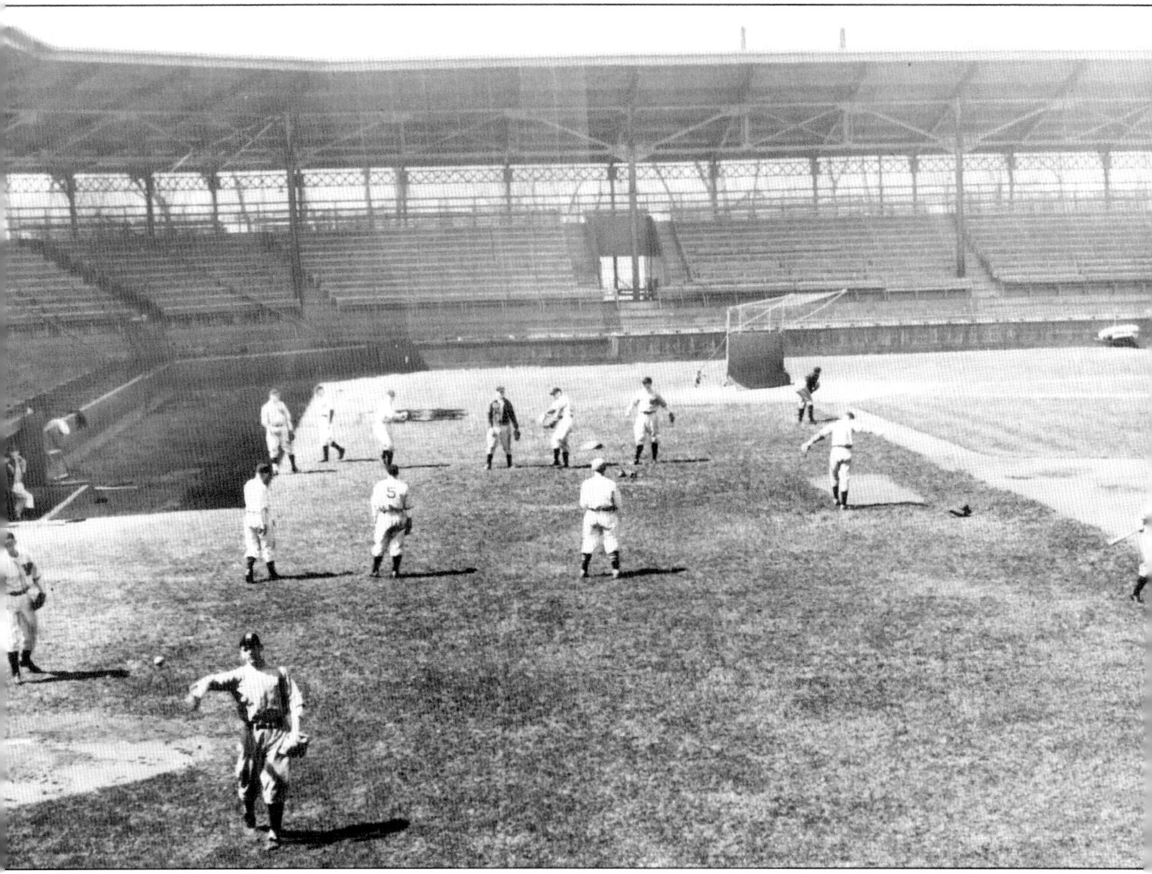

Williamsport Grays' Practice Session (1937). Members of the Williamsport Grays' baseball club limber up and play catch at the beginning of a grueling practice session prior to the start of the New York-Pennsylvania League season. During this period, the local club conducted an extended spring training at Bowman Field and often played several exhibition games before the regular season commenced. For photographer D. Vincent Smith, the ballpark was always the chief focus, with the players relegated to a minor role. Bowman Field and its distinctive grandstand served as an enclosed landscape for Smith. (*GRIT*.)

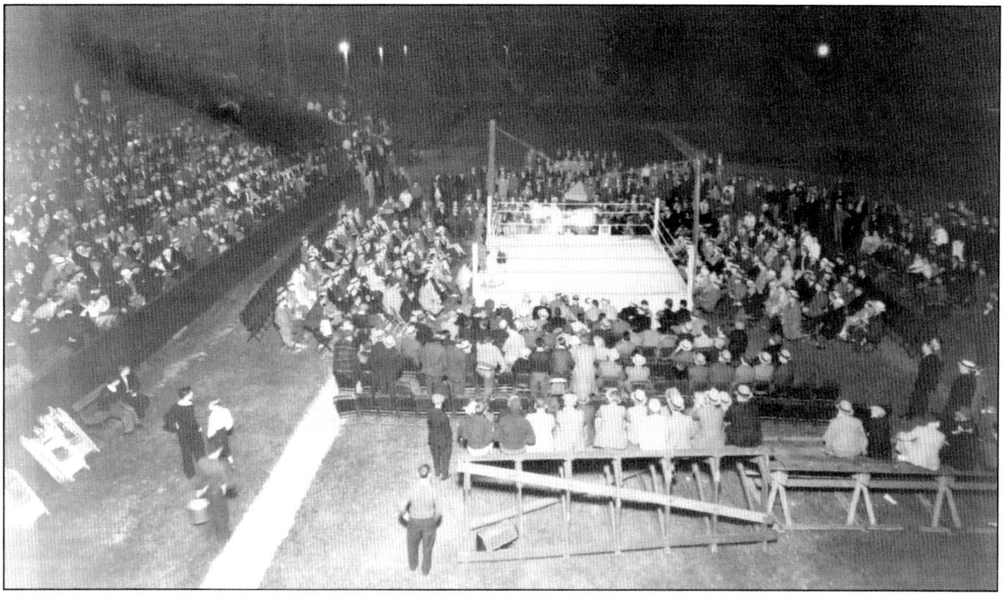

Boxing Match, Bowman Field (1930s). Outdoor amateur and professional boxing cards, and exhibitions by ring legends, drew large crowds to the uptown ballpark during the pre-World War II era. The boxing ring was positioned in full view of the right field bleacher area. For avid boxing fans the portable bleachers surrounding the ring were the best seats to view the action. (*GRIT*.)

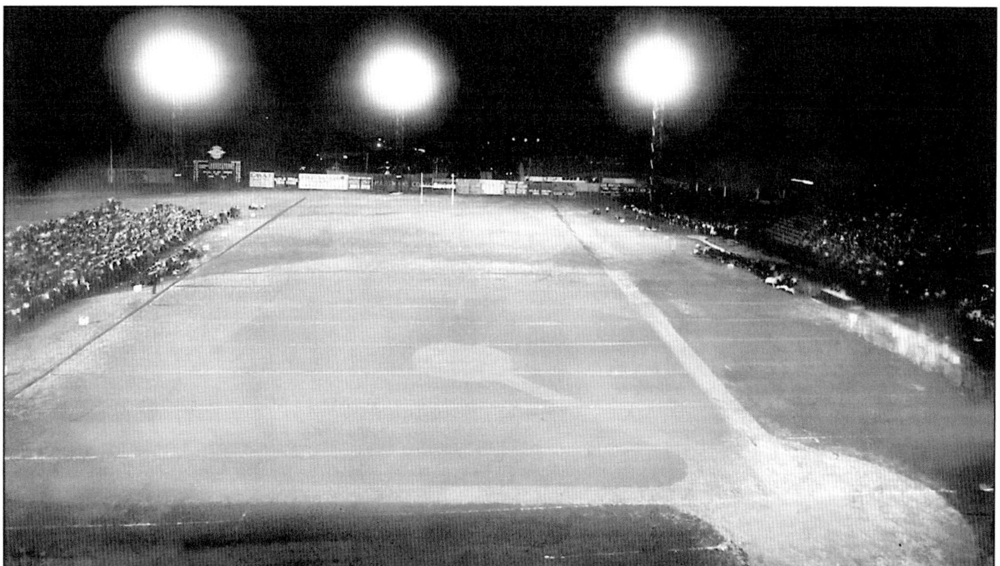

Williamsport High School Football Game (1930s). Bowman Field served as a multipurpose stadium long before the concept came in vogue. This rare image shows the ballpark reconfigured for Williamsport High School football games. The high school became a Bowman Field tenant shortly after the school district and the Grays' baseball directors jointly funded the erection of light towers for evening sporting events in 1932. Lycoming College also played some of its home football games at Bowman during the 1950s prior to the construction of Consistory (Person) Field. (JVB.)

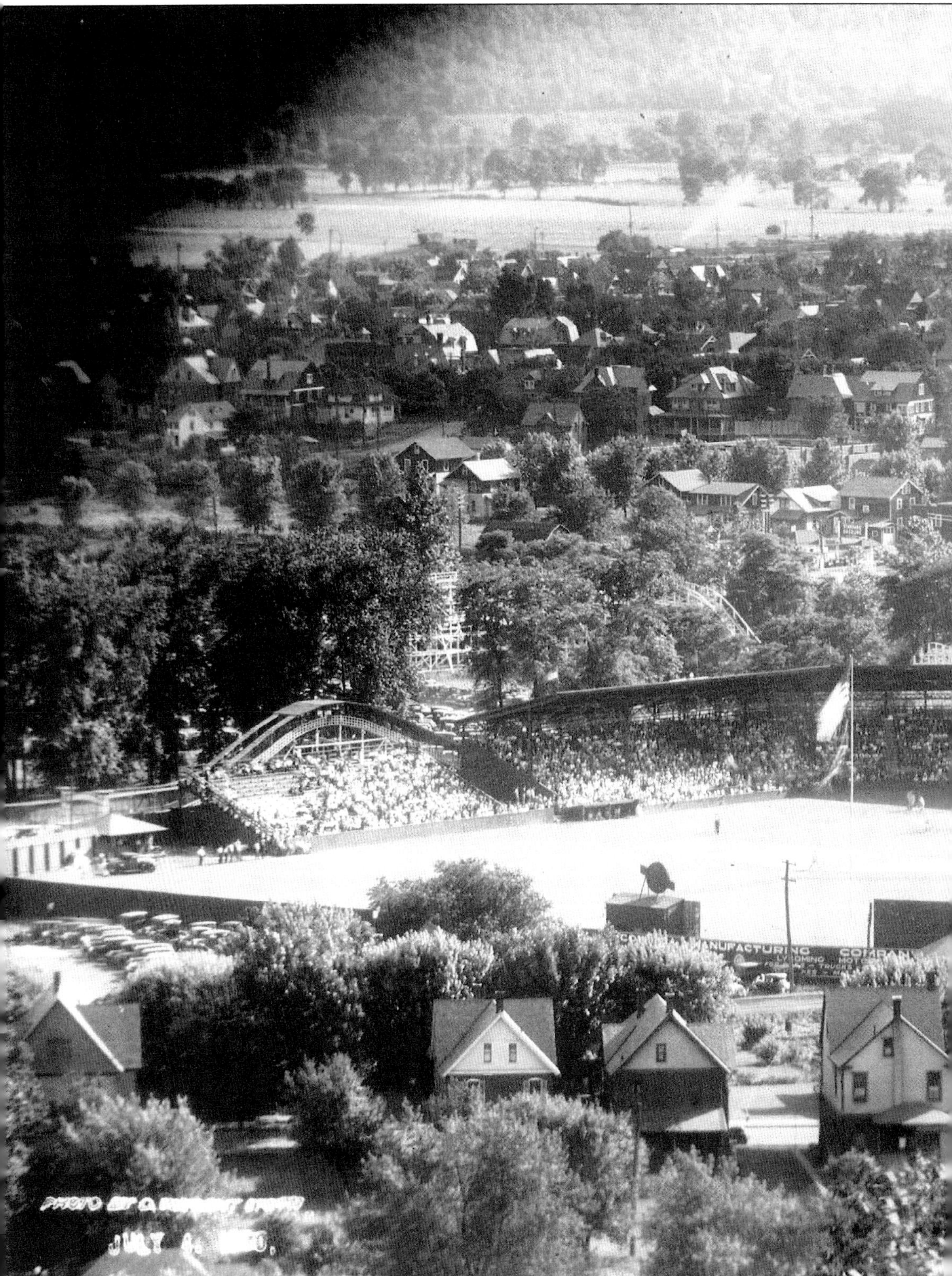
MANUFACTURING
LYCOMING MOTO
TRUCKS

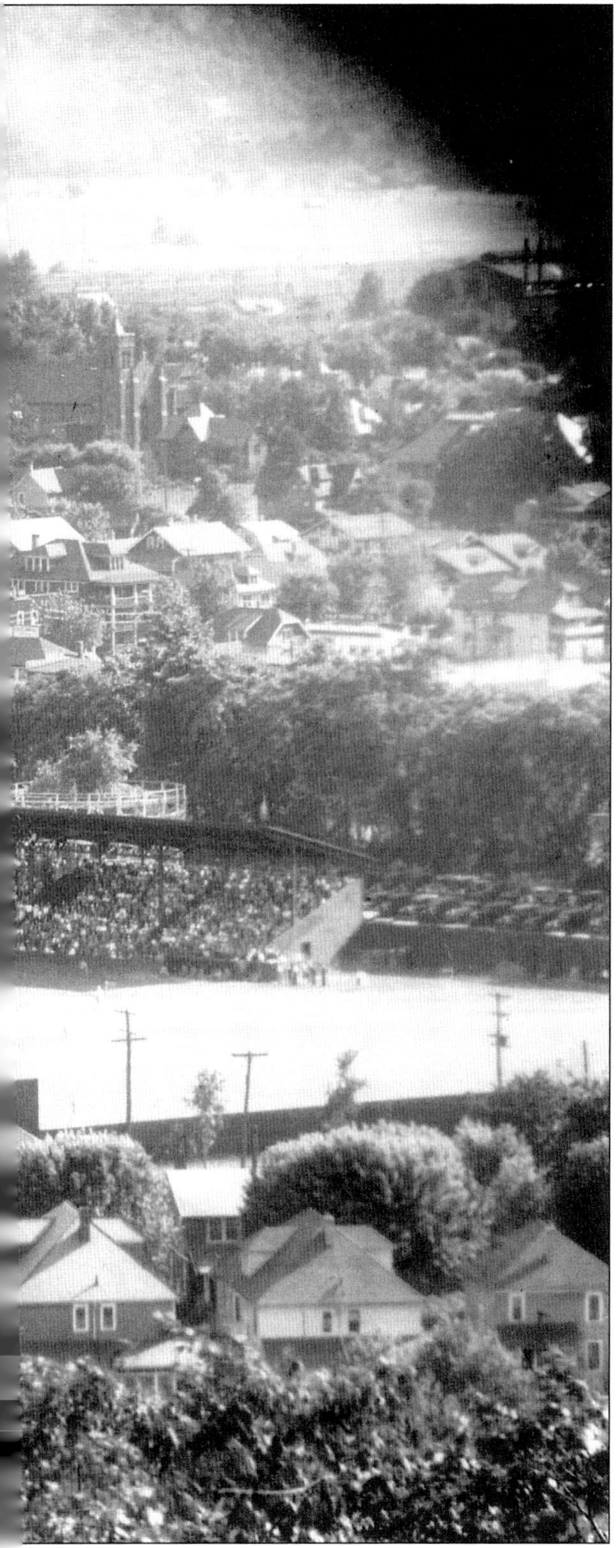

Bowman Field, Independence Day (July 4, 1930). Prominent Williamsport area photographer D. Vincent Smith, whose career spanned from the 1890s to the 1950s, delighted in photographing landscapes, residences, and historic buildings throughout the north-central Pennsylvania region. He considered Bowman Field a camera-worthy subject. This is perhaps his best, and most memorable, image of Williamsport's venerable ball field, captured from the heights of Wildwood Cemetery Ridge overlooking the ballpark and its environs. Note Memorial Park's amusement park and roller coaster looming in the background. The park complex was a popular recreational spot for the city's emerging middle class. (DVS-LCHS.)

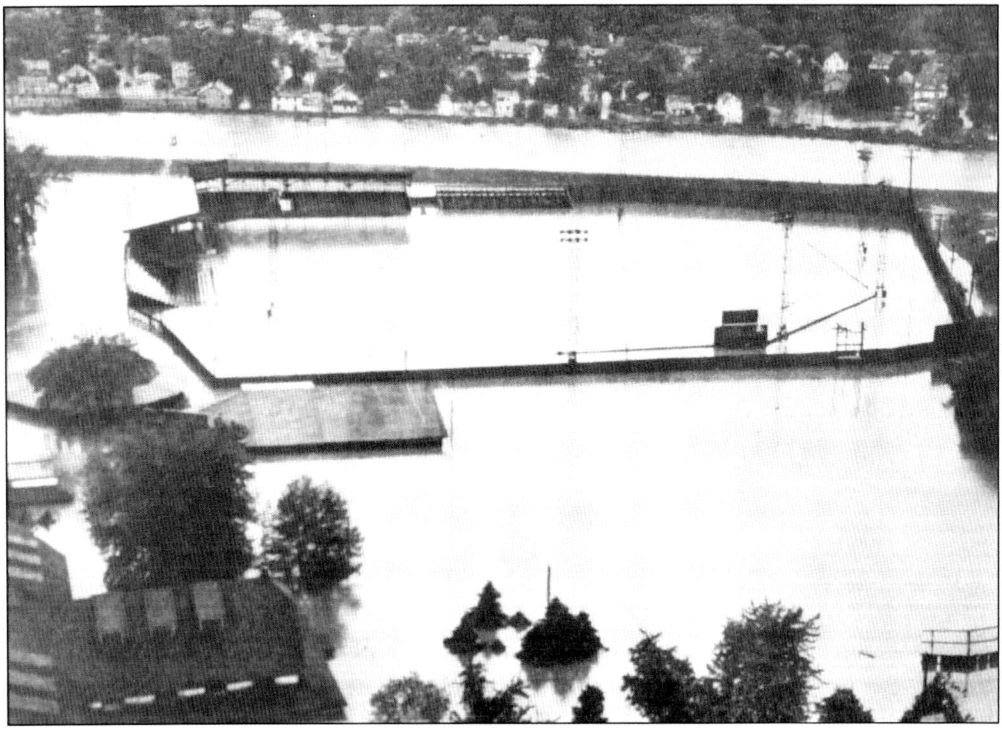

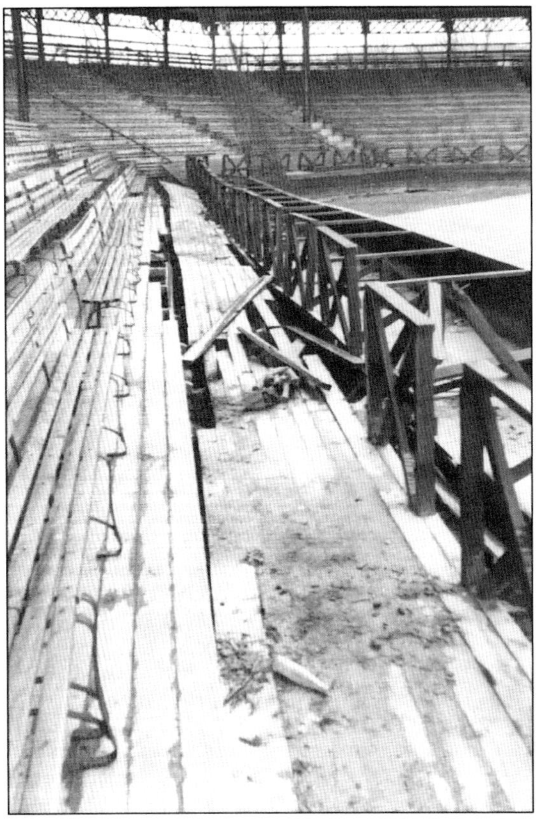

Bowman Field under Water (March 1936). Lycoming Creek waters engulf Bowman Field at the high watermark of the epic 1936 flood. Lying directly in the flood plain, the ballpark suffered extensive structural damage. A decade later, the flood of 1946 also hit with a vengeance. Construction of an elaborate dike and levy flood-control system (completed by the Army Corps of Engineers during the 1950s) helped to mitigate, but not eliminate, the threat of future flooding. (*GRIT*.)

Aftermath of a Flood (March 1936). The flood waters eventually receded, leaving Bowman Field's box seating area totally destroyed and portions of the grandstand extensively damaged. Williamsport Grays' directors and city officials argued over responsibility for financing the necessary repairs, amounting to thousands of dollars. Fortunately, the city enlisted the resources of the New Deal's Works Progress Administration to complete the repairs in time for the home opener in May. (*GRIT*.)

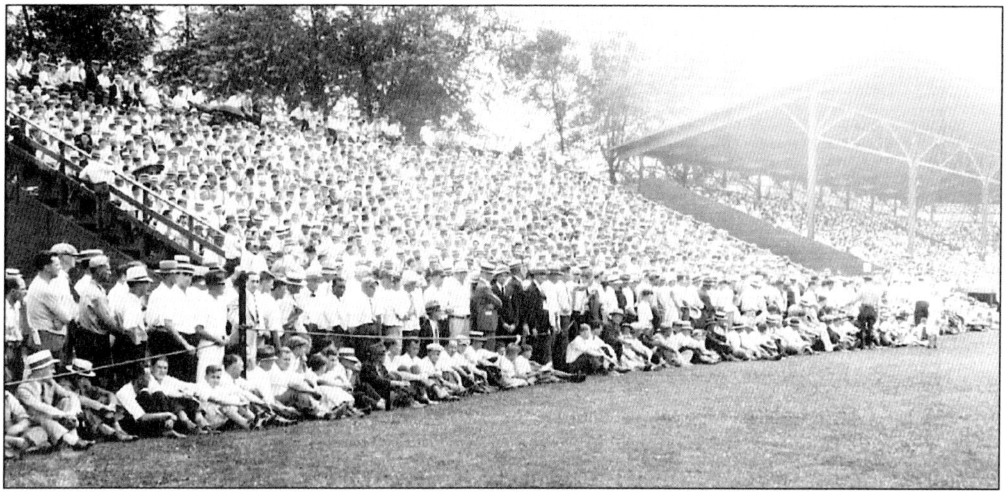

BOWMAN FIELD, PACKED HOUSE (LATE 1930S). Large overflow crowds were common at Bowman Field during the 1930s and early 1940s, especially when Williamsport was engaged in a tight pennant race, or when area merchants sponsored popular promotional giveaway events. One of the most popular promotions was a raffle for a new automobile, generously donated by Tommy Richardson's Buick Dealership. This photograph shows a standing-room-only crowd (some patrons with straw boat hats) assembled along the right field bleachers and roped-off foul territory area. (*GRIT*.)

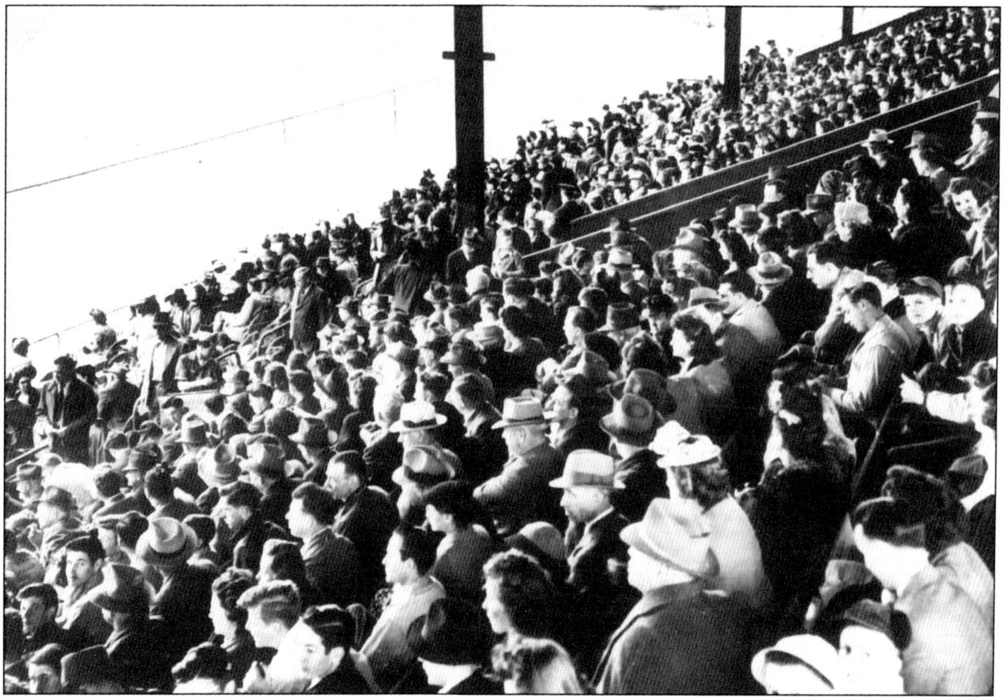

OPENING DAY (APRIL 1947). Bundled Williamsport fans take in the action from the grandstands as the Tigers and Elmira Pioneers play ball on a chilly Eastern League opening day. Williamsport (Boom Town) and Elmira, New York (Queen City of the Southern Tier), enjoyed a long association and rivalry in the league. In the past these two teams vied for the "Challenge Cup," awarded to the winner of the season series. (*GRIT*.)

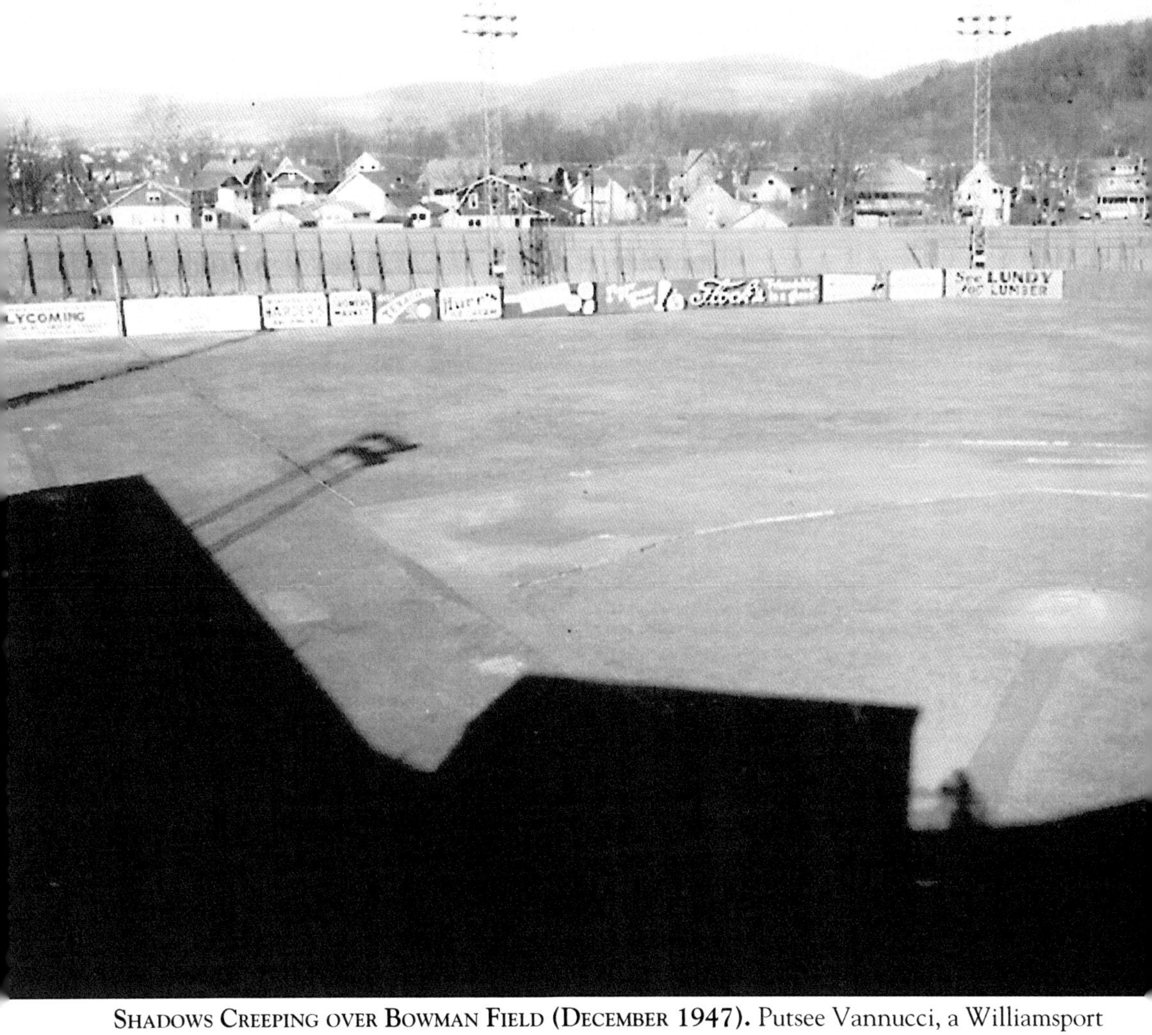

SHADOWS CREEPING OVER BOWMAN FIELD (DECEMBER 1947). Putsee Vannucci, a Williamsport commercial photographer, captured this stunning panorama of Bowman Field and the surrounding vista from atop the stadium grandstand roof. Commissioned by the Detroit Tigers (the parent club of the Williamsport Tigers) to photograph the stadium for insurance and property valuation, Vannucci produced a series of images that documented the pristine ballpark's distinctive retro-look. One of the more noticeable features of Bowman Field was the

original outfield (buttressed) wall lying well beyond the "newer" inner fence. This outer wall, resembling a fort palisade, was finally removed in 1961. The billboard advertisements on the inner fence will rekindle memories of businesses, stores, and companies, long since gone. One of the most popular ballpark billboards of this era was the Flock's Brewery sign in left-center field promoting its beer as "Friendship in a Glass." (PV-LCHS.)

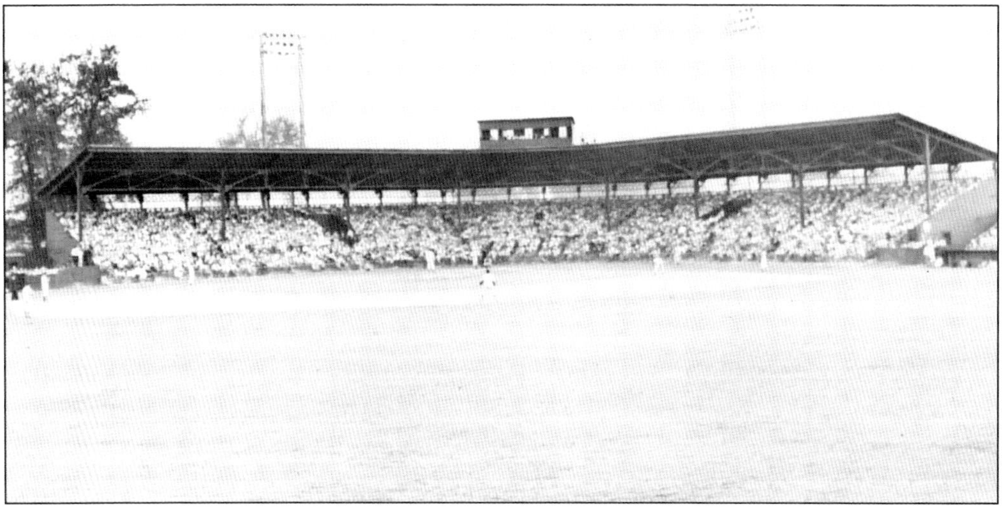

WILLIAMSPORT VS. SCRANTON, BOWMAN FIELD (SUMMER 1947). This stunning view of the game in progress was most likely taken by a *Grit* staff photographer from a catwalk on the scoreboard or center field fence. A crowd of 7,265 vocal fans—one of the largest ever at Bowman Field—witnessed this day game between the Grays and the Red Sox. Scranton, Wilkes-Barre, and Elmira were Williamsport's chief rivals in the Eastern League and always drew well at the home gate. (*GRIT*.)

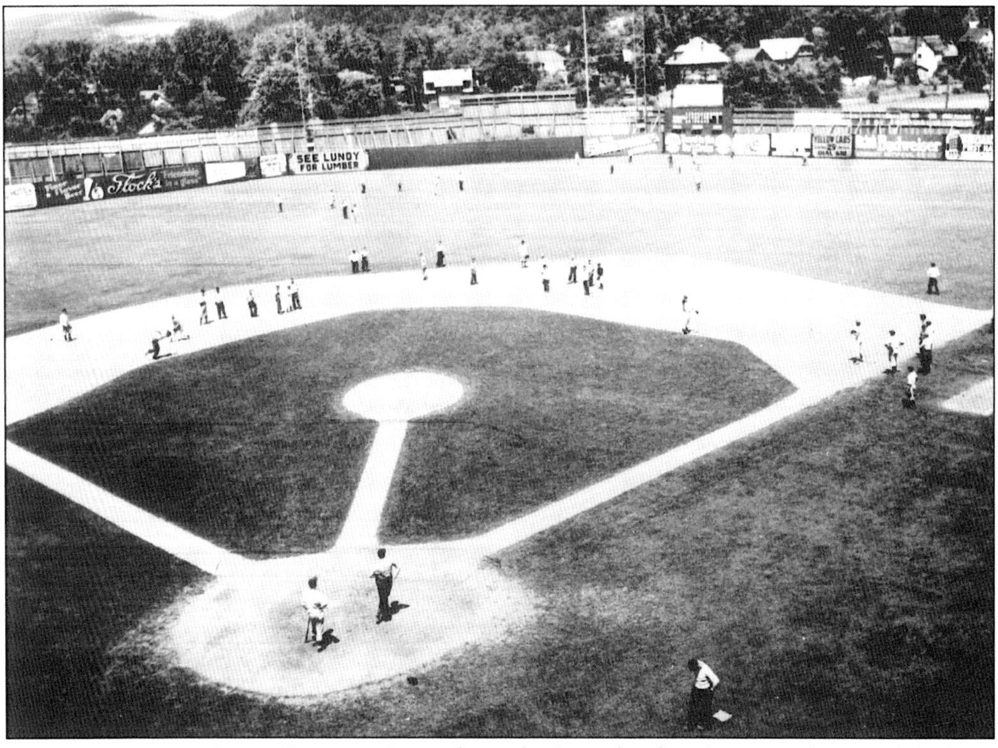

BASEBALL TRYOUT CAMP, BOWMAN FIELD (1945). Over the decades major-league clubs have held tryout camps at Bowman Field hoping to discover and sign talented local prospects. These young hopefuls are put through the paces under the watchful eye of baseball scouts. The image captures the ballpark's spacious interior as seen from Bowman Field's grandstand roof. (*GRIT*.)

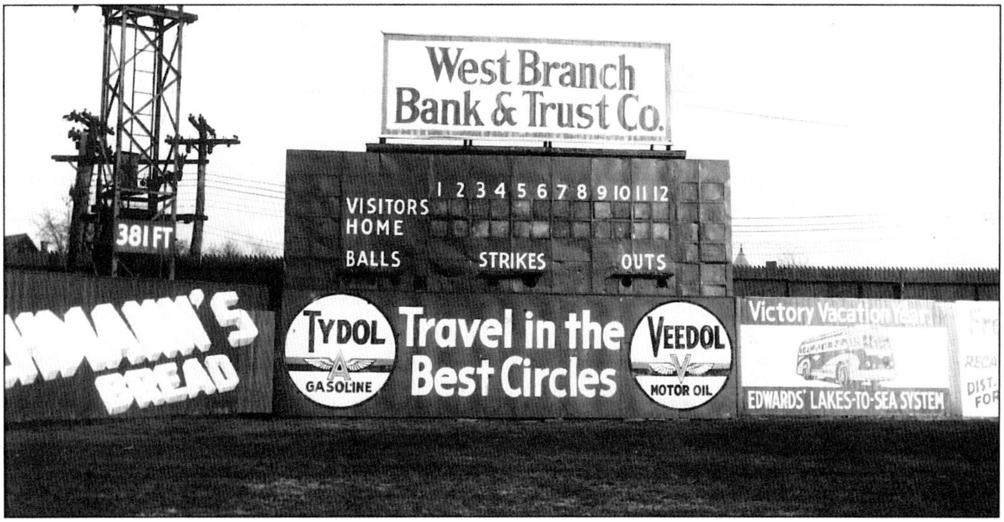

West Branch Bank Scoreboard (1947). Longtime Williamsport baseball fans fondly remember Bowman Field's distinctive center field scoreboard and the West Branch Bank advertisement that adorned it. The scoreboard offered an inviting target for hitters and a pleasant visual background for spectators. It is believed to be the first electronic scoreboard installed at Bowman Field. (PV-LCHS.)

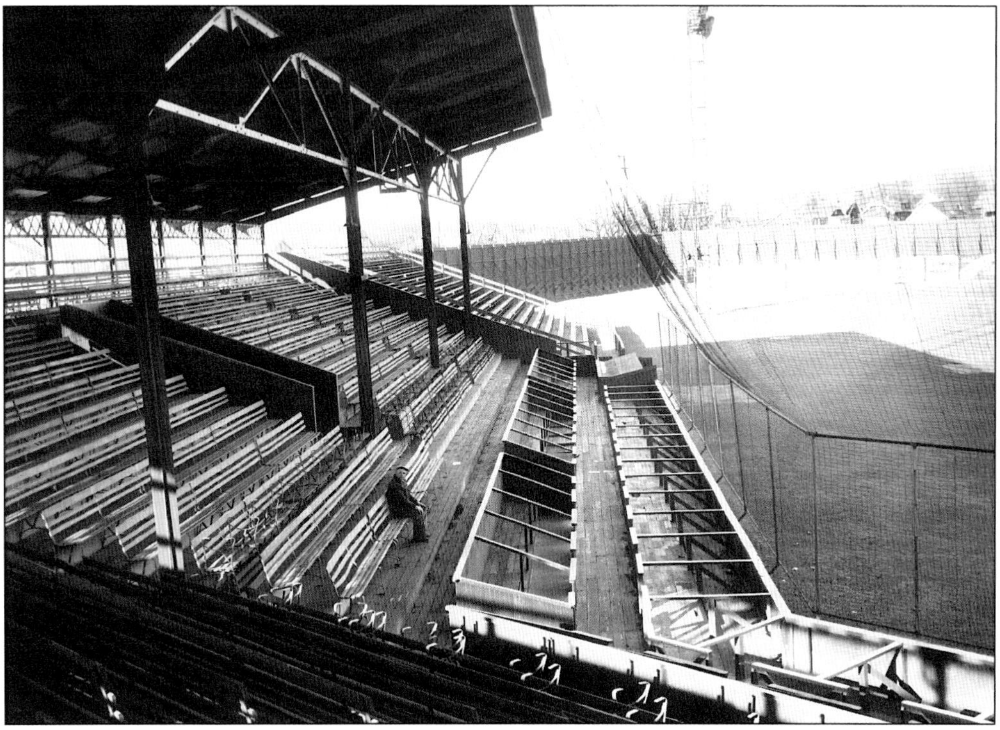

Bowman Field, Winter (1947). This Putsee Vannucci image of the third base side of Bowman Field's grandstand captures the solitude of the ballpark on a mild December day. The figure sitting in the grandstands is unknown. Ray Keyes, the long-departed venerable Williamsport sports scribe, drew inspiration for his "Hot Stove League" columns by visiting Bowman on such days. (PV-LCHS.)

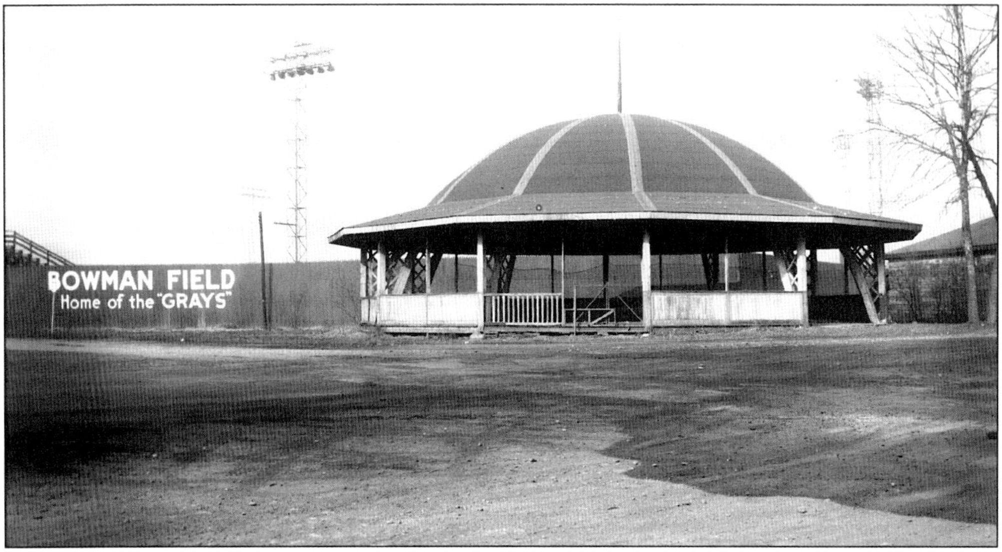

MEMORIAL PARK MERRY-GO-ROUND (1947). Other familiar Bowman Field and Memorial Park landmarks were the merry-go-round and fun house (background) that lay just beyond the shadows of the right field fence. Both were popular diversions for picnicking families, and many children left the park with a brass ring or souvenir home run ball. (PV-LCHS.)

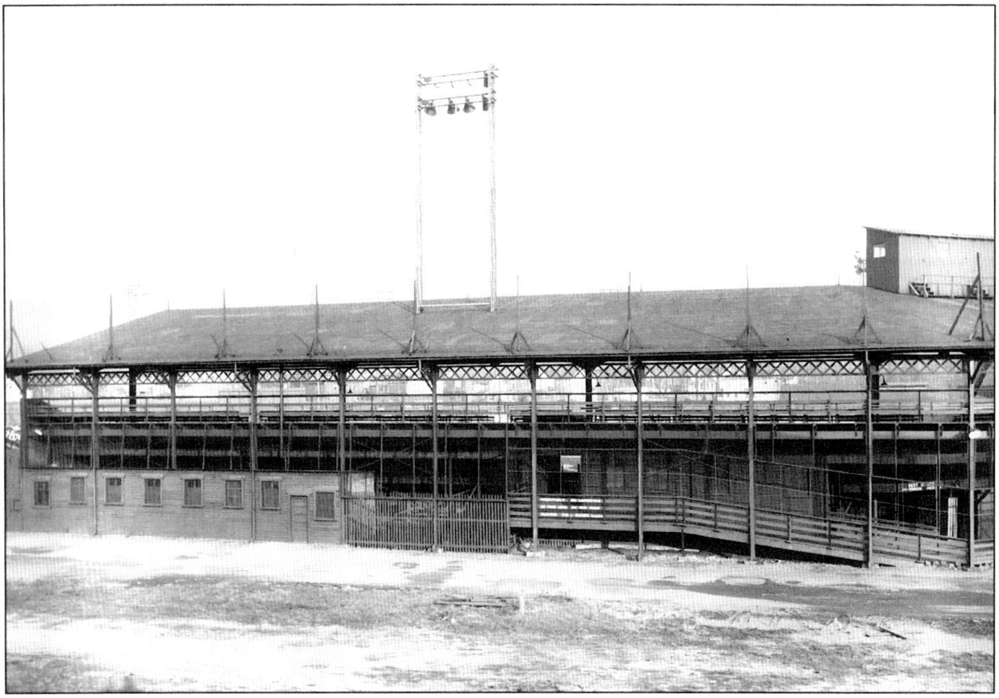

MAIN ENTRANCE GATES TO BOWMAN FIELD (1947). As this picture illustrates, Bowman Field's outer edifice has undergone little structural change since 1947. With the exception of the present-day office and ticket booth partitions that outcrop from the grandstand, this view would be immediately recognizable to current fans lining up to purchase tickets for a ballgame. Bowman Field's signature wooden ramps leading to the stands are visible in this image. (PV-LCHS.)

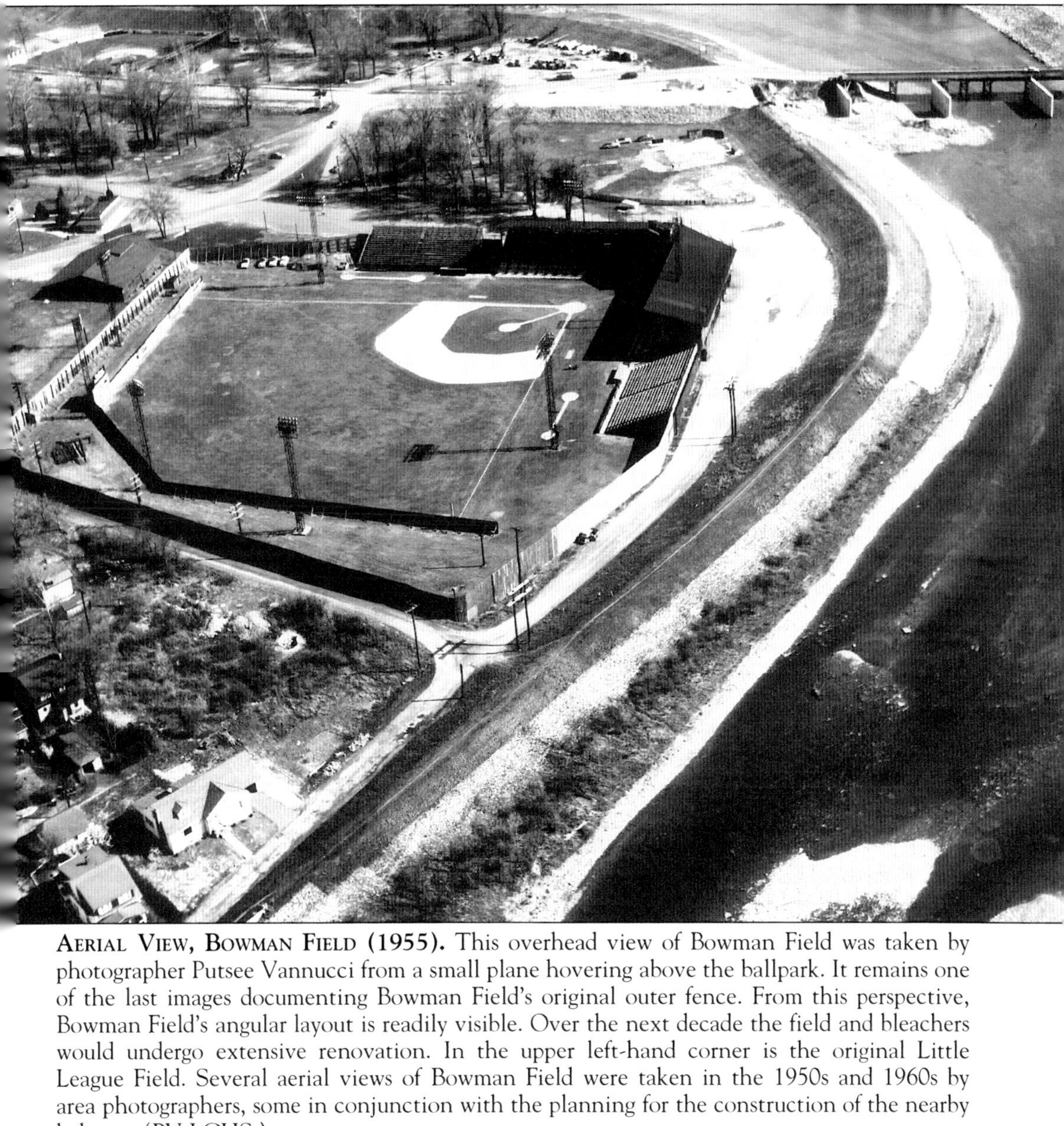

AERIAL VIEW, BOWMAN FIELD (1955). This overhead view of Bowman Field was taken by photographer Putsee Vannucci from a small plane hovering above the ballpark. It remains one of the last images documenting Bowman Field's original outer fence. From this perspective, Bowman Field's angular layout is readily visible. Over the next decade the field and bleachers would undergo extensive renovation. In the upper left-hand corner is the original Little League Field. Several aerial views of Bowman Field were taken in the 1950s and 1960s by area photographers, some in conjunction with the planning for the construction of the nearby beltway. (PV-LCHS.)

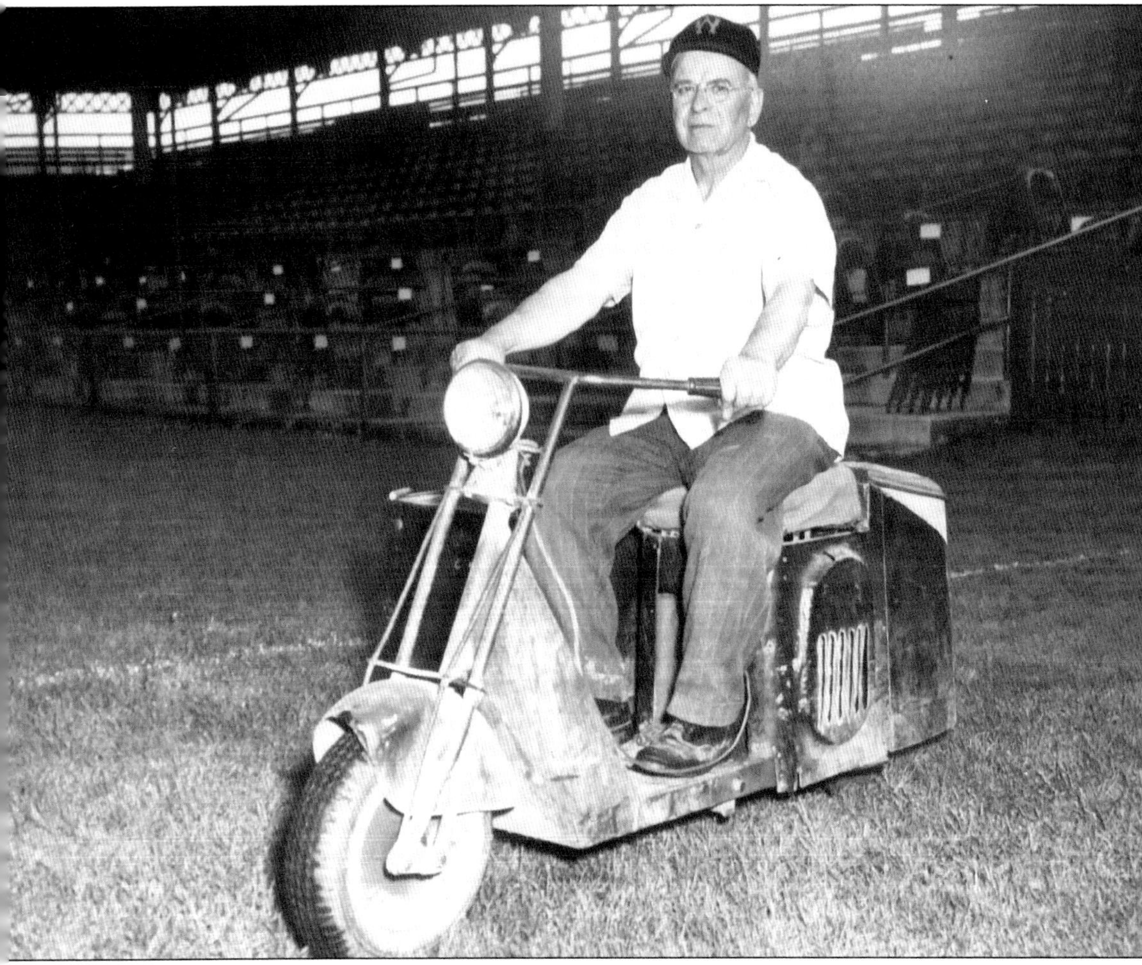

AL BELLANDI'S GARDEN (EARLY 1950S). Head groundskeeper Al Bellandi strikes a jaunty pose upon his motor scooter while tending to his duties at Bowman Field. Regarded as one of the best groundskeepers in the country, Bellandi transformed Bowman Field into the "Garden Spot of the Minor Leagues." Originally hired in 1935 to dig posts for Bowman Field's new inner fence, the Italian immigrant so impressed the Grays' management that they appointed him head groundskeeper the following year. From 1936 to 1961, Bellandi gave his full devotion to the ballpark, and Bowman Field never had a finer caretaker. He reduced turf management to its essential elements—"hard work, plenty of water and sunshine, plus the right kind of grass seed will do the trick." Though offered jobs by the Detroit Tigers and Baltimore Orioles, Bellandi never strayed from his beloved Bowman Field. On July 15, 1961, the Grays and the Sons of Italy honored him with a special night at the ballpark. (*GRIT*.)

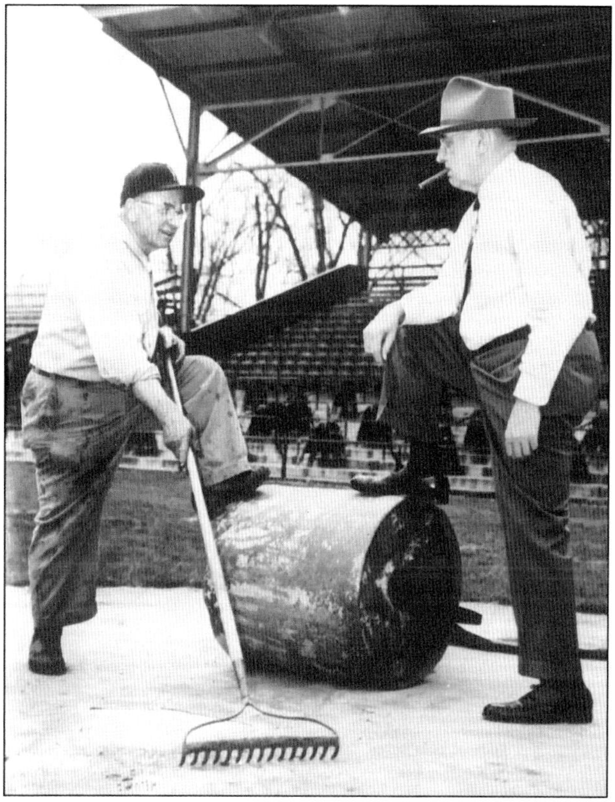

MEETING OF THE FIELD GENERALS (1954). Groundskeeper Al Bellandi (left) confers with Williamsport Grays' business manager J. Roy Clunk (right) prior to a game. The feisty Italian and the gruff, cigar-smoking baseball administrator made quite a pair, successfully performing their daily ballpark tasks on a shoestring budget. Upon Clunk's death in November 1961, Bellandi came out of retirement one last time to sweep-up the remaining cigar ashes in his dear friend's Bowman field office. (*GRIT*.)

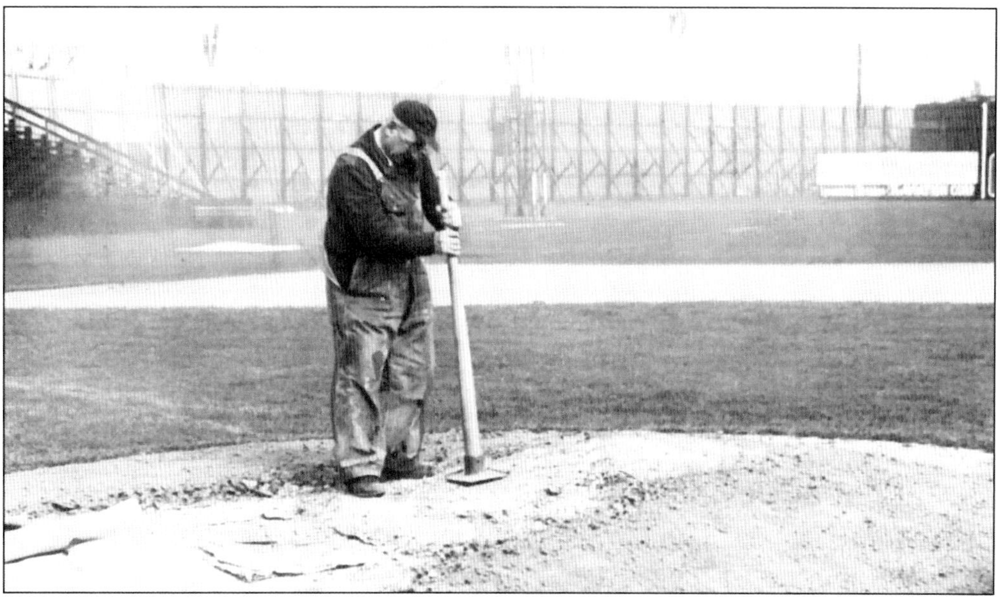

MOLDED TO PERFECTION (1954). One of the most important tasks performed by the head groundskeeper involved the tamping and sculpting of the pitcher's mound. Here, master craftsman Al Bellandi goes about his work oblivious to the camera. Bellandi worked 18-hour days at the ballpark. He often returned to the field in the early morning hours to inspect it after rain storms, or to tend to the sprinkler system. (*GRIT*.)

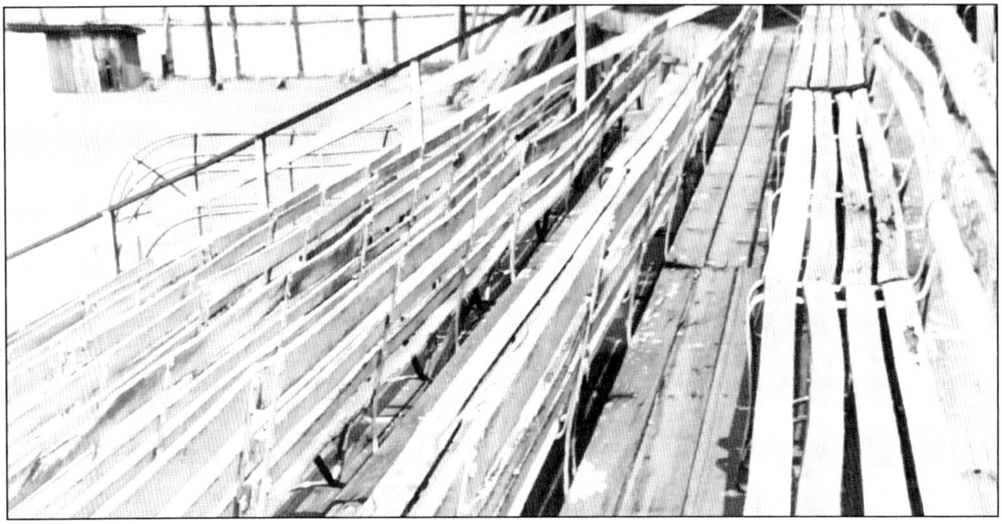

Dormant Bowman Field (1957). By 1957 Bowman Field had fallen into such a state of neglect that the Pennsylvania Department of Labor and Industry condemned the bleachers as unsafe for use. Without a minor-league tenant, city officials proposed the sale of the stadium to the Little League Incorporated as a permanent site for the annual Little League World Series. Little League rejected the proposal. Fortunately, professional baseball returned the following year. (*GRIT*.)

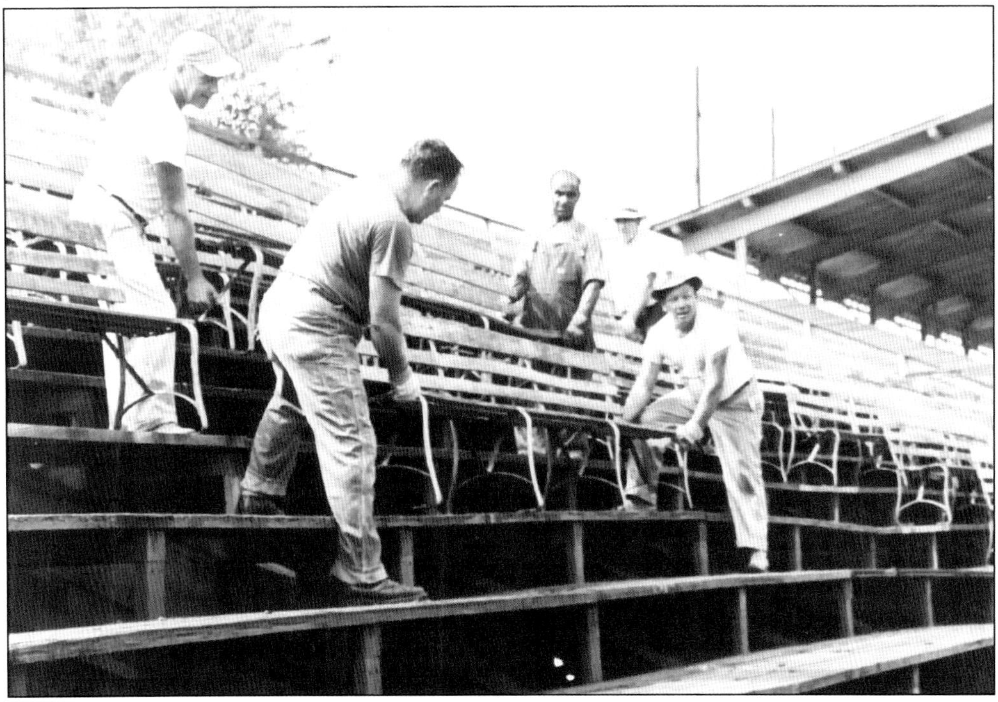

Replacing the Bleachers (1958). With the return of minor-league baseball in 1958 the city undertook extensive renovations to Bowman Field. Here a city work crew removes rotted bleachers in preparation for the new season. The warped bleacher planks seen in this photograph were also replaced. Working in tandem, the city and the Bowman Field Commission lured the Phillies' Class AA Eastern League franchise to Williamsport. (*GRIT*.)

Gateway to the Majors (1954). Since 1936, fans entering the West Fourth Street entrance to Memorial Park and Bowman Field have been greeted by a signboard proclaiming Williamsport's team and league affiliation. Between the late 1940s and 1950s the most memorable sign inscription read "Bowman Field: Gateway to the Majors." Here is a rare image of the sign, partially obstructed by the Women's Christian Temperance Union Memorial Fountain. (*GRIT.*)

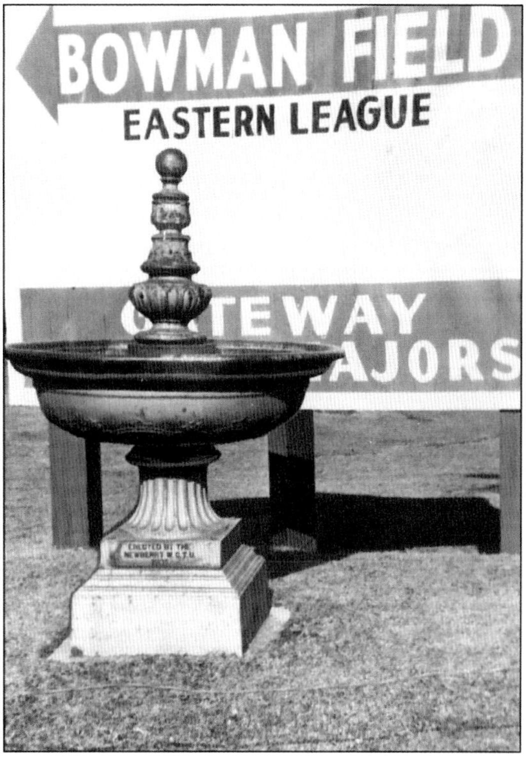

Installation of Polo Grounds Lights (1964). A little bit of history was erected at Bowman Field when the New York Mets, Williamsport's new parent club, graciously donated the light towers that had illuminated the old Polo Grounds for many years. Workers are shown installing and adjusting the light fixtures for proper illumination—no small feat as they were nearly 60 feet off the ground and had to negotiate the tower's narrow catwalk. (*GRIT.*)

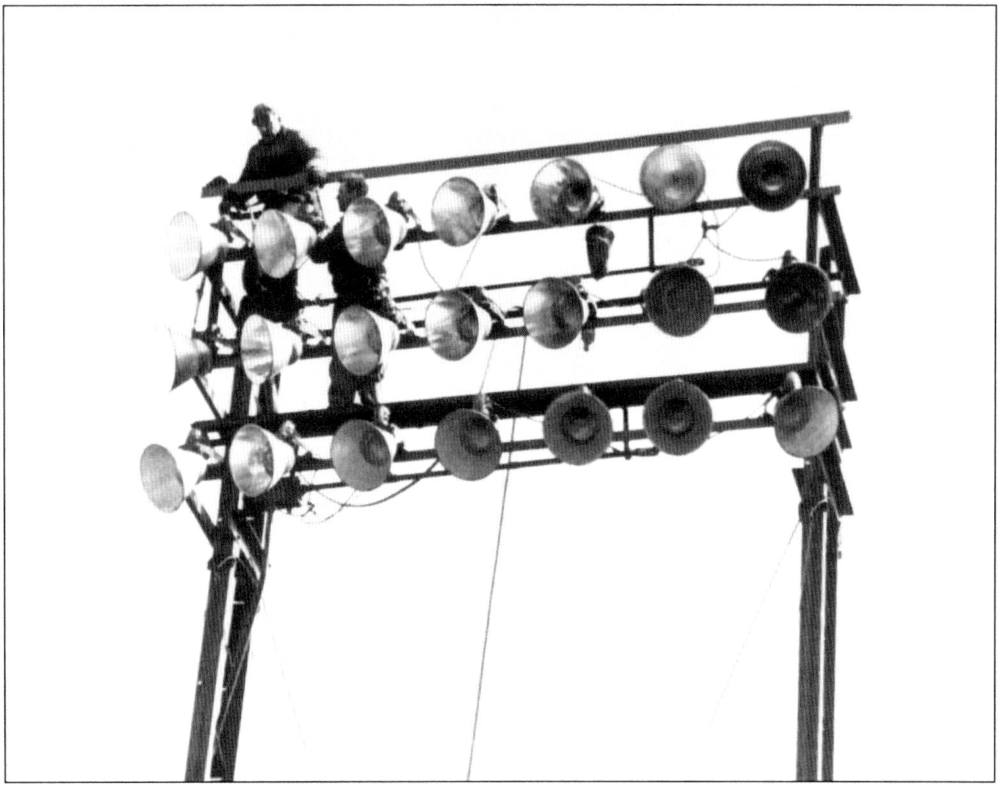

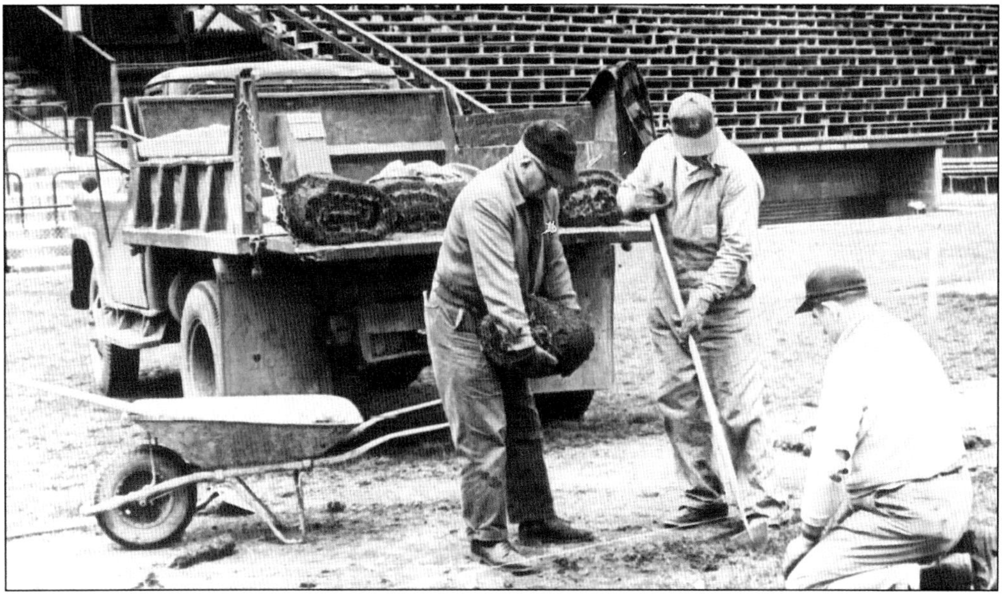

Resodding Bowman Field (1966). As part of the preparations for another baseball season, the Bowman Field grounds crew patches up the infield with new rolls of turf. One worker holds the next turf strip to be rolled out, another tamps the new sod in place, and a third crew member inspects the seams for a flawless match. An annual spring rite, resodding heralded the return of baseball. (*GRIT*.)

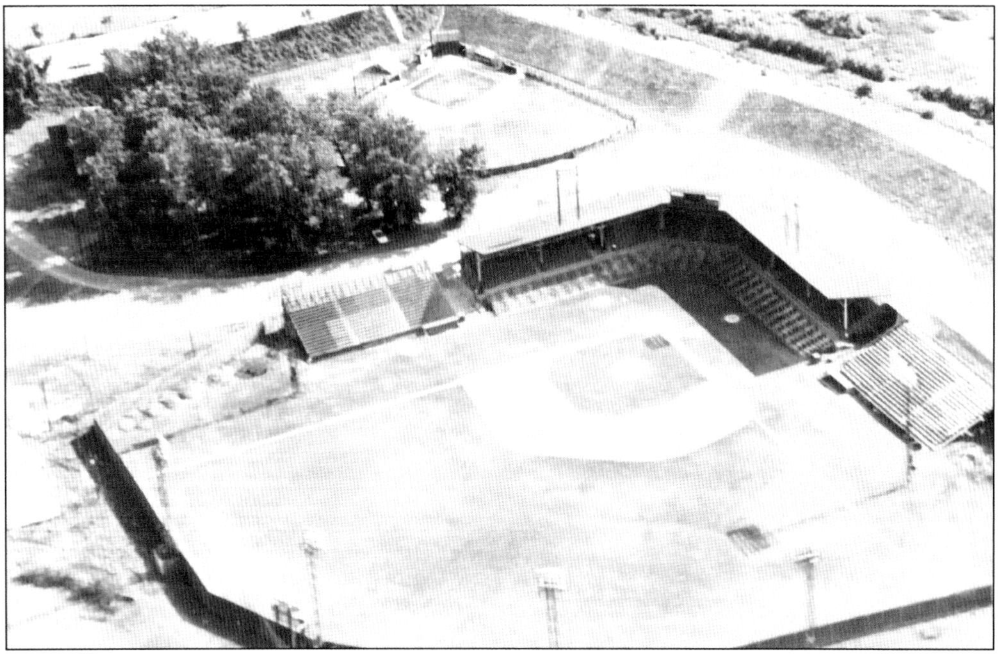

Aerial View of Bowman Field (1967). This interesting aerial shot of Bowman Field, looking from the outfield toward the grandstand, captured the ballpark prior to the permanent removal of the left field bleachers a few years later. A concession and picnic area now occupies that space. Note the position of the light stanchions in the foul territory areas. The towers presented a formidable obstacle for left and right fielders pursuing foul fly balls. (*GRIT*.)

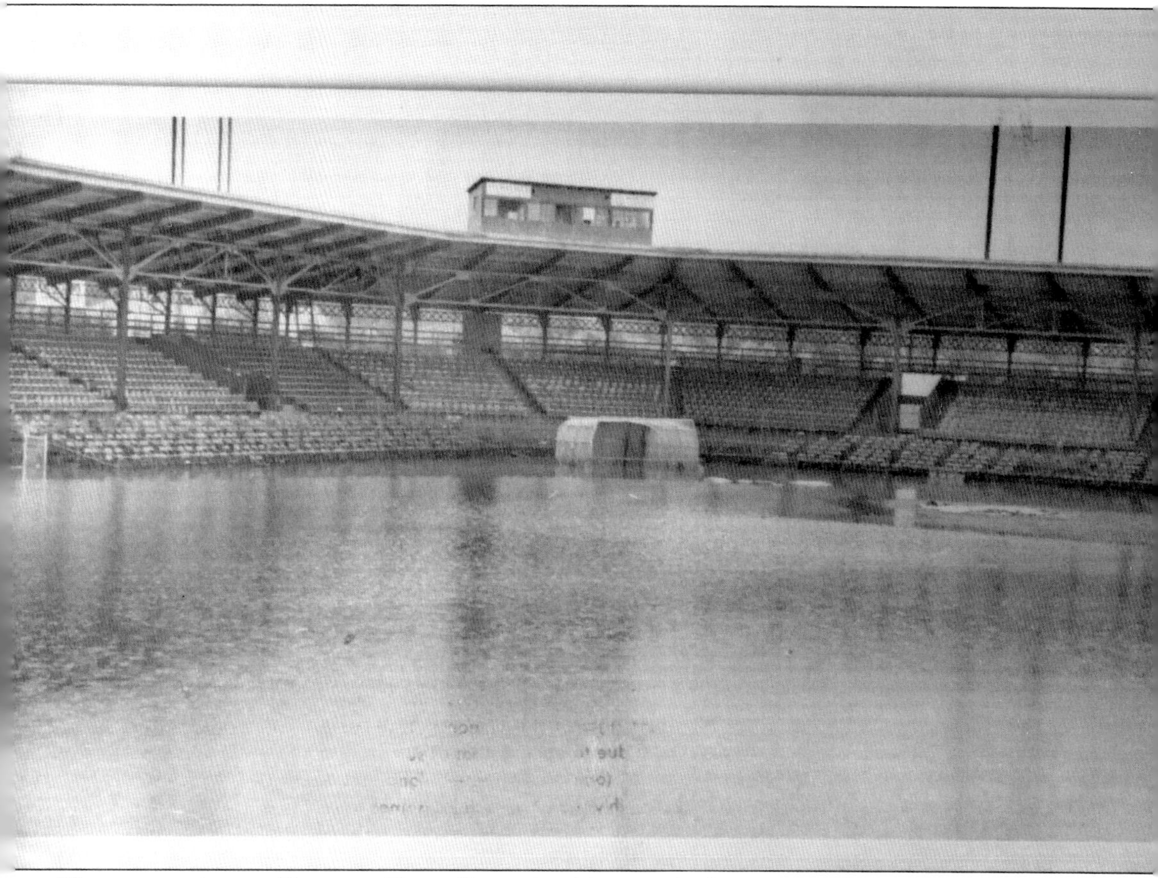

Hurricane Agnes, Bowman Field (June 21–23, 1972). Once again the uptown ballpark was ravaged by flooding—this time by torrential downpours spawned by Hurricane Agnes. This view of flooded Bowman Field, looking inward from the right center field scoreboard area, was taken at the crest of the flood. Agnes caused extensive damage to the ballpark, though not on the same scale as the floods of 1936 and 1946. The water played havoc with the New York-Penn League season, forcing Williamsport and other clubs to open the season late. The Williamsport Billsox did not play their home opener until July 10, and the season attendance mark of 19,038 was the lowest achieved in this century. One casualty of the flood was the scheduled historic debut of professional baseball's first female umpire, Bernice Gera, at Bowman Field. She later umpired the Auburn-Geneva game and promptly quit after one game. (*GRIT*.)

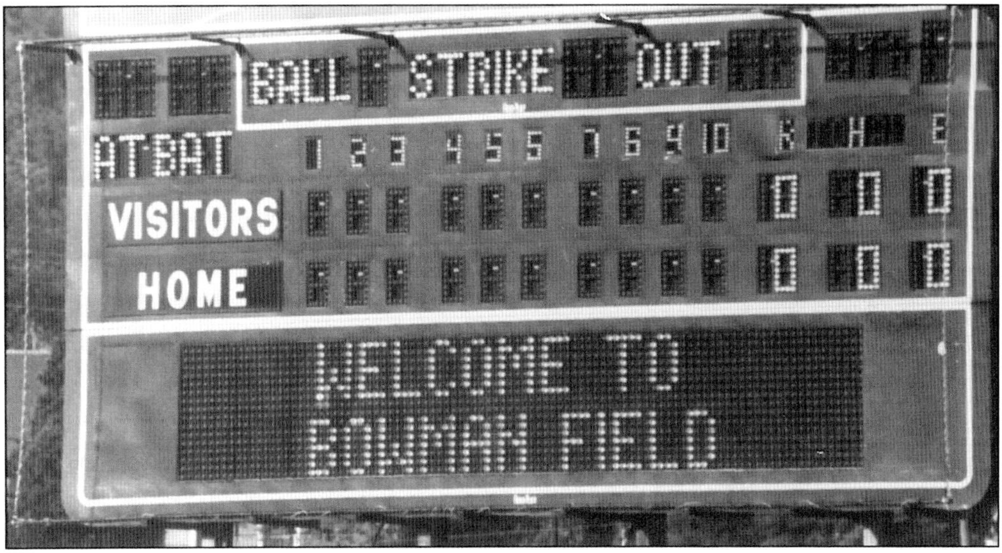

Bowman Field Scoreboard Greeting. The Miller Scoreboard electronic message board has been a familiar sight to fans attending games in recent years. The scoreboard once graced Buffalo's old War Memorial Stadium before it was dismantled and shipped to Williamsport's Bowman Field. It now has become a ballpark fixture. The protective net covering the face of the scoreboard helped to minimize damage from the impact of tape-measure home runs. (*GRIT*.)

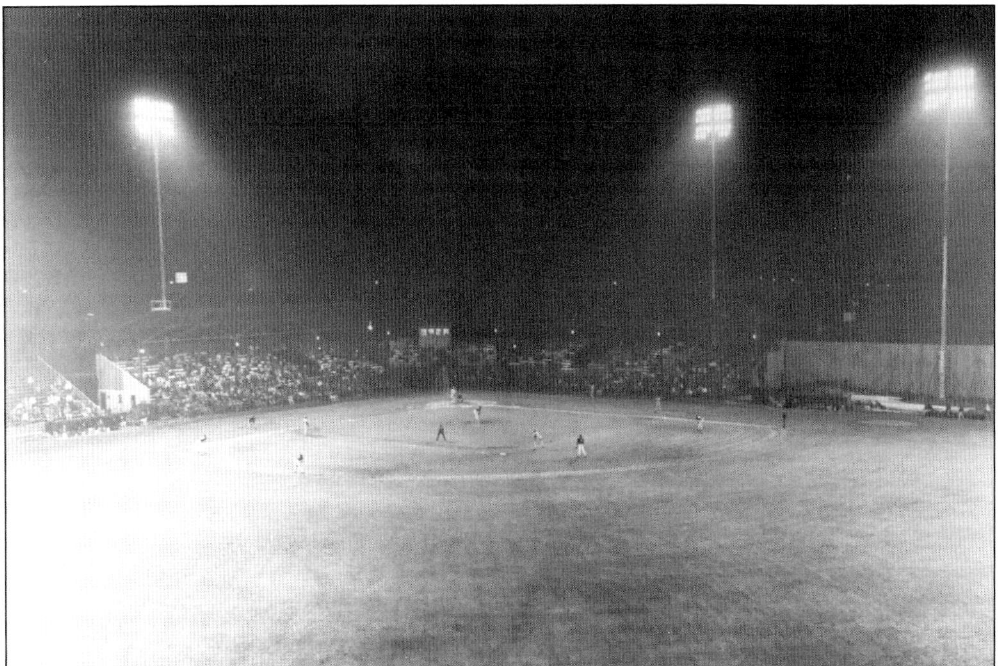

Bowman under the Lights. A homage to D. Vincent Smith's well-known July 4, 1930 panorama of Bowman Field, this photograph of a more recent night game completes the circle, linking the past and present eras of minor-league baseball in Williamsport. Hopefully, scenes such as this one will endure into the next century. (*WS-G*.)

Two

Players, Teams, and Managers

Over the passing decades, a signboard located at the West Fourth Street entrance to Williamsport's Memorial Park and Bowman Field has greeted baseball fans entering the environs. Each season it has identified Williamsport's current parent club and league affiliation—standing as a humble tribute to all the great players, teams, and managers who made Williamsport their home, if only for a fleeting summer. During those rare years when Williamsport did not have baseball and the ballpark was dormant, the sign's presence held out the promise of a future season for local fans.

From the late 1940s to the early 1960s one of the most memorable signs to grace the park entrance boldly proclaimed: "Bowman Field: Gateway to the Majors." This statement was no exaggeration. Over the past century nearly 400 former Williamsport players graduated to the ranks of the Major Leagues. The list spans the 19th century (including such greats as Harry Stovey and John Montgomery Ward) up to the current Williamsport franchise (Jeremi Gonzalez and Kerry Wood) of the short-season Class A New York-Penn League. Hall of Famers Jim Bunning and Nolan Ryan (soon to be elected) had brief stays in Williamsport before achieving big league stardom. Many well-known players toiled here in the minors before establishing solid careers in the majors, including Dale Long, Bill Nicholson, Bill Mazeroski, Curt Simmons, Danny Cater, Dick Allen, Ron Swoboda, Ray Culp, Jim Rice, Larry Anderson, and Tino Martinez. Managers Harry Hinchman, Mike McNally, Glen Killinger, Spence Abbott, "School Boy" Rowe, Frank Lucchesi, and Bill Virdon passed through town on the way up (or down) the minor-league managerial chain.

Fittingly, several local players, plucked off the sandlot, lived out their dream of playing as a professional ballplayer before the hometown fans. Among the more notable former Williamsport Grays were city natives Don Manno (Boston Braves), Dick Welteroth (Washington Senators), and Bill Witmer. Other ex-Williamsport Grays and Tigers players, including A. Rankin Johnson Jr. (Philadelphia A's), Dewey Waugh, and Norm Scott, made the city their permanent home after their respective professional playing days were over.

Championship seasons have been few and far between for Williamsport fans. Still, this has not dampened fans' support for minor-league baseball and the teams that represented the city. The bond between the city and its adopted players and managers remains strong. No doubt, the names of more former Williamsport ballplayers will be added to the major-league encyclopedia in coming years.

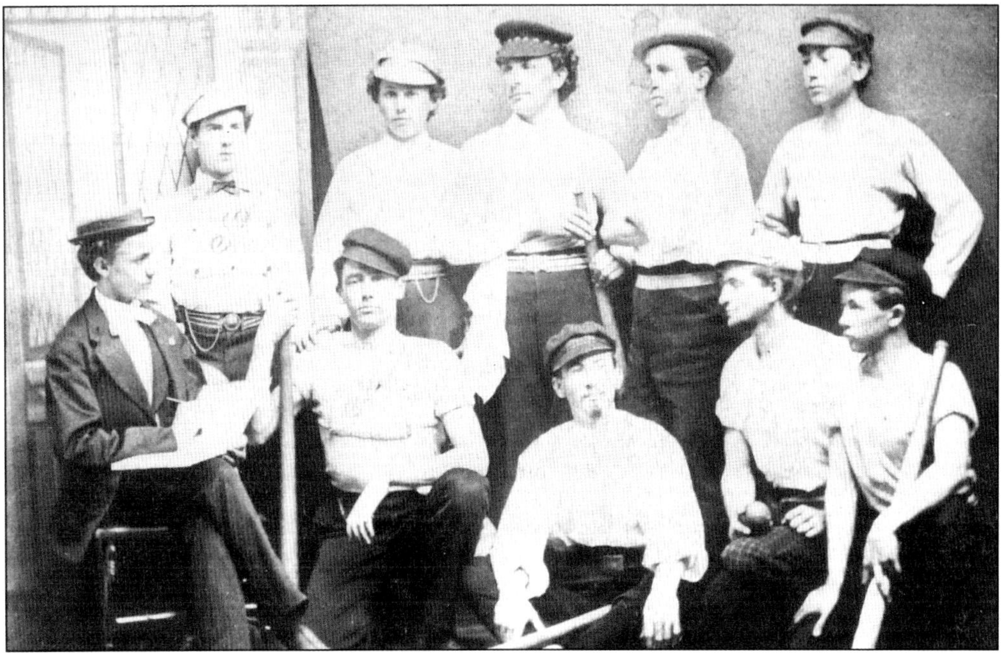

EARLY WILLIAMSPORT BASEBALL TEAM (1860s). Though not the storied Williamsport Athletic [Baseball] Club, this photograph of a local amateur team from the era constitutes the earliest-known image pertaining to baseball in Williamsport. The young gentleman in the suit might have been a team manager or club secretary. Many 19th-century teams functioned as fraternal organizations or gentlemen's clubs. (Photograph by E. Stuart, LCHS.)

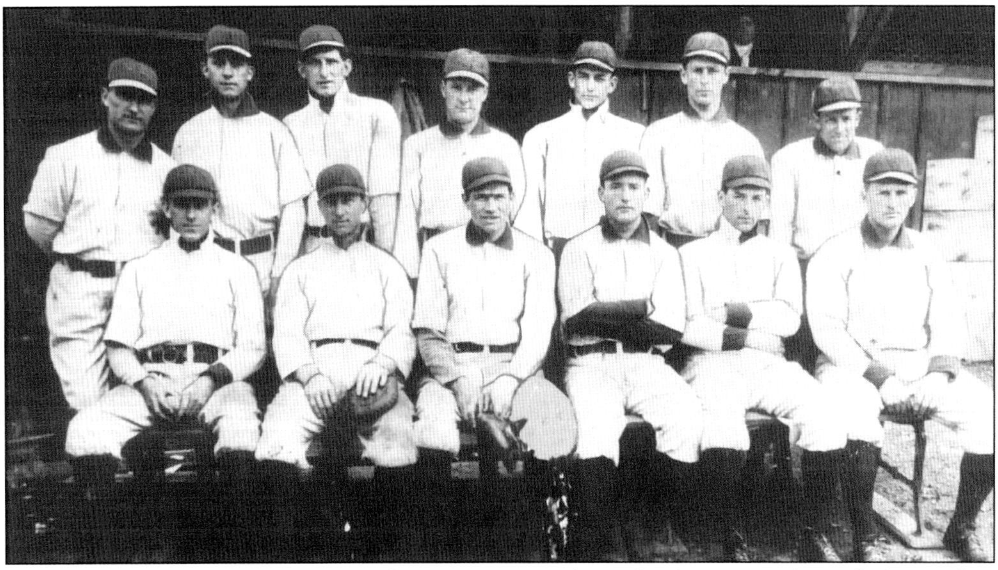

WILLIAMSPORT MILLIONAIRES, TRI-STATE LEAGUE (1906). As a member of the outlaw professional Tri-State League in 1906, Williamsport finished in second place behind the York White Roses. The team, managed by Harry Wolverton and Jimmy Sebring (player-managers), included several players who had either played in the big leagues (Sebring and Bob Unglaub), or were destined for the Majors. Among the notable players were catcher Charles "Gabby" Street, pitcher Rube Bressler, and shortstop Harry "Rabbit" Gleason. (*GRIT*.)

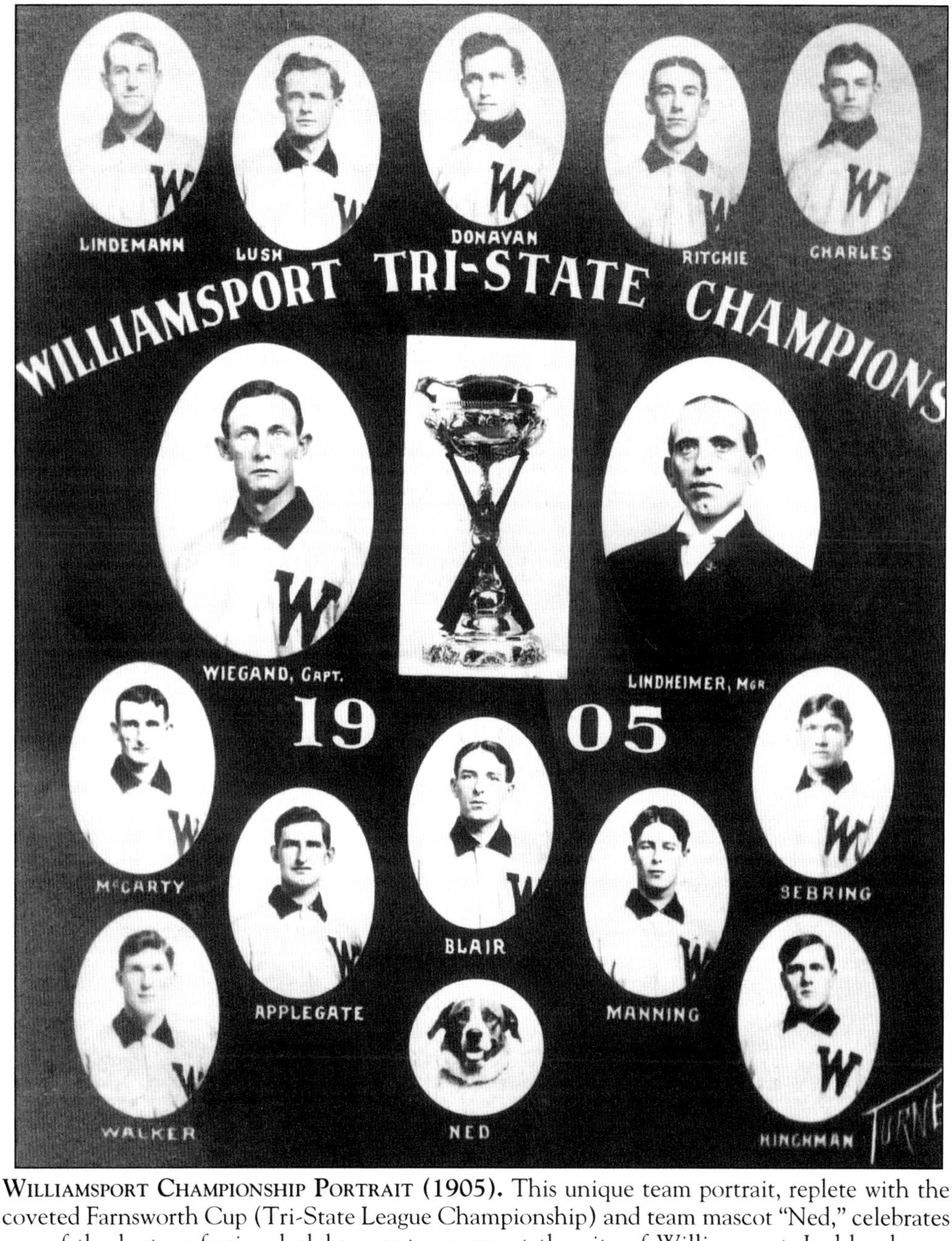

Williamsport Championship Portrait (1905). This unique team portrait, replete with the coveted Farnsworth Cup (Tri-State League Championship) and team mascot "Ned," celebrates one of the best professional clubs ever to represent the city of Williamsport. Led by slugger Jimmy Sebring (acquired from the Cincinnati Red Stockings), Williamsport overtook York and the Johnstown Johnnies in one of the most exciting pennant races witnessed by local fans during the era. The Millionaires were paced by the hard-hitting trio of Sebring (.329), Johnny Lush (.326), and Bill Hinchman (.283), and pitchers Lou Ritchie (24-9), Rube Manning (17-11), and Lush (16-13). The team also included Williamsport's own native son, Fred "Snitz" Applegate. Manager Max Lindheimer and the players were the recipients of a raucous parade and pennant celebration attended by 8,000 spectators at Athletic Park. Williamsport's famous Repasz Band led the procession to the ballpark. (*GRIT*.)

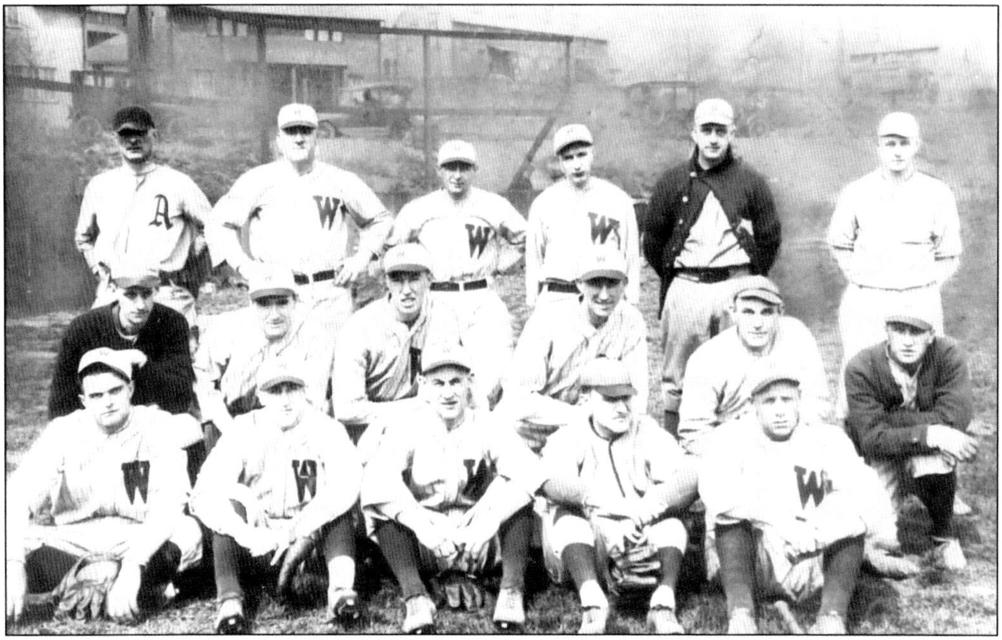

WILLIAMSPORT BILLIES (1923). This is a rare team photograph of the 1923 "Billies" prior to an early season workout at the old high school field. Managed by Harry Hinchman, the "Portboys" captured the New York Pennsylvania League pennant in their inaugural campaign. Notable team members included George "Mule" Haas (later a member of the Philadelphia A's), Dudley Foulk, Walter French, and city natives Arnold "Bucky" Poole and "Punch" Miller. (*GRIT.*)

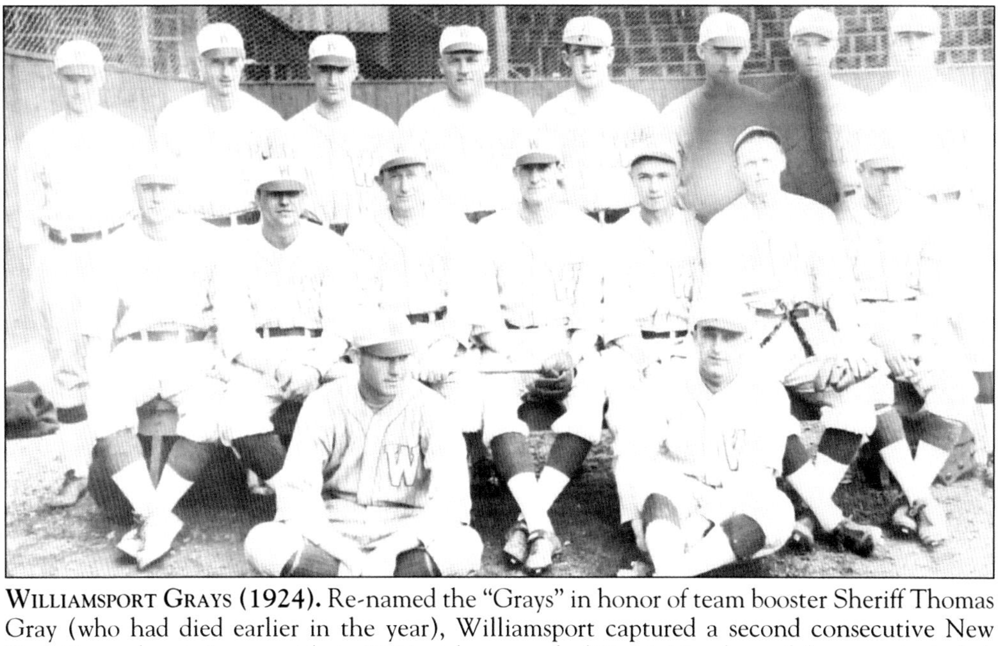

WILLIAMSPORT GRAYS (1924). Re-named the "Grays" in honor of team booster Sheriff Thomas Gray (who had died earlier in the year), Williamsport captured a second consecutive New York-Pennsylvania League title in 1924 with a record of 87-46. Members of the team included, from left to right: (front row) Burns and Ringwood; (seated) Davis, Poole, Boland, Fulweiler, Dorman, Hunnefield, and Johnson; (standing) Hughes, Grassck, Leavitt, Manager Hinchman, Mahady, Cooper, Demerest, and an unknown player. (*GRIT.*)

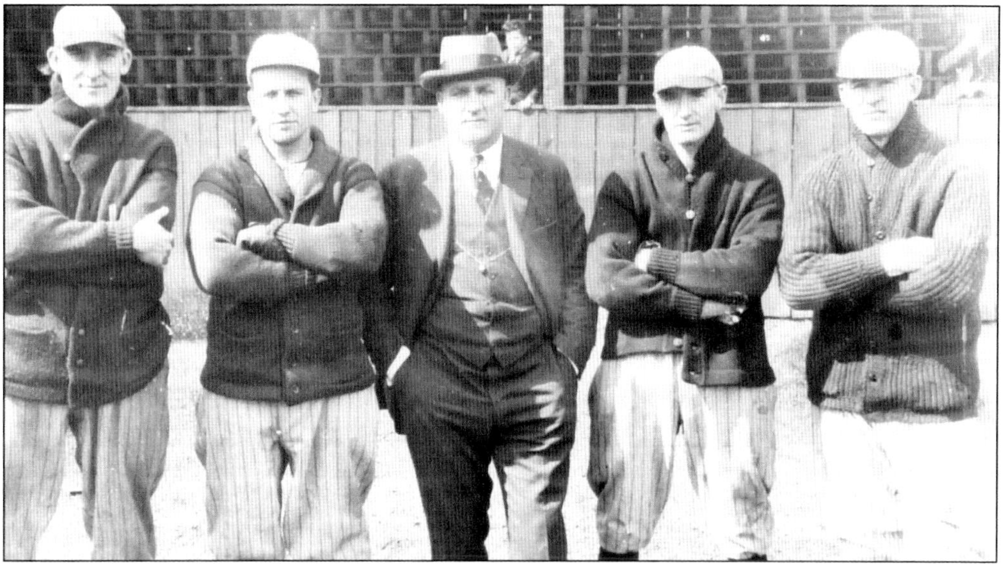

Manager Harry Hinchman (1924). Wearing his best suit, manager Hinchman poses with four members of the 1924 Grays at the Williamsport High School Athletic Field. Upon the recommendation of his brother, Bill Hinchman, chief scout for the Pittsburgh Pirates, Hinchman took the helm of the Williamsport club. Harry Hinchman had played briefly for the Cleveland Indians before embarking on a lengthy minor-league managerial career with stints in the American Association, Virginia, Southern, and Blue Grass Leagues. (*GRIT*.)

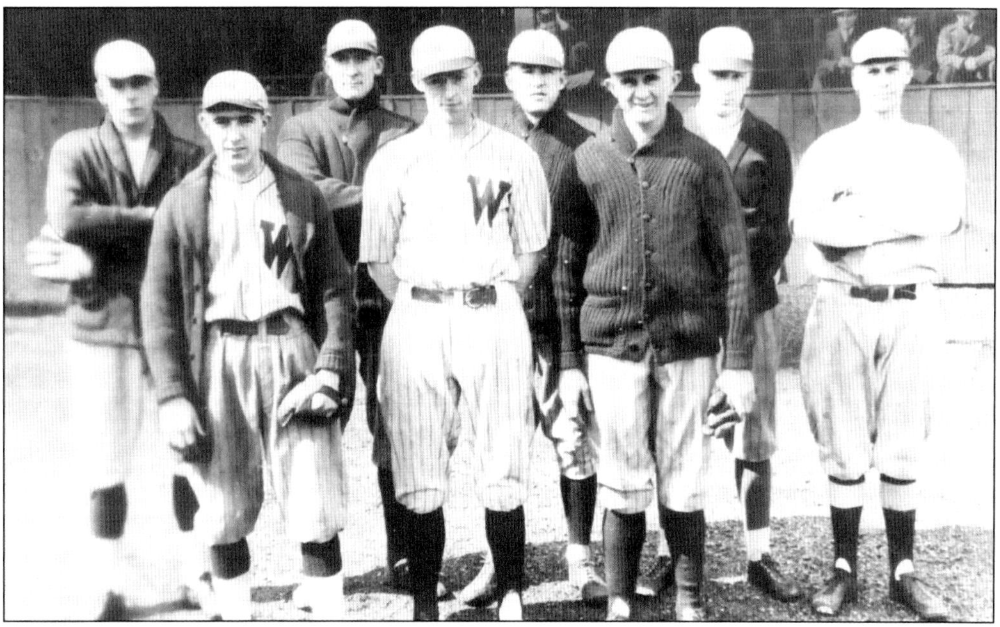

Pitchers Trying for Berth on Hinchman's Squad (April 20, 1924). These stalwart Grays hurlers were assembled for a group portrait prior to the opening of the 1924 season. Several contributed to Williamsport's pennant-winning season. Pictured here from left to right are Lefty Hoffman, Henry Huffman, Harold Fulweiler, Harry Holsclaw, Jim Mahady, ? Stammerman, ? Reed, and ? Frey. Henry Hoffman compiled a record of 18-9 and Holsclaw went 16-11 to pace the Billtowners that year. (*GRIT*.)

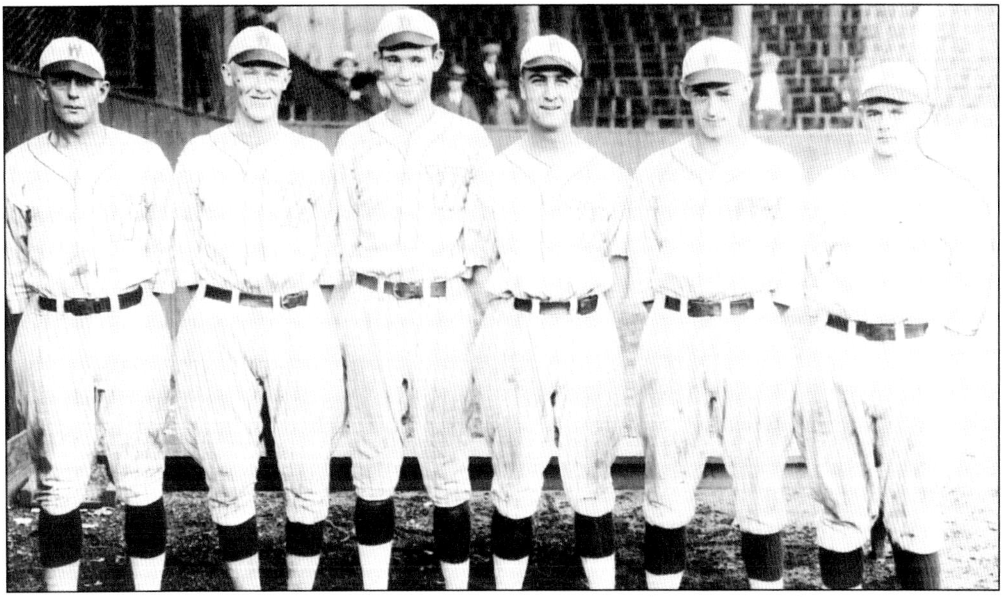

CLUB'S SEXTET OF YOUTHFUL PITCHERS (SEPTEMBER 14, 1924). Several pitching acquisitions by the Williamsport Grays' club directors helped the team during the 1924 pennant stretch. None was more important than young Carlton Demarest (third from right), who compiled a sterling 18-6 record for the Grays that year. His mound mates included, from left to right, Sammy Jones, Jack Matthews, Bobby Burns, Harry Holsclaw, and Henry "Lefty" Hoffman. (*GRIT*.)

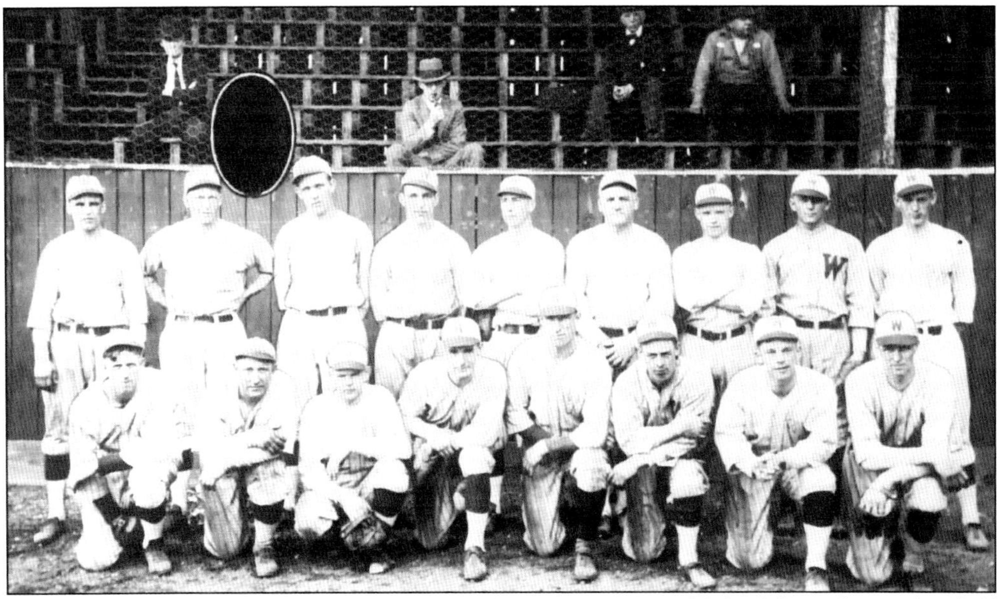

1925 WILLIAMSPORT GRAYS (MAY 2, 1925). The 1925 Grays established their place in baseball history when they finished the regular season in a first-place tie with York, the first ever in organized baseball. However, the locals lost a heart-wrenching five-game playoff series to the White Roses. Members of that squad included Ted Donovan (first person, kneeling on left), who hit a sizzling .349 for the season, and pitcher Walter Tauscher (standing, third from left), a 19-game winner that year. (*GRIT*.)

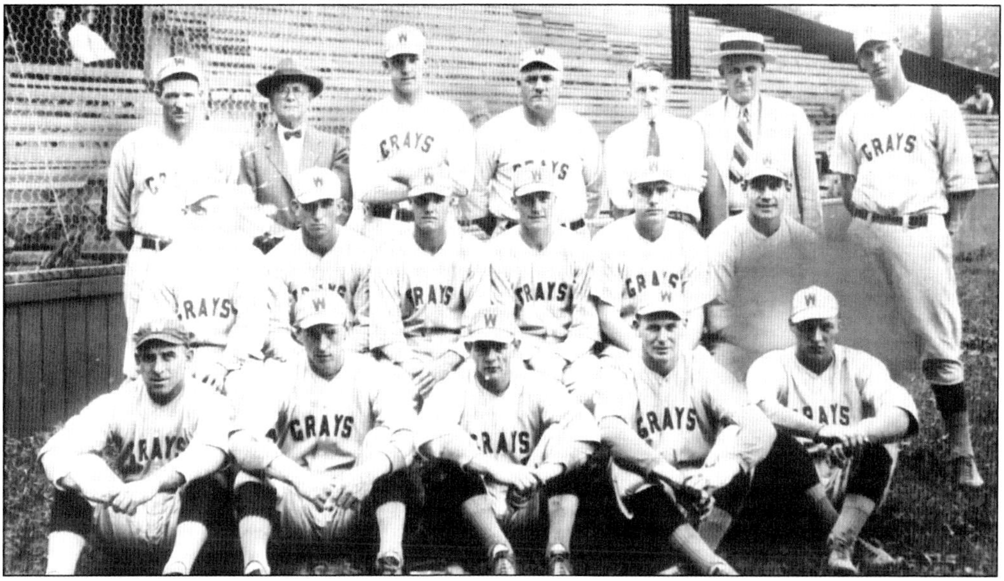

1926 Grays Fight for League Honors (August 15, 1926). This was one of the first team portraits taken at new Memorial (Bowman) Field in 1926. The 1926 Grays, a poor hitting club, finished the season at 69-65, 15 games behind the pennant-winning York team. Among the notables pictured here are slugger Adam Comorosky (front row, last person, right) and several Grays' officials—J. Walton Bowman, Manager Hinchman, Edgar Maitland, and Joseph Mosser—in the back row. (*GRIT.*)

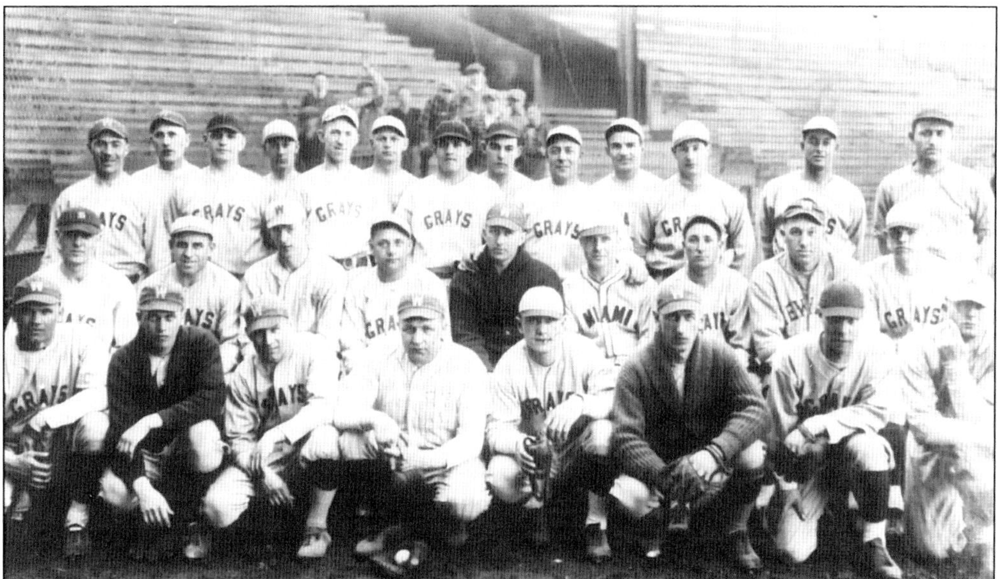

1927 Williamsport Grays (April 17, 1927). The 1927 Grays, managed by George J. Burns (standing, fifth person from right), finished in the cellar of the New York-Pennsylvania League with a dismal 56-80 record. Pittsburgh's termination of its working agreement with Williamsport contributed greatly to the local team's demise. Highlights of the season included catcher Art Mueller (seated, fourth from left) batting .330, and Phil Voyles (kneeling, fourth from right) hitting at a .312 clip. Player-manager Burns led the team in stolen bases with 18. (*GRIT.*)

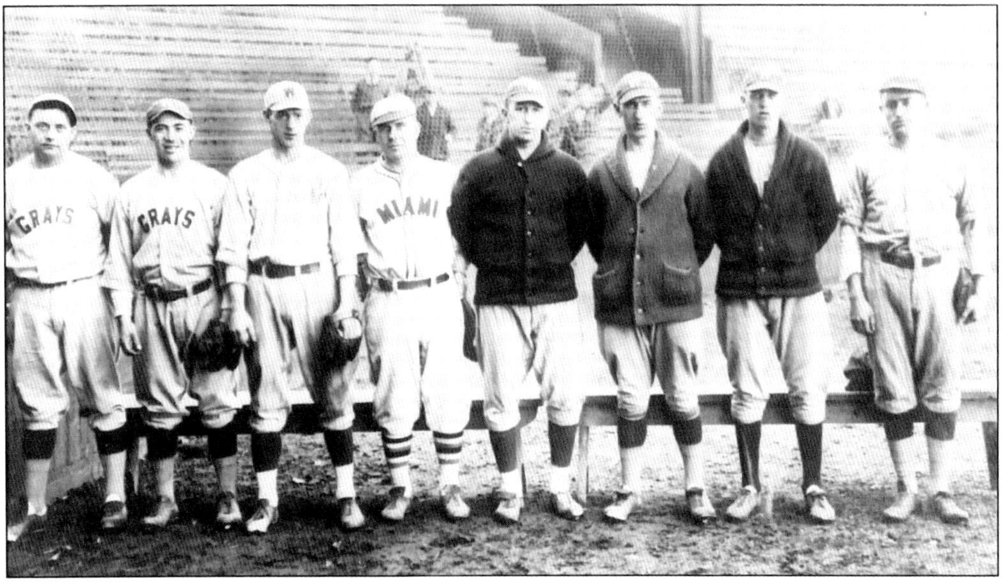

PITCHING STAFF (APRIL 17, 1927). Among the members of the 1927 Grays' pitching staff who suffered through a long draining season were, from left to right, Knowlton, Bustina, Holsclaw, Lynch, Kinnere, Minosky, Grove, and Gallegos. Bill Knowlton was the Grays' top hurler that year, compiling a respectable 13-10 record. Pitcher "King" Lehr, not included in this picture, suffered a hard luck 13-20 record despite tossing a team-high 276 innings. (*GRIT.*)

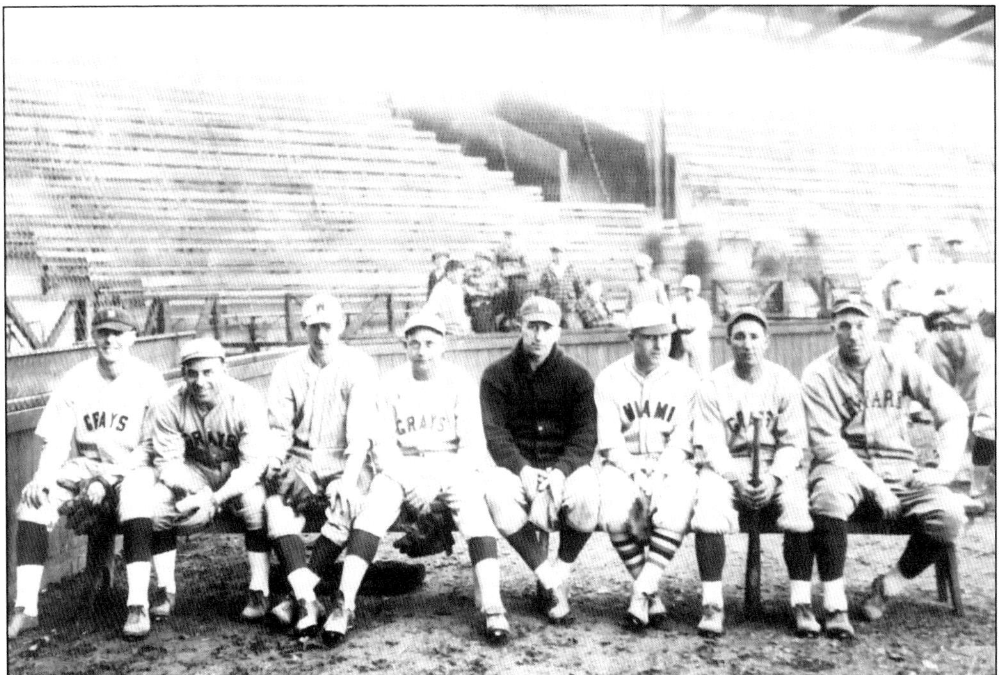

FIGURES FAMILIAR TO WILLIAMSPORT FANS (APRIL 24, 1927). These returning veterans from the 1926 team, shown here from left to right prior to opening day of the 1927 season, are as follows: Tapson, shortstop; Kelley, second base; pitchers Holsclaw, Knowlton, Kinnere, Lynch, and Hurley; and catcher Mueller. (*GRIT.*)

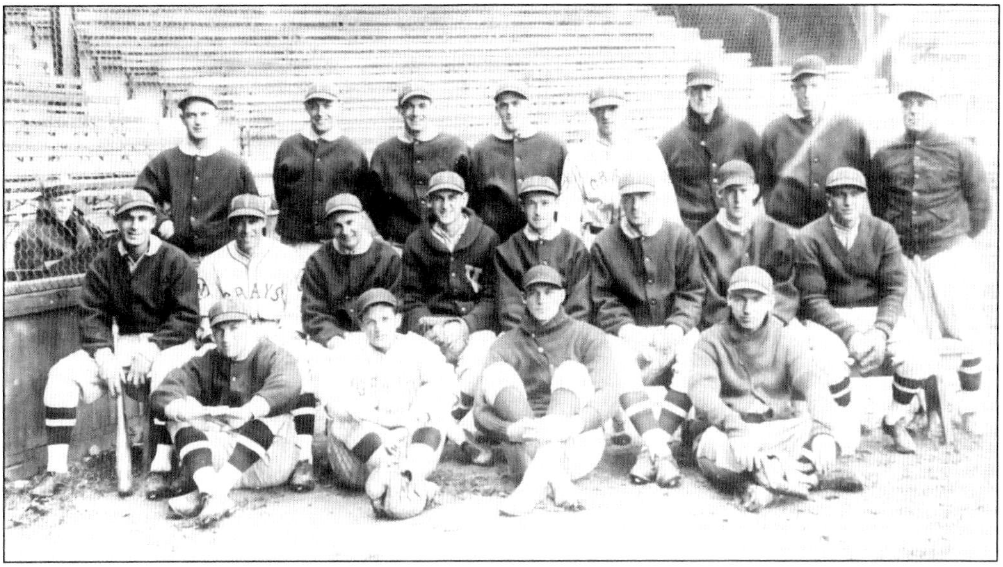

1928 Williamsport Grays. The Grays suffered another humbling season, finishing 69-71. Player-manager George Burns, one of the teams leading hitters (.332), resigned in August, and Baxter Jordan, the league leader in triples (20) that year, was recalled by the New York Giants. Both departures hurt the team. Team members included the following, from left to right: (front row) Ernst, Steech, Stone, and Farquhar; (middle row) Blessing, McDonnell, Capes, Jordan, Dorman, Menard, Doyle, and Poole; (back row) Voyles, Tapson, Lehr, Wilson, Holsclaw, Fulweiler, Porter, and Manager Burns. (*GRIT*.)

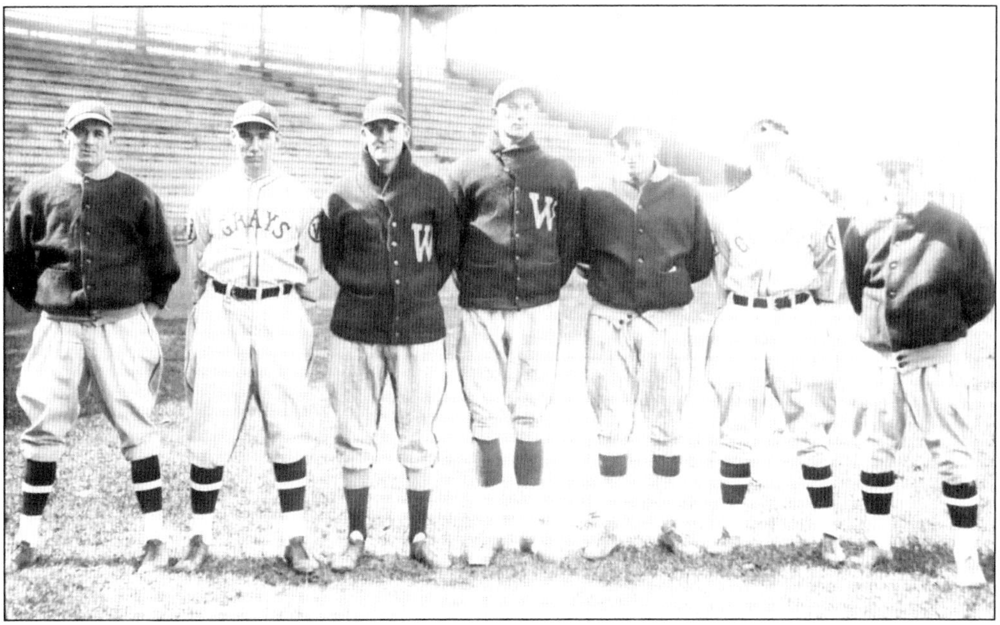

Seven Pitchers Called for Duty (April 29, 1928). The heart of the Grays' 1928 pitching rotation assembled on a blustery spring morning for this photo opportunity. Note the classic wool cardigan sweaters donned by, from left to right, Norm "King" Lehr, Farquhar, Fulweiler, Stone, Porter, Holsclaw, and McDonnell. Lehr sported a 13-8 record in 1928 and veteran Harry Holsclaw, pitching his last season in Williamsport, led the Grays in strikeouts with 89. (*GRIT*.)

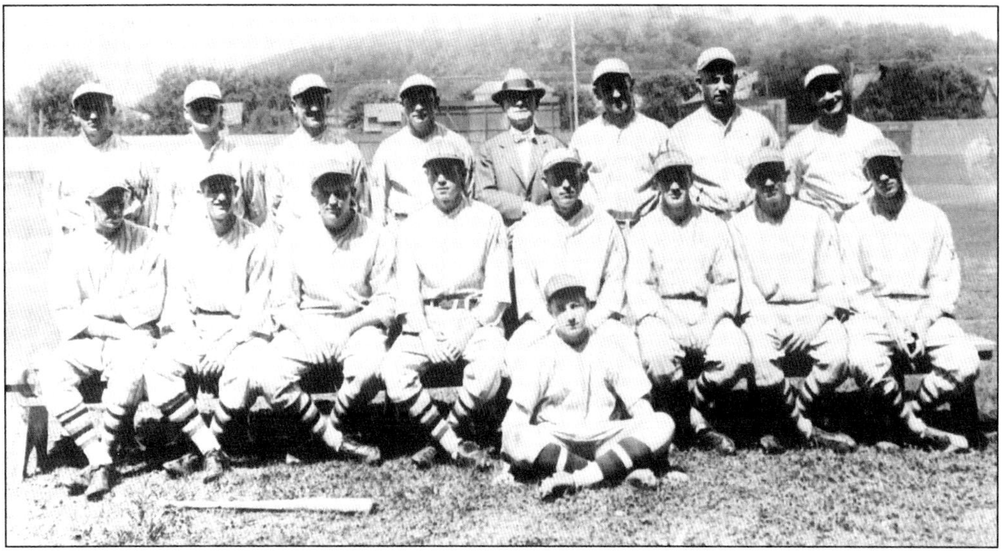

1929 WILLIAMSPORT GRAYS. The 1929 Grays, pictured here with club president J. Walton Bowman (center, back row), enjoyed their best season since 1925—finishing 79-60, four games behind the champion Binghamton Triplets. Williamsport's Cy Anderson captured the league batting crown by hitting a sizzling .382, and the Grays' pitching staff compiled a string of 62 scoreless innings and four consecutive shutouts during one stretch of the season. (*GRIT.*)

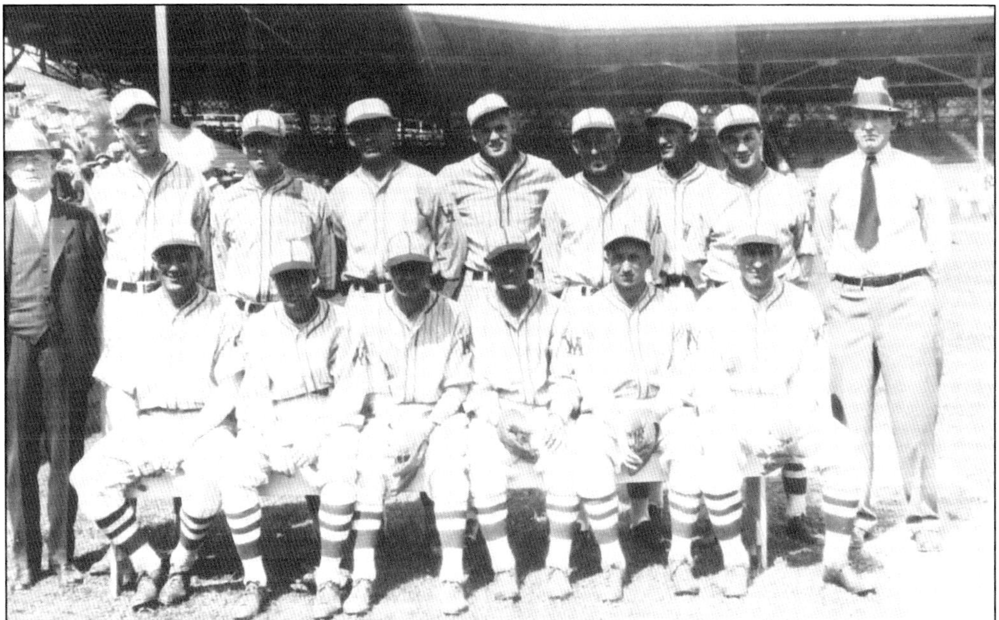

1930 WILLIAMSPORT GRAYS. Player-manager Glenn Killinger guided the team to a respectable third place finish, 74-65, five games behind Wilkes-Barre. He also was the Grays' leading hitter that season (.342). Pictured from left to right are the following: (seated) Hollis McLaughlin, ? Vachal, Wally Novak, ? Shatzer, ? Morgan, and ? Killinger; (standing) J. Walton Bowman, Jim Lyle, ? Brunier, ? Johnson, ? Carroll, Cy Anderson, Carr Smith, Jack Ernst, and J. Roy Clunk. Jack Ernst, who hit .290 for the year, quarterbacked the NFL's Frankford Yellow Jackets in the fall of 1930. (*GRIT.*)

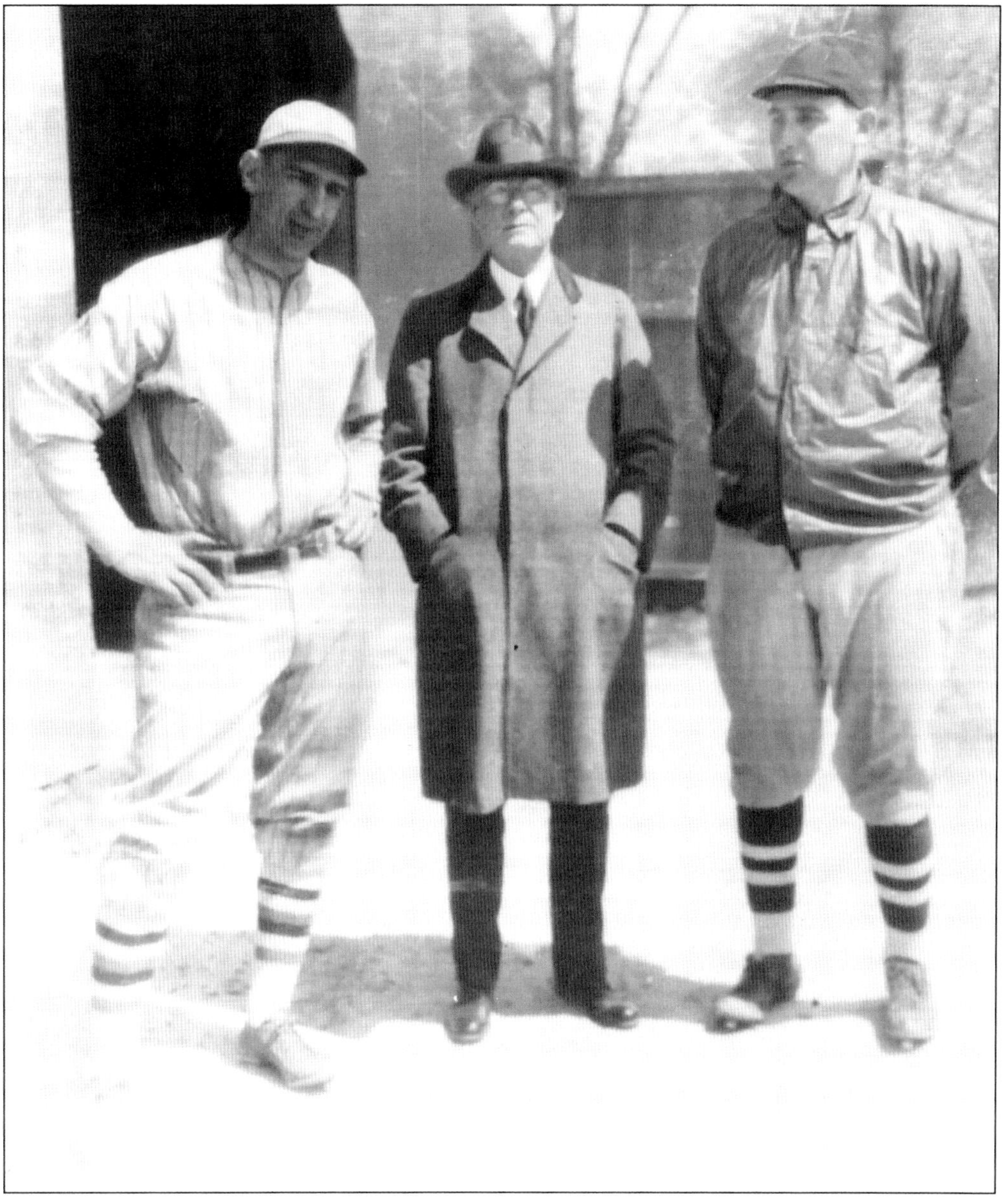

MANAGER GLENN KILLINGER, J. WALTON BOWMAN, AND J. ROY CLUNK (APRIL 13, 1930). The Grays' top brass is pictured here prior to a spring workout at Bowman Field in early April. J. Walton Bowman and his brother Frank had been longtime supporters of professional baseball in Williamsport. The Bowman family fortune, built on lumber manufacturing, banking, and other commercial endeavors, contributed greatly to the financial underpinning of the Grays. Bowman spearheaded the fund-raising campaign to construct the stadium that bears his name. J. Roy Clunk, a former minor leaguer and organizer of local semi-professional teams, made the transition to the Grays' front office in 1930 and became one of the longest serving business managers in Williamsport franchise history, lasting well into the 1950s. Glenn Killinger, a former Penn State football All-American, had played for the Williamsport Grays in 1925 and returned as a player-manager in 1929. The hard-nosed veteran inspired his younger teammates with his energy, discipline, and professional demeanor. (*GRIT*.)

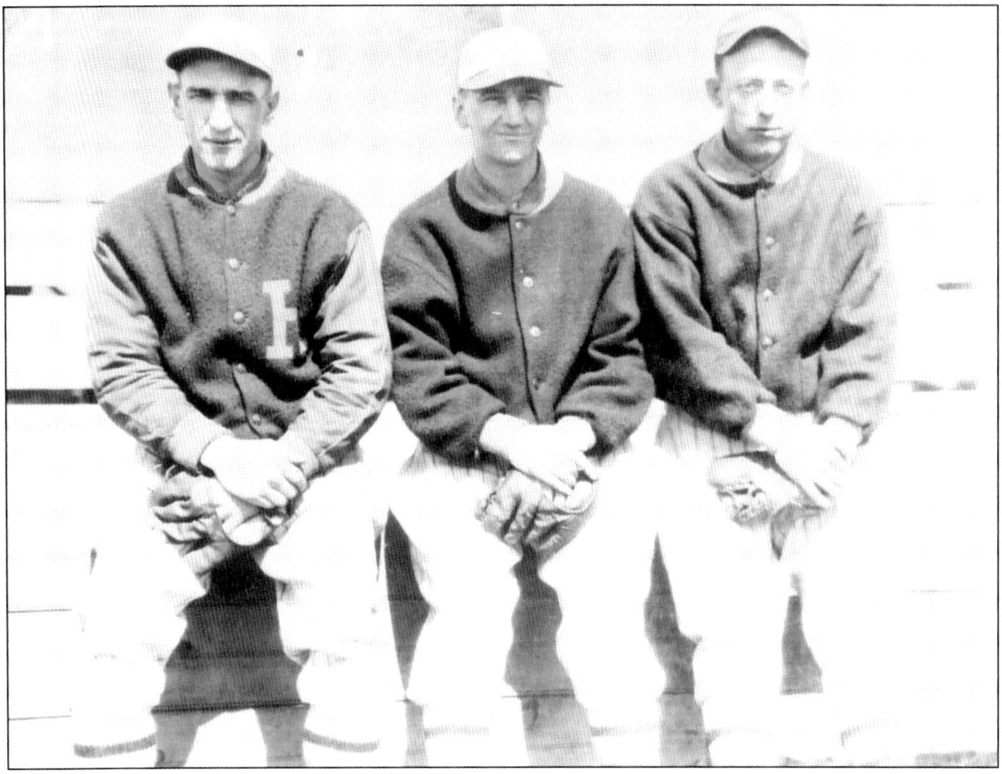

Heart of the early 1930s Grays' Infield. From left to right are player-manager Glenn Killinger, Wally Novak, and Cy Anderson. In addition to their fine fielding the trio also compiled impressive offensive statistics. Killinger and Anderson were consistent .300 hitters and garnered New York-Pennsylvania League All-Star honors. (*GRIT*.)

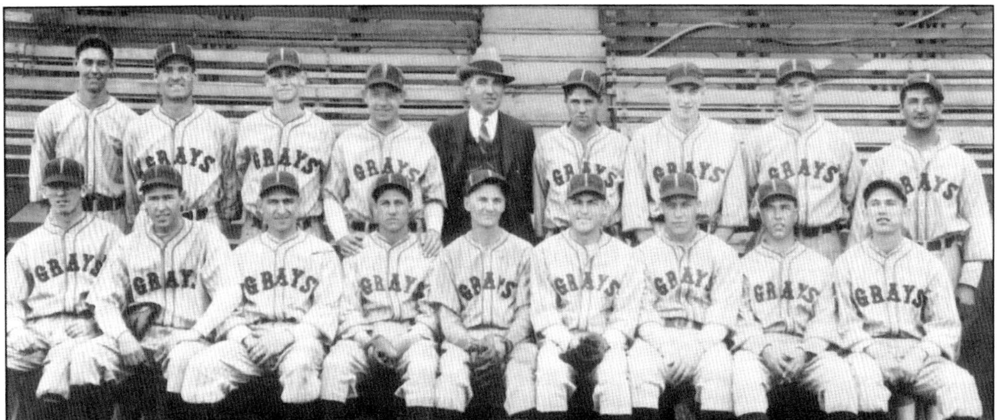

1931 Williamsport Grays. Though contending for much of the season, the team faltered in August and ended up finishing in third place with a record of 76-64. Third baseman Bucky Walters (later a pitcher in the Major Leagues) paced the club in batting with a .316 average. Dick Tangeman was voted the Grays' MVP in 1931. Members of the 1931 team included the following, from left to right: (front row) Parkes, Brown, Killinger, Tangeman, Novak, Mauney, Prichard, C. Brannon, and Gwathney; (back row) White, Wilson, R. Brannon, an unidentified player, J. Roy Clunk, Walters, Johnson, and Mike "Dirty Neck" Martineck. (*GRIT*.)

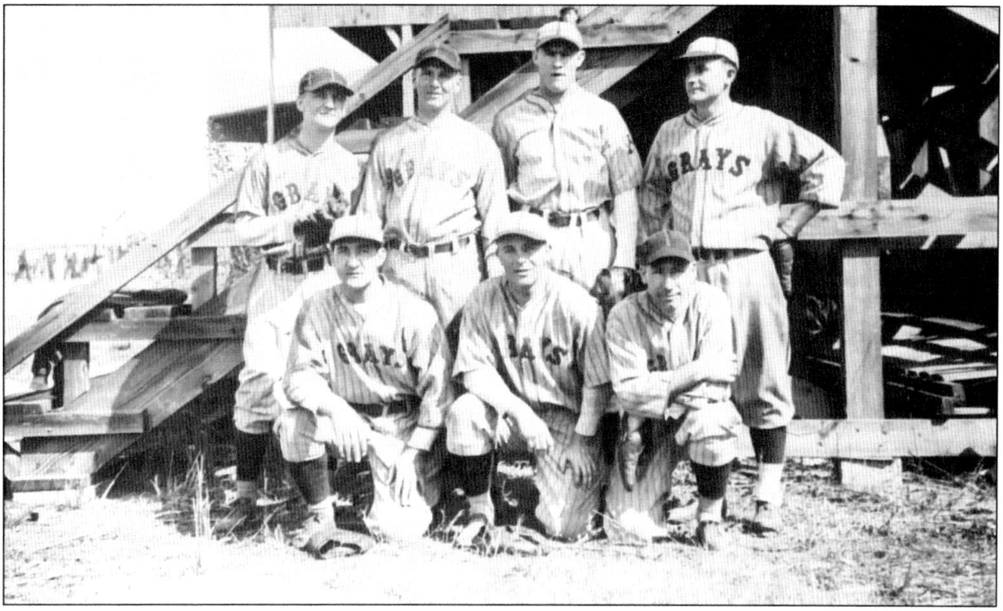

GRAYS' PRESEASON WORKOUT (1932). Unidentified members of the 1932 Grays pose near the bleachers during a brief respite from practice. Grueling preseason practices, often held in inclement spring weather, acclimated the team to the long season ahead. (*GRIT*.)

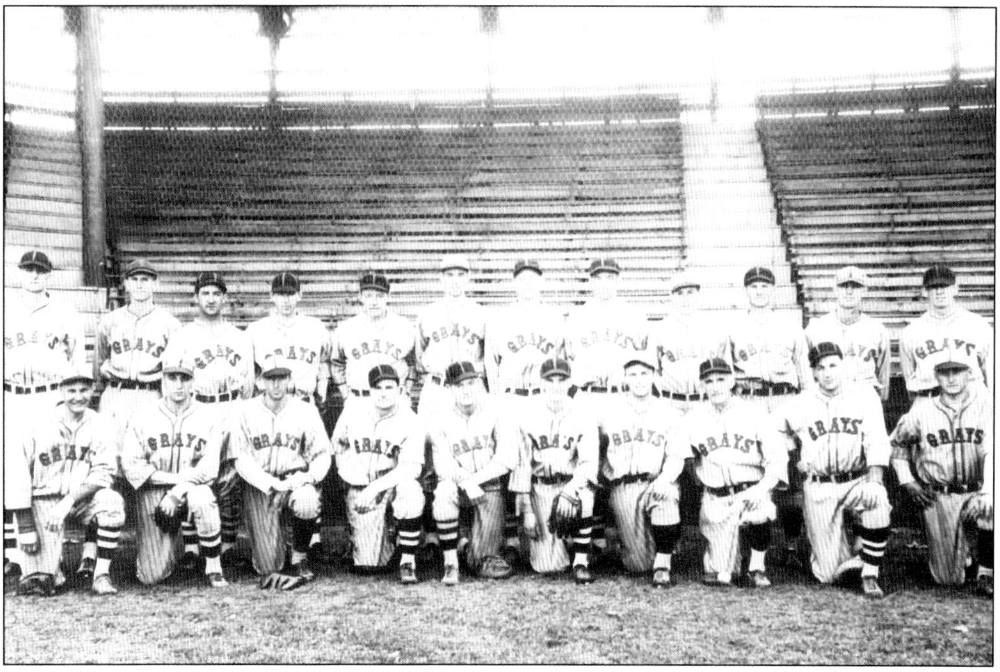

1932 WILLIAMSPORT GRAYS. The 1932 Grays experienced turmoil on the field and economic woes at the gate during the throes of the Great Depression. Manager Herb Moran (front row, third person from right) was fired in mid-May and his successor, Harry Hinchman, failed to reverse the team's lackluster play. Glenn Killinger finished out the season with Williamsport after the Allentown franchise in the old Eastern League folded. The Grays ended up in seventh place with a record of 63-76. (*GRIT*.)

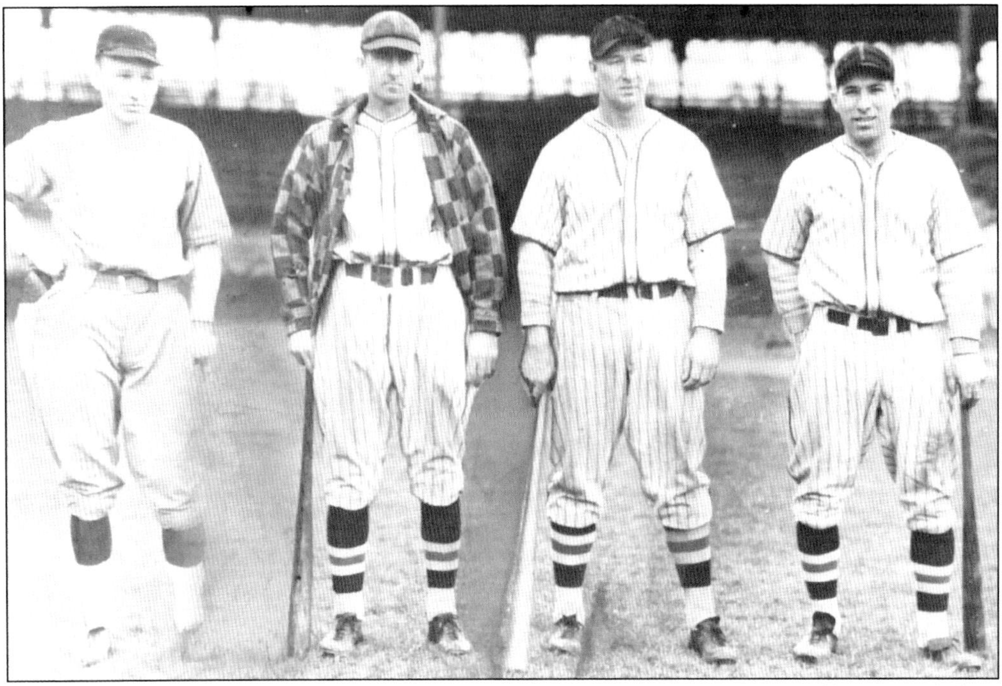

Grays' Infield (April 10, 1932). Members of the Williamsport Grays' infield pose with bats before the start of the 1932 baseball campaign. (*GRIT.*)

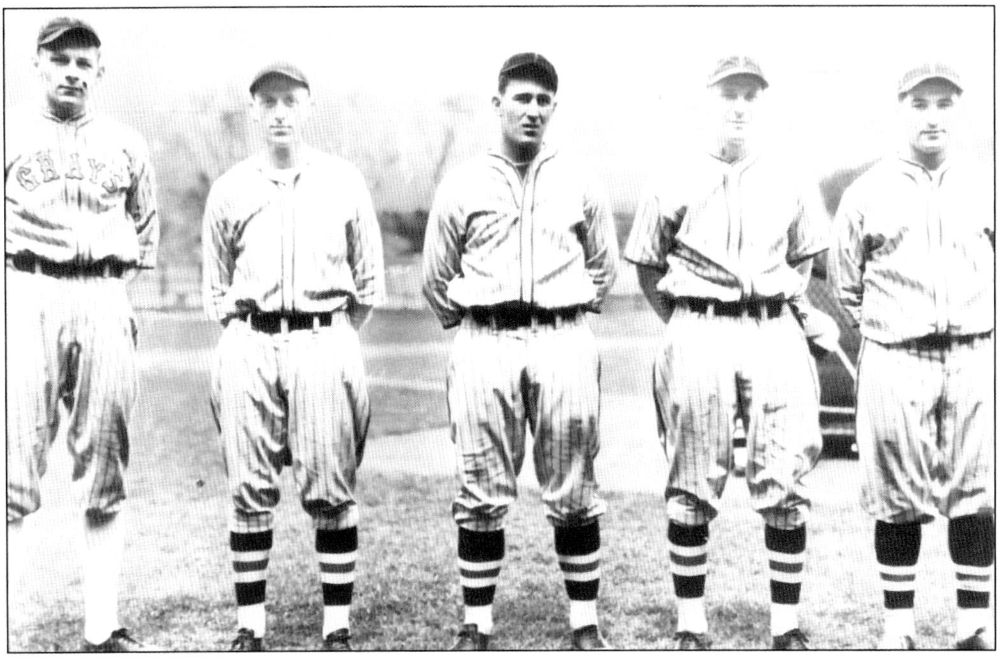

Grays' Pitching Staff (April 1932). The Grays' 1932 pitching corps poses in their new striped socks prior to opening day. The staff was paced by Chant "Red" Parkes (third person from left), who recorded 21 victories and led the New York-Pennsylvania League in innings (289) pitched. After Parkes, Charley Reddock (not pictured) tallied the next highest win total for the Grays—only six victories. (*GRIT.*)

Shortstop Bernie Snyder (1934). One of the rare surviving images from the heralded 1934 Grays' championship season is this portrait of Snyder. He and second baseman Ollie Marquart formed Williamsport's keystone combination in 1934. Snyder was also one of the heroes in the Grays' exhibition victory over the Philadelphia A's that year, driving in two runs. Paced by sluggers Horace "Red" McBride, Joe Bonowitz, and Joe Cicero, the Grays defeated the Binghamton Triplets for the 1934 New York-Pennsylvania League title. (*GRIT.*)

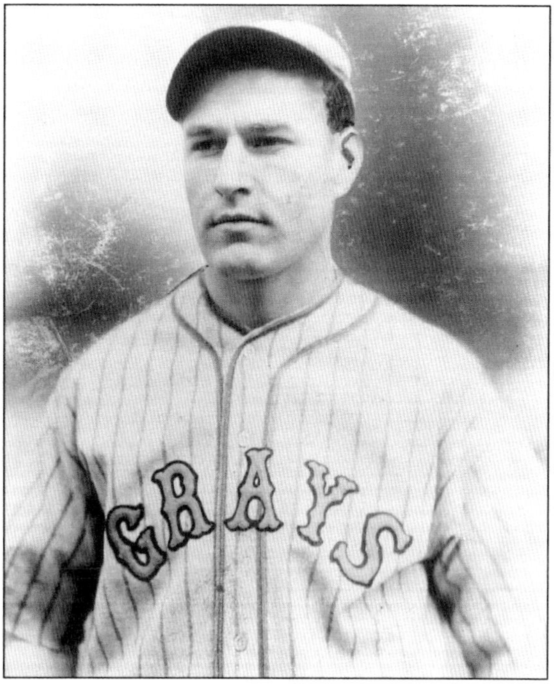

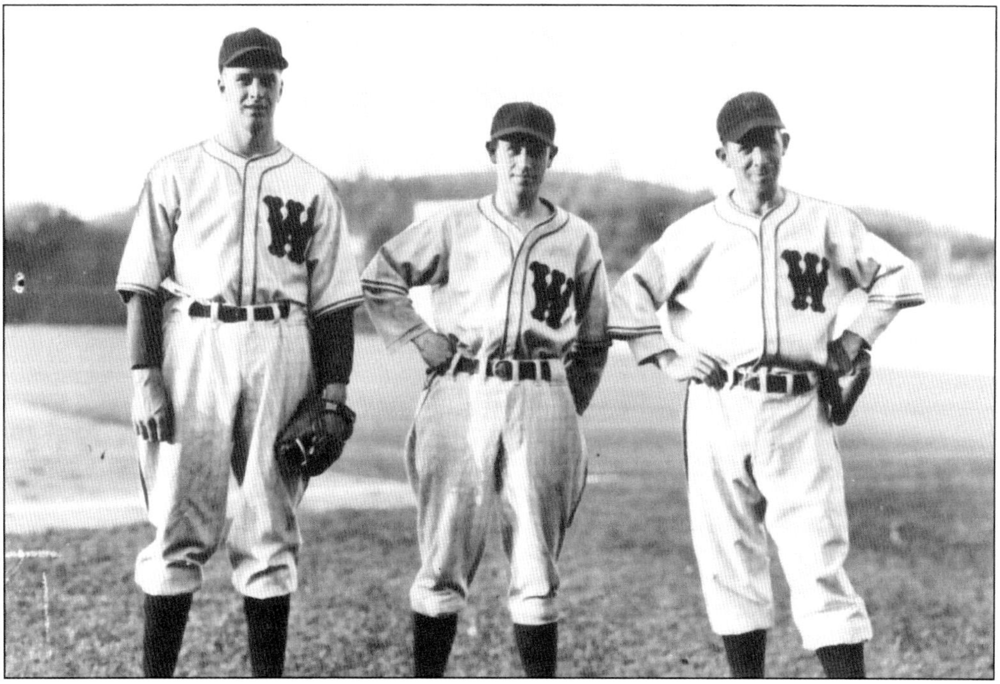

Patrolling the Outer Gardens, 1935 Williamsport Grays' Outfielders. Starting Grays outfielders ? Fisher, Tony Kubek Sr., and Fred Browning strike a confident pose prior to the start of the 1935 season. Kubek was the father of Tony Kubek Jr., the well-known New York Yankee shortstop and baseball broadcaster. One of the highlights of the 1935 season was Kubek's tape-measure grand slam home run off the top of Bowman Field's center field scoreboard that sparked Williamsport's dramatic ninth-inning victory over the Harrisburg Senators. (*GRIT.*)

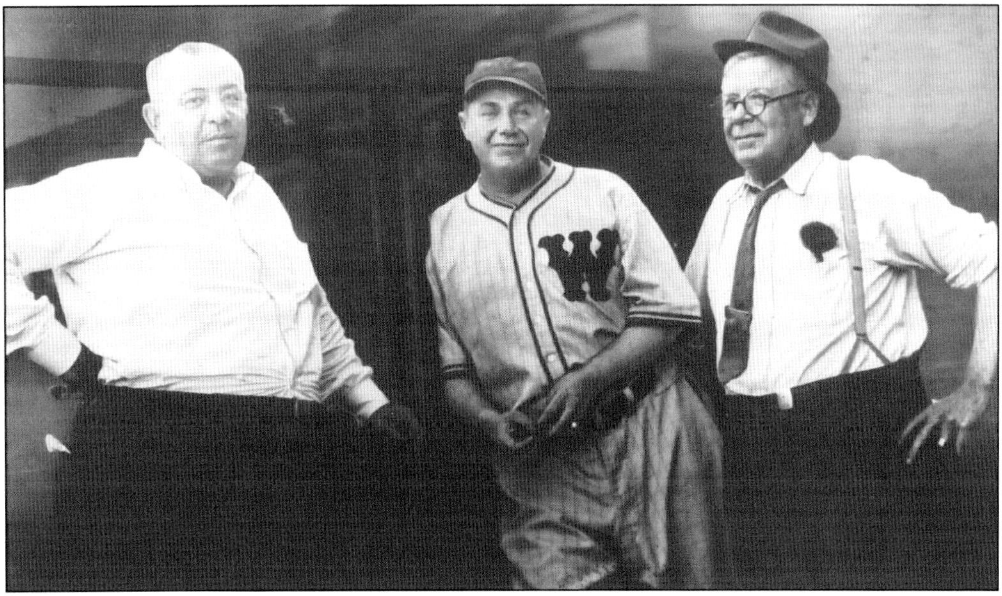

WILLIAMSPORT MANAGER MIKE MCNALLY (JULY 14, 1935). Grays' popular manager Mike "Minooka" McNally poses with Mr. Swift, president of the Wilkes-Barre team, and the Grays' business manager, Irv Gleason, before a game. McNally, a veteran minor-league manager, was adored by local fans for his hustling brand of baseball. He left the Grays in 1937 to manage the Wilkes-Barre Barons and later landed a front office position with the Cleveland Indians. (*GRIT*.)

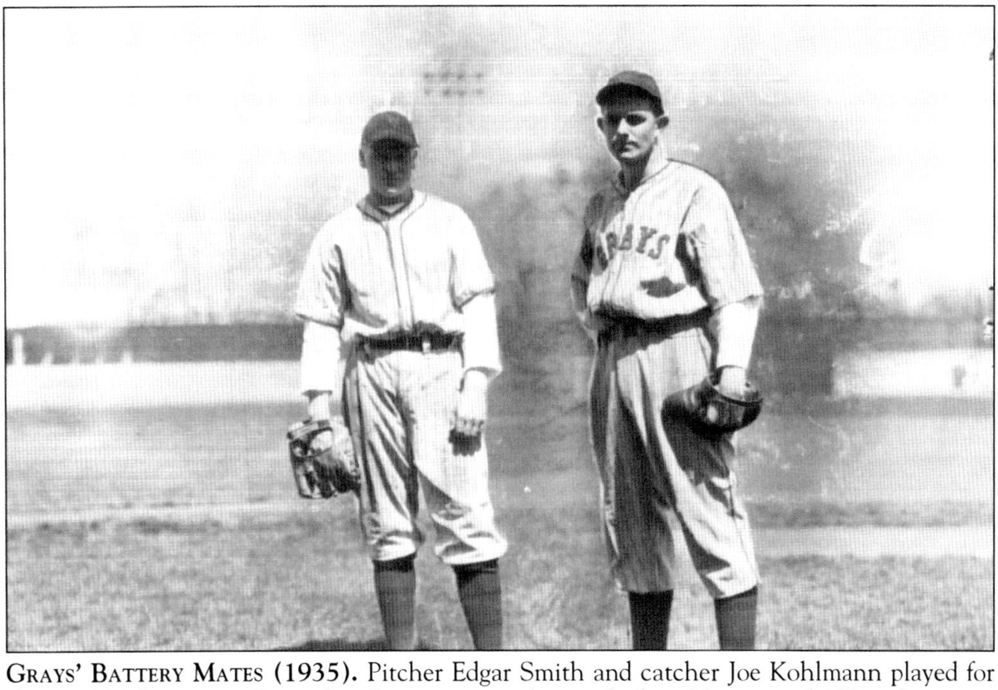

GRAYS' BATTERY MATES (1935). Pitcher Edgar Smith and catcher Joe Kohlmann played for the 1935 Williamsport Grays. Smith, a power pitcher, racked up 20 wins and 158 strikeouts to lead the team in 1936. He later played for the Philadelphia A's and Chicago White Sox, and was dubbed the "Yankee Killer" for his success against the "Bronx Bombers." (*GRIT*.)

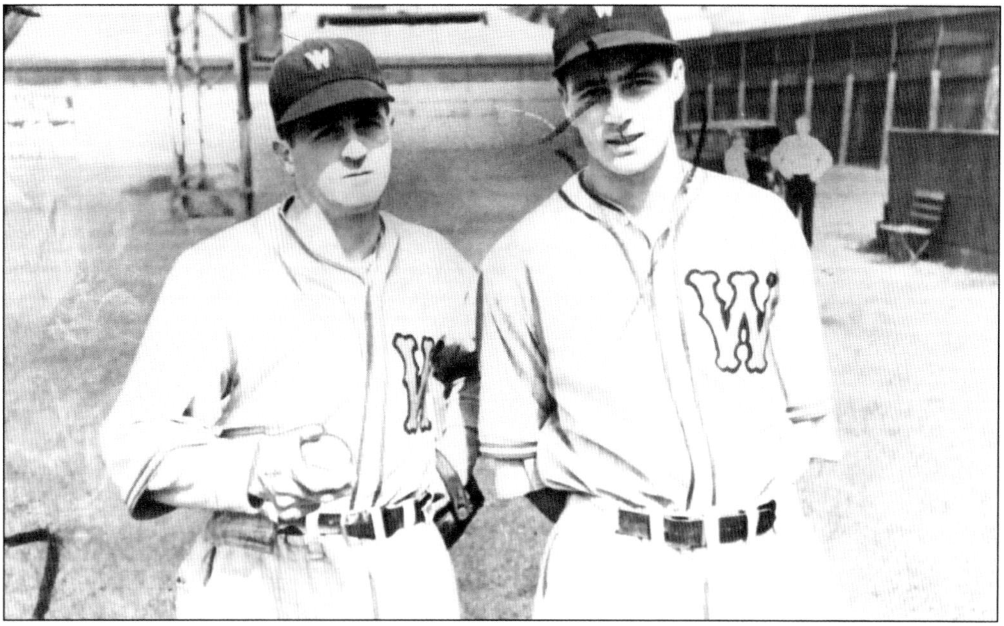

GRAYS' PITCHERS (APRIL 14, 1936). Williamsport Grays' pitchers Smith and Kohluskau strike a pre-season pose for the local press shortly before the start of the 1936 season. The Grays' home jersey, replete with the large tiffany red "W," was one of the most distinctive uniforms of the New York-Pennsylvania League that year. (*GRIT*.)

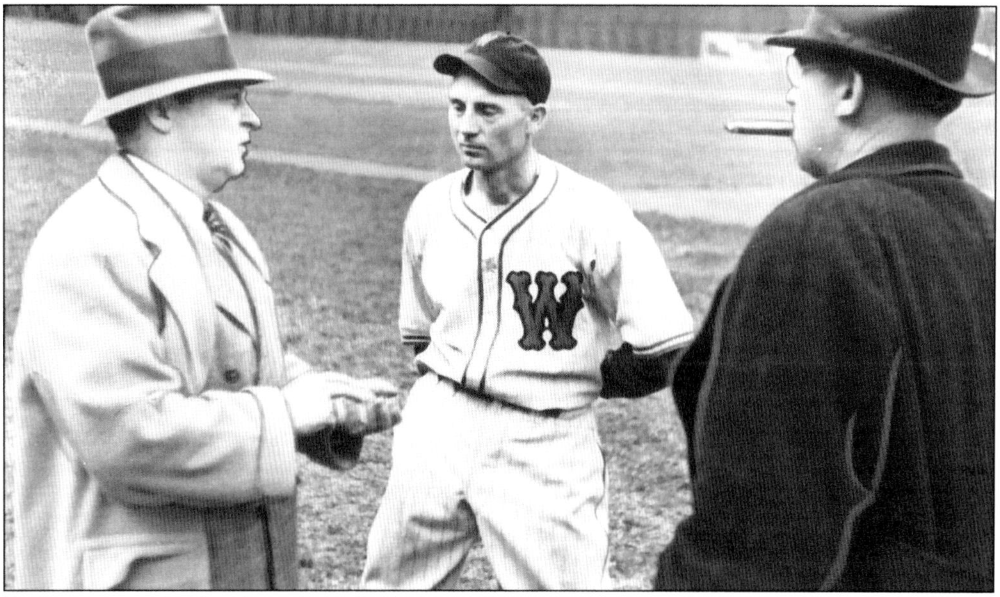

WILLIAMSPORT'S TOP BASEBALL MEN DISCUSSING PROSPECTS (1937). Grays' club director Tommy Richardson (left), manager Ollie Marquart (center), and business manager J. Roy Clunk (right) discuss plans for the upcoming season. In 1937 Richardson gained the presidency of the New York-Pennsylvania League with the support of his influential friend, the legendary Connie Mack. Marquart, a firebrand, had been a key member of the Grays' 1934 championship team. During a game against Hazleton in 1937, he punched opposing manager George "Specs" Torporcer in a disagreement over a dropped foul ball. (*GRIT*.)

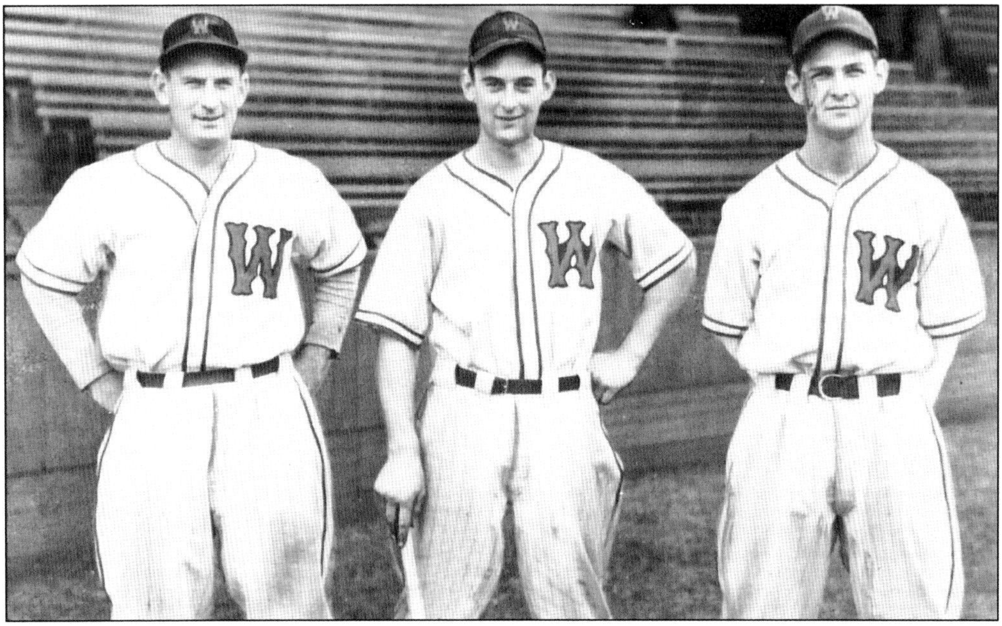

1938 GRAYS' TRIO (MAY 22, 1938). These 1938 Williamsport Grays' players, from left to right, are "Spud" Nachand, Hal Tyler, and Eddie Yount. Yount, a speedster on the base paths and an excellent bunter, led the Billtowners in hitting in 1937 with a .295 average. (*GRIT.*)

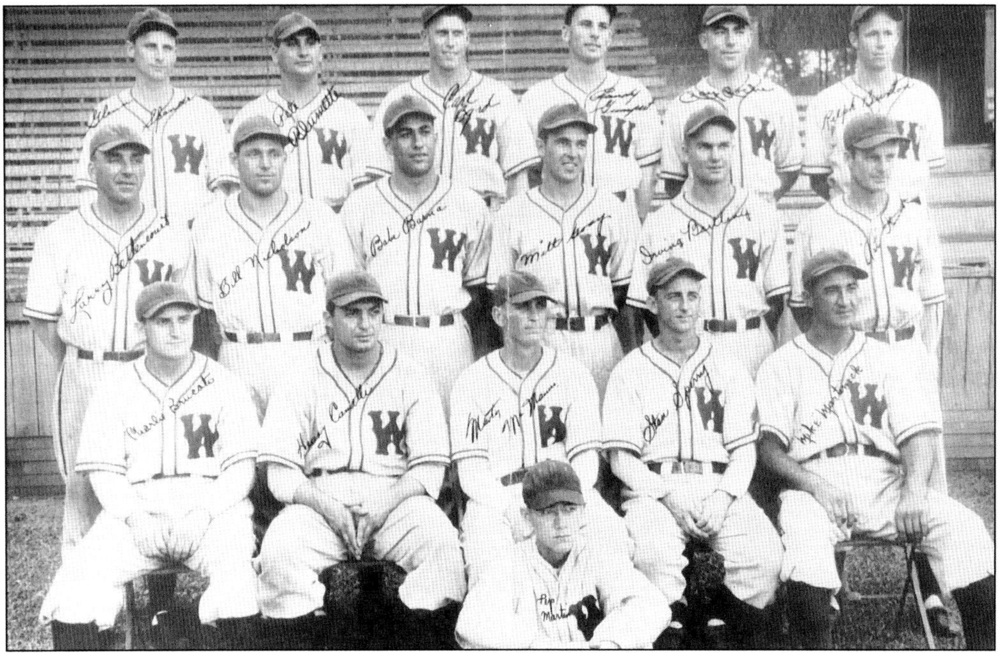

1938 WILLIAMSPORT GRAYS (1938). Managed by Marty McManus (a former member of the St. Louis Browns and one-time manager of the Boston Red Sox), the Grays finished sixth with a record of 65-74. However, local fans witnessed the slugging feats of Bill "Swish" Nicholson, who led the league in home runs with 22. Nicholson later played on two World Series teams, the 1945 Chicago Cubs and the 1950 Phillies. Babe Barna paced the 1938 Grays in hitting with a .304 batting average and Irv Bartling batted .301. (*GRIT.*)

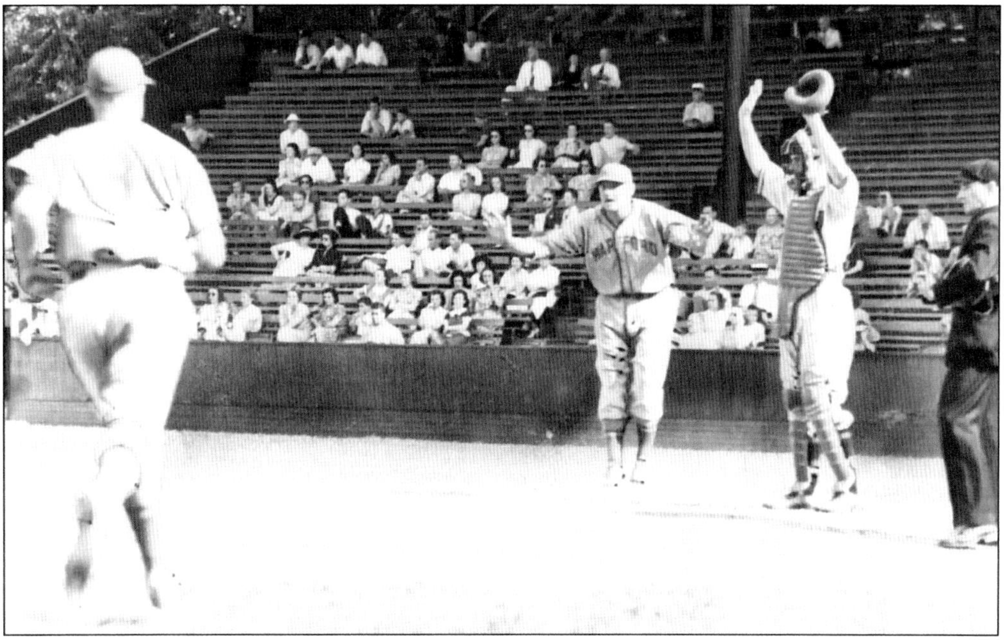

Williamsport vs. Hartford Chiefs (August 7, 1938). This rare image of a game in progress during the 1930s shows Hartford Chiefs pitcher Art Doll motioning for a teammate not to slide at home plate. Doll was later traded to the Williamsport Grays. It must have been a long day for the sparse Bowman Field crowd. (*GRIT*.)

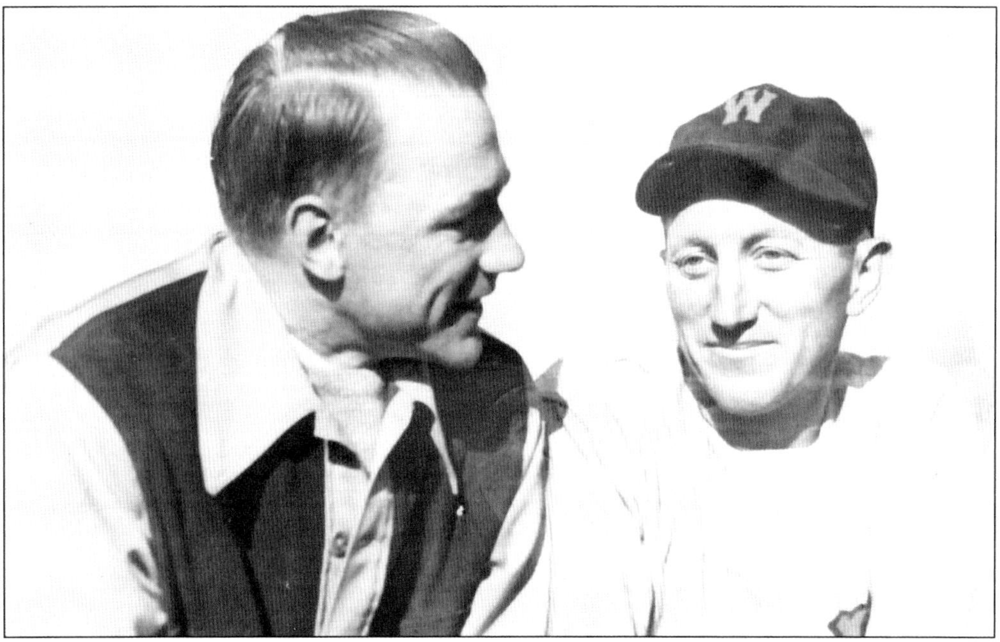

Spring Training, Tarboro, North Carolina (1939). Pitcher Doc Bowers and outfielder Buford Rhea enjoy a quiet moment during a break in practice at the Grays' spring training complex in North Carolina. Rather than traveling to Florida, many minor-league teams trained in the Carolinas and gravitated northward during the exhibition portion of the baseball season. (*GRIT*.)

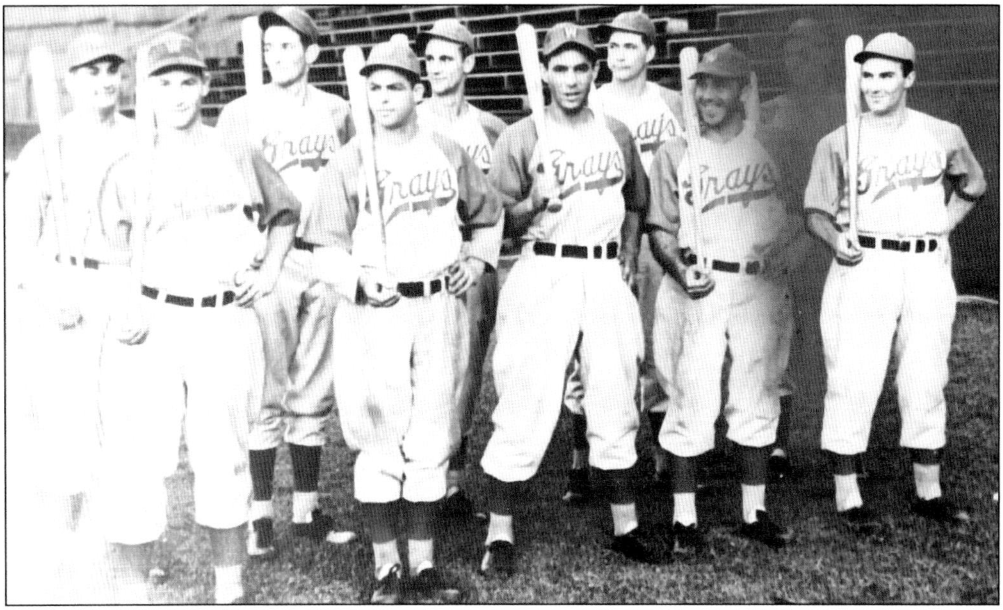

GRAYS PASS MUSTER (AUGUST 4, 1940). In keeping with the theme of military preparedness, members of the 1940 Grays assemble for muster. They are, from left to right, as follows: (front row) Harry Simpson, Jerry Lynn, Bartola, Ralph Rhein, and Ron Northey; (back row) Pete Blumette, Johnny Cordell, Nick Butcher, Harris, and Irv Kohlberg. (*GRIT.*)

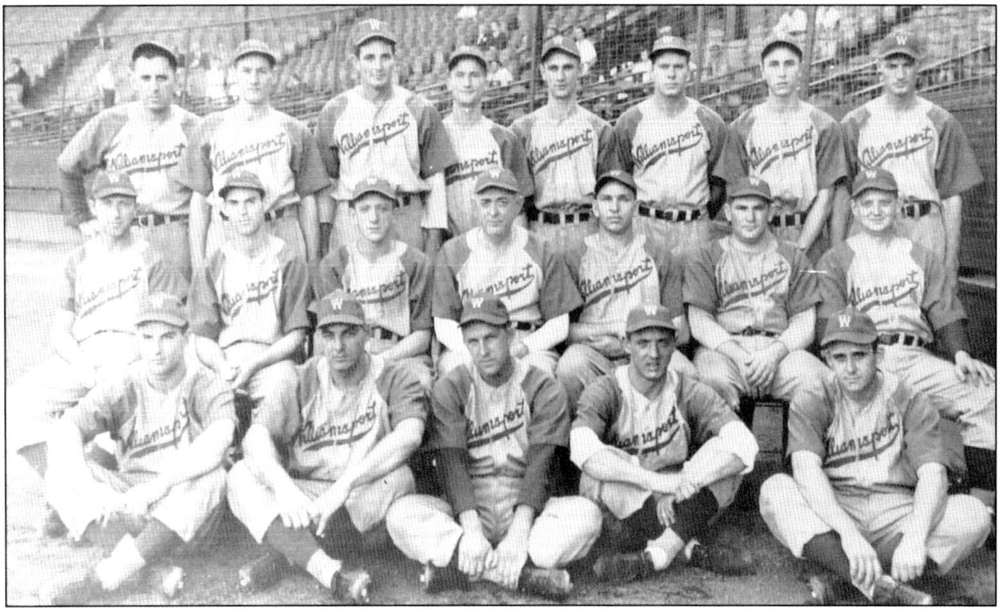

WILLIAMSPORT GRAYS. This team portrait, taken on the road at Elmira's Dunn Field, captures the Grays before the beginning of the Governor's Cup Series for the Eastern League championship. Manager Spence Abbott's charges lost to Elmira in the decisive seventh game. Arguably Williamsport's best team since the 1934 championship team, the 1941 team graduated 15 members to the big league ranks. Among the more noteworthy players were sluggers Ron Northey, Irv Kohlberg, Alex Mustaikis, Don Richmond, Ken Richardson, and pitchers Roger Wolff, John Cordell, and Orrie Arntzen. (*GRIT.*)

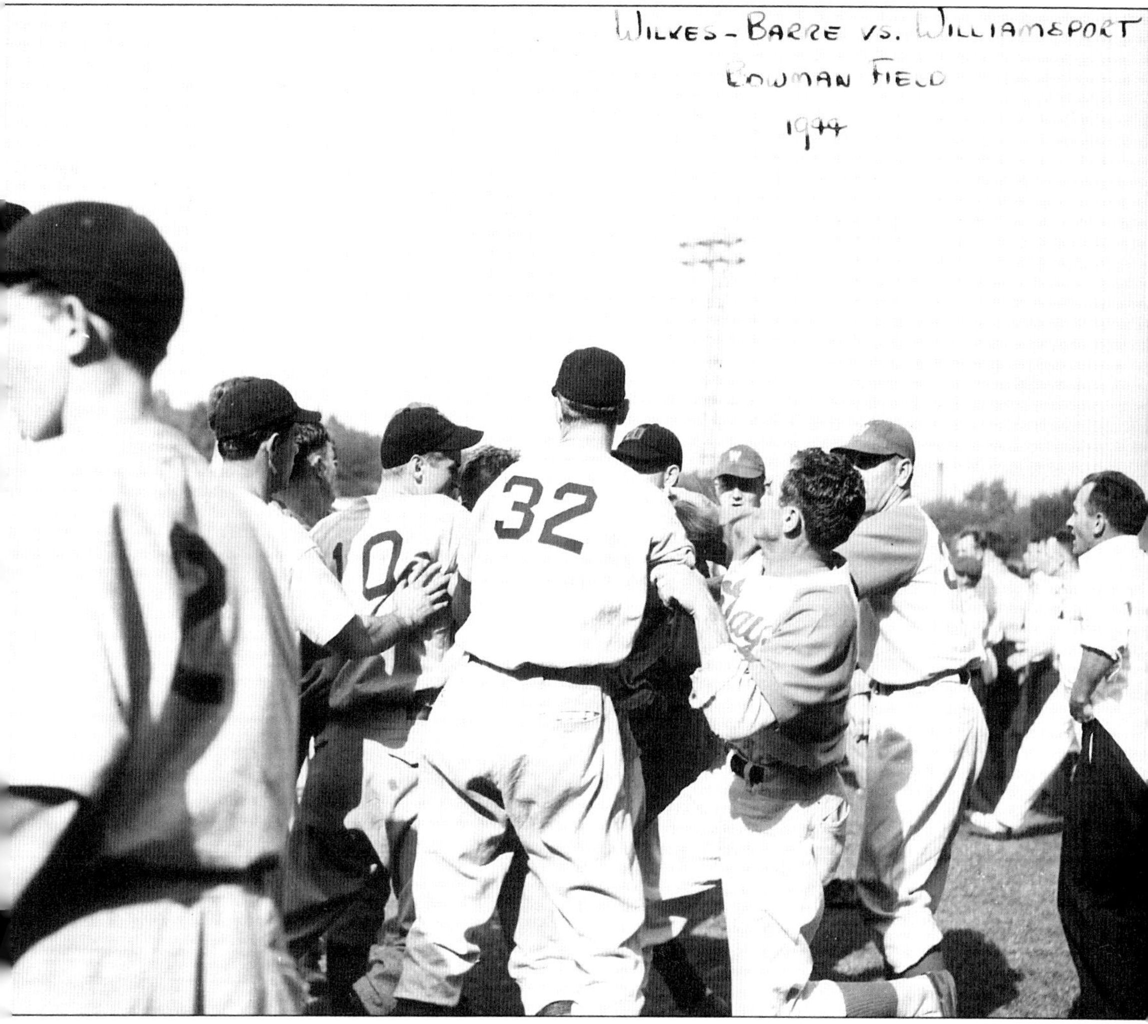

BASEBALL BRAWL, WILLIAMSPORT VS. WILKES-BARRE (AUGUST 24, 1941). One of the most memorable games of the spectacular season of 1941 was the infamous "riot game" involving the Grays and the Wilkes-Barre Barons. All season long the two teams engaged in intense competition for first place. Tensions mounted in late August when the Barons traveled to Bowman Field to play three doubleheaders over the weekend series. The riot was sparked by the ejection of Grays' pitcher Art Jones for arguing balls and strikes. When Barons' manager Earl Wolgamot refused a request from Grays' manager Spence Abbott for warm-up time for Jones's replacement, the two engaged in a heated argument that led to fisticuffs. A wild free-for-all broke out as benches emptied and fans poured onto the field to participate in the melee. Williamsport police were called to the ballpark to restore order. Alex Mustaikis pitched the remainder of the game for the Grays and hit a dramatic game-winning home run in the 13th inning. Note the wrong inscription date attributed to this image. (TR.)

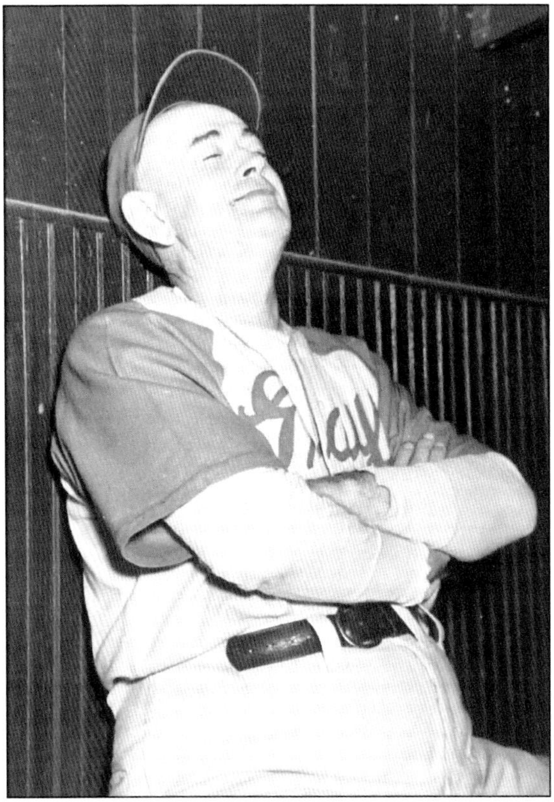

The Many Moods of Spence Abbott (1941). Grays' manager Spence Abbott hams it up for the camera prior to a game. Dubbed the "John McGraw of the Minor Leagues," Abbott's managerial career spanned 43 years, from 1903 to 1946. In that time he won over 2,000 games and managed ten pennant-winning teams. Hard-nosed, aggressive, and shrewd, Abbott instilled in the 1941 Grays a fighting spirit not seen since the 1934 team. The Grays' animated manager was very popular with local fans and the sports press. (*GRIT*.)

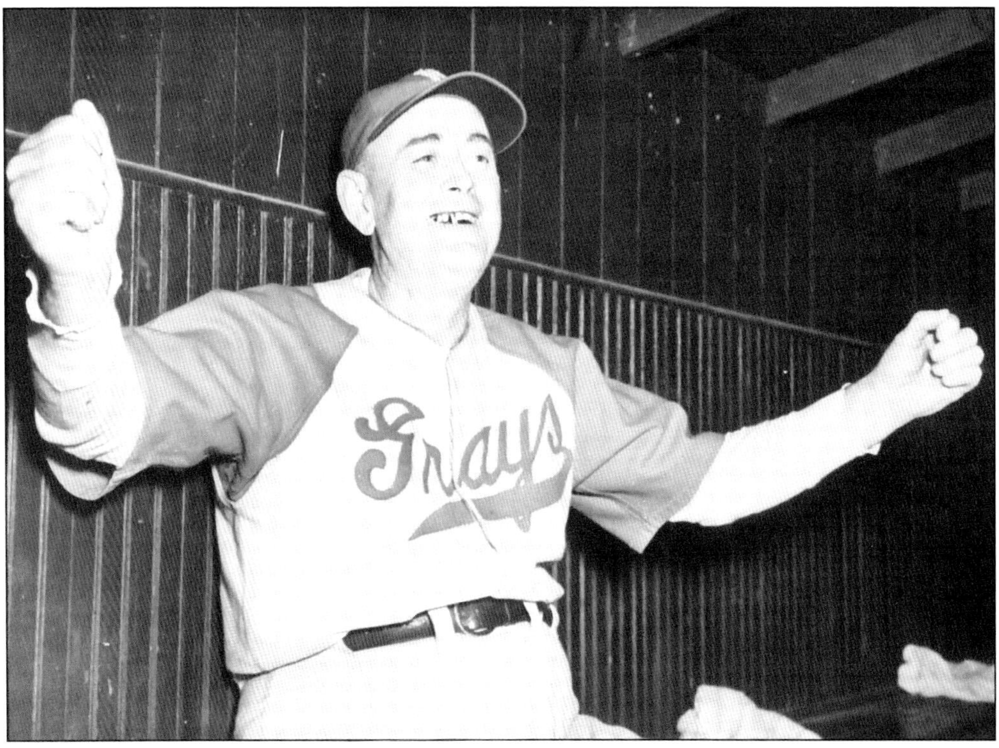

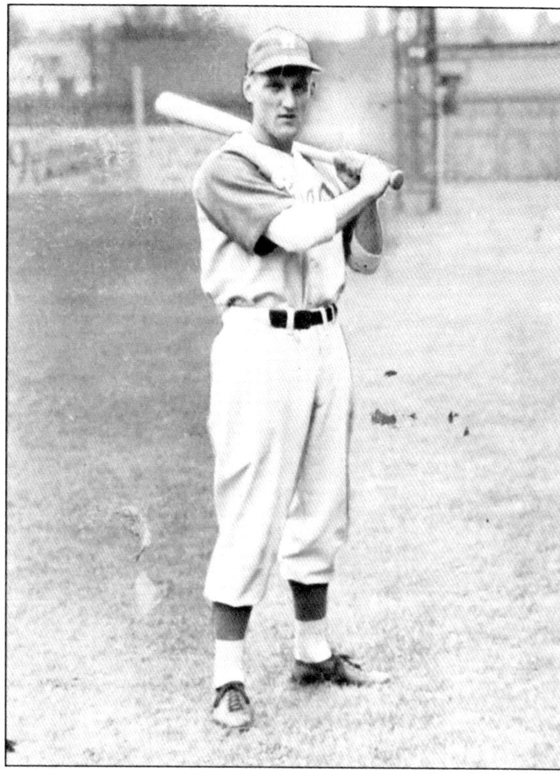

Williamsport Slugger Irv Kohlberg (1941). One of the Grays' leading left-handed hitters during the early 1940s, Kohlberg was always near the top in home run and RBI totals. He was also a very good defensive first baseman. (*GRIT*.)

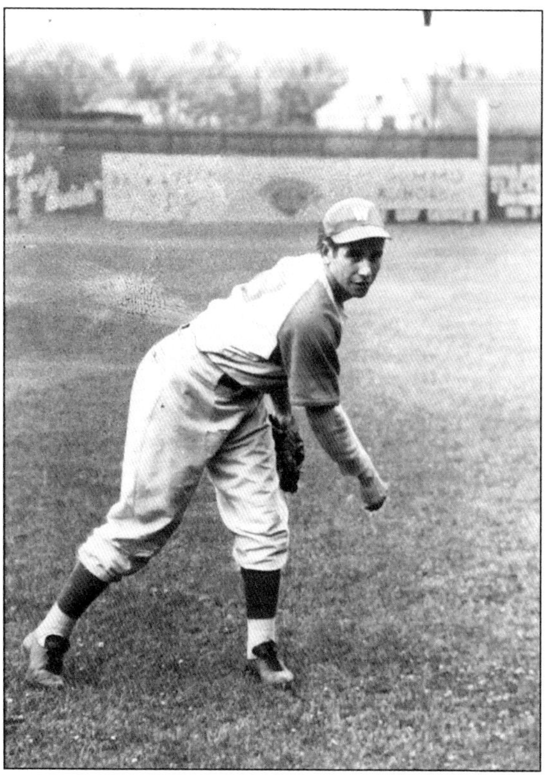

Grays' Pitcher Sam Scarriot (June 1, 1941). Scarriot displays his delivery form for posterity during a warm-up session prior to an Eastern League game. Called up to the Grays during mid-season, Scarriot saw only limited action during the 1941 season. (*GRIT*.)

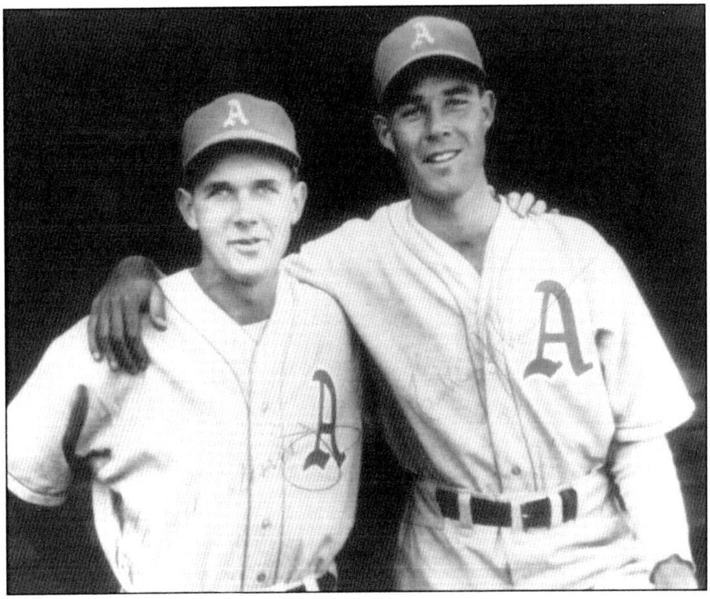

EDDIE COLLINS JR. AND RANKIN JOHNSON JR. (1941). Young Rankin Johnson Jr. towers over his Philadelphia A's teammate and friend in this dugout portrait. Johnson got his first taste of big league life during the 1941 season with the A's and was particularly well liked by A's owner Connie Mack. (Photograph courtesy of A. Rankin Johnson Ji.)

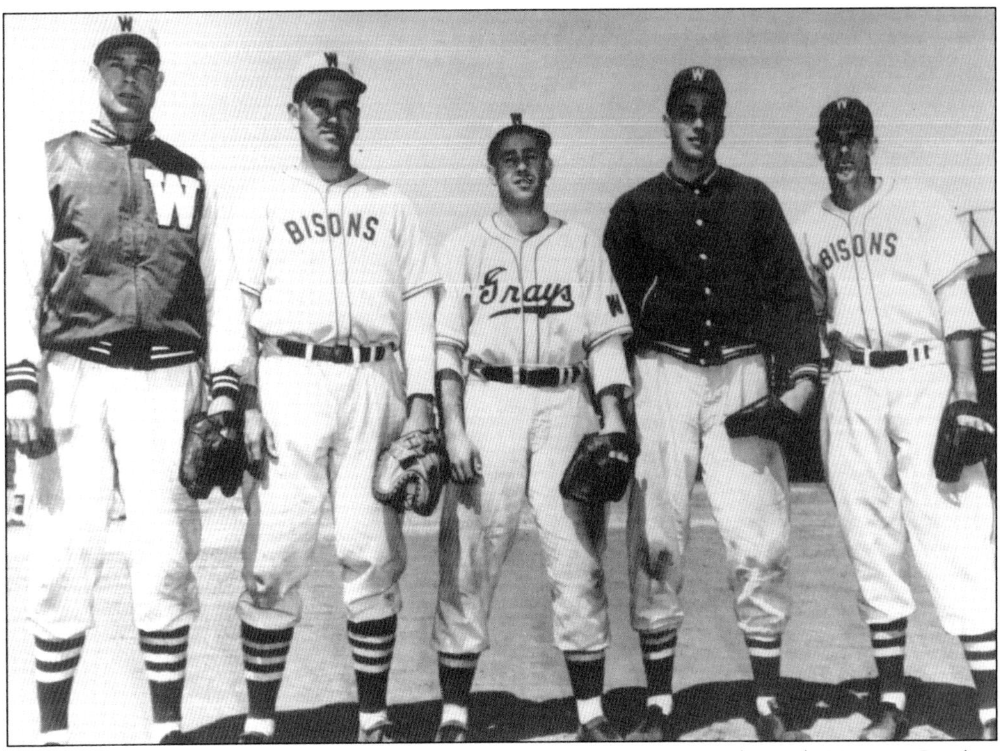

RANKIN JOHNSON JR. WITH GRAYS TEAMMATES AT SPRING TRAINING (1946). Veteran Rankin Johnson Jr., wearing a "W" warm-up jacket, lines up with other Grays' pitching prospects before the start of the season. (Photograph courtesy of A. Rankin Johnson Jr.)

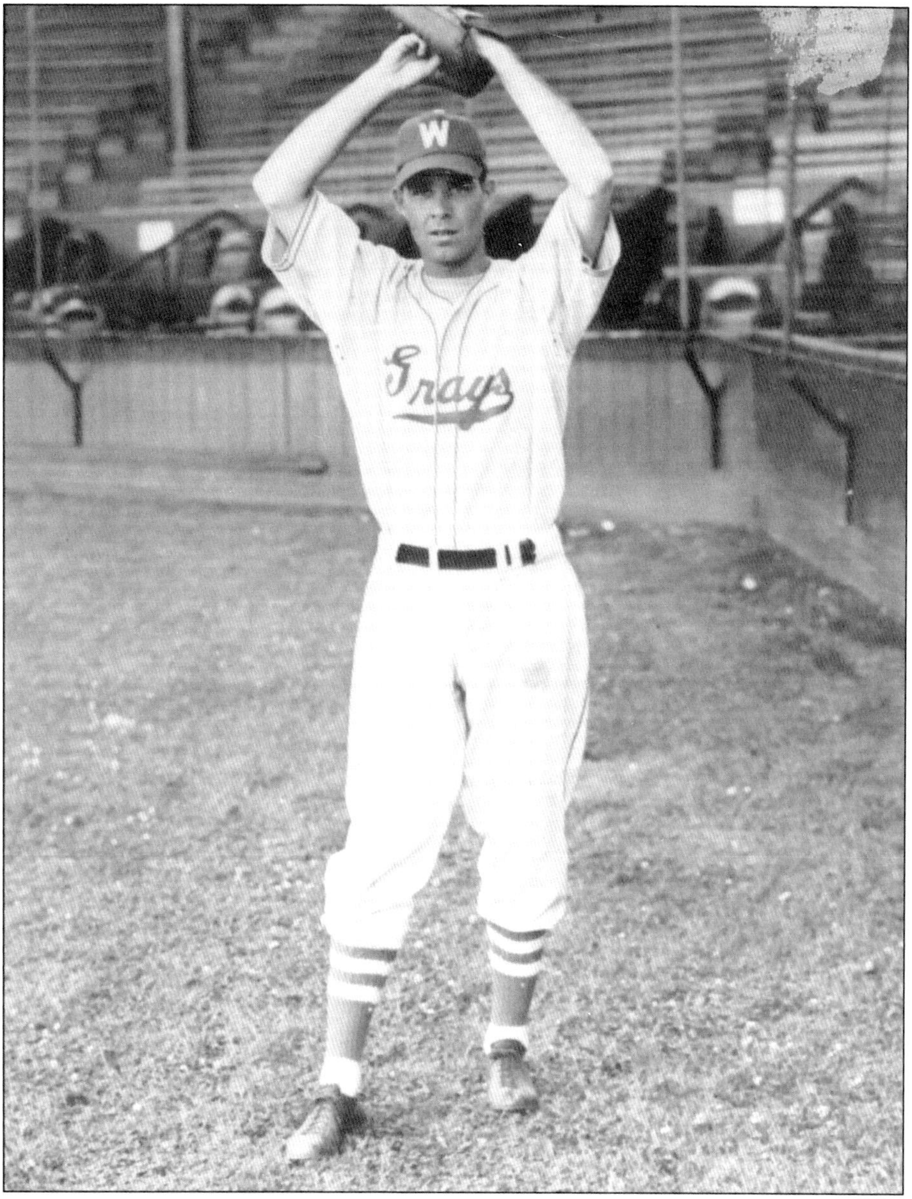

Rankin Johnson Jr. (1940s). Rankin Johnson Jr. has been a permanent fixture on the Williamsport baseball scene for over 50 years as a professional ball player, club business manager, Eastern League president, and avid fan. The lanky Texan was originally signed as a pitcher by the Yankees and later worked his way up the minor-league chain with the Chicago Cubs and Philadelphia A's. In 1941 he pitched in several games with the A's. Sent down to the Grays during the early 1940s, Johnson dated and married Joan, a city native. In the intervening war years Johnson joined the Navy and served in the Pacific. After the war Johnson made Williamsport his permanent home and finished his playing career with the Grays and Tigers in 1946 and 1947. Recruited by Eastern League President Tommy Richardson to serve as a personal assistant in 1953, Johnson embarked upon a front office career with the Williamsport franchise that lasted until the early 1970s. Johnson also served as president of the Eastern League from 1961 to 1967. (Photograph courtesy of A. Rankin Johnson Jr.)

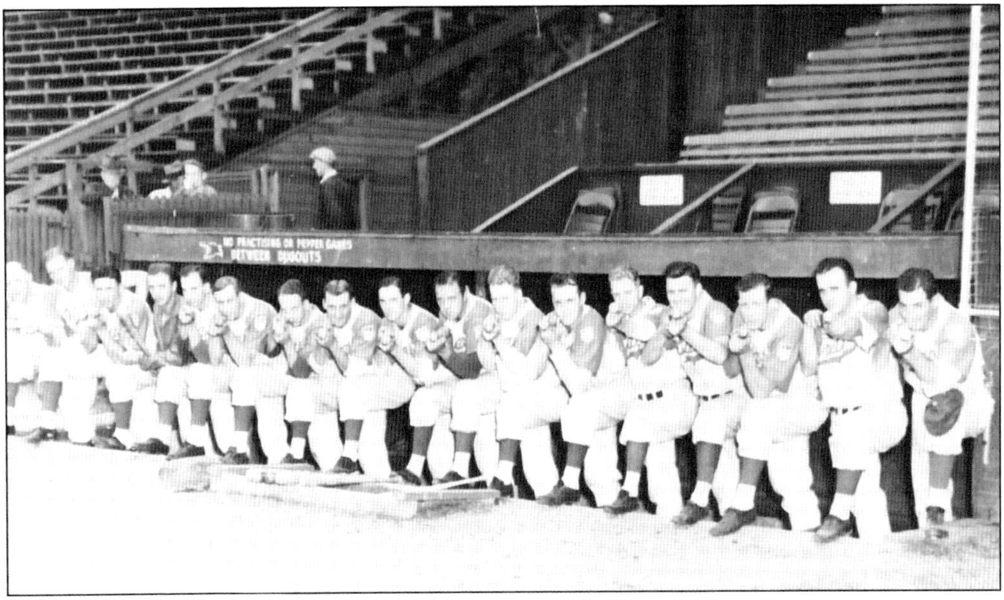

Grays Growing Stronger (May 31, 1942). The Grays take aim with their bats as they pursue the Eastern League pennant in 1942. Pictured here, from left to right, are Manger Spence Abbott, Alex Mustaikis, Bill Burch, Sam Zoldak, Bill Curry, Irv Kohlberg, Barney Lutz, Stan Stencel, Irv Hall, Gene Hasson, Carl Twyble, Gus Hixon, Nate Pelter, John McCarthy, Bill Peterman, Ken Richardson, and John Cordell. The Grays sported the wartime "America Health" patches worn on the left sleeve of the jersey. (*GRIT*.)

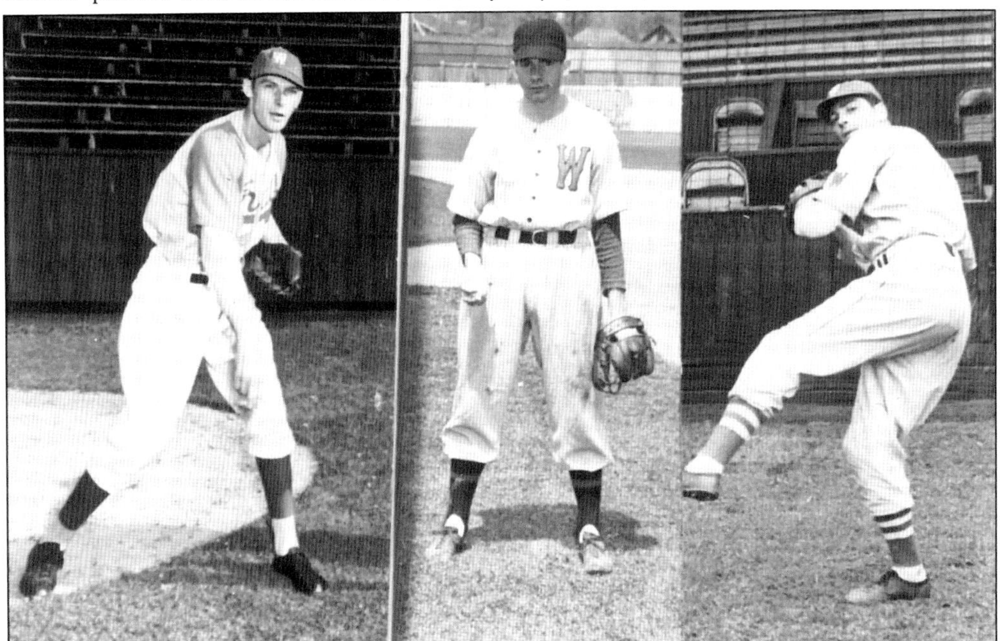

Williamsport Grays' Players (1942). Leo Pukas, Nate Pelter, and Herm Bishop were well-known pitchers during the 1940s era of the Grays. Pelter beat future Yankee great Allie Reynolds (then pitching for Wilkes-Barre) in a 5-0 shutout on August 11, 1942. He sported a 15-11 record and led the Grays' pitching staff with 95 strikeouts in 1943. (*GRIT*.)

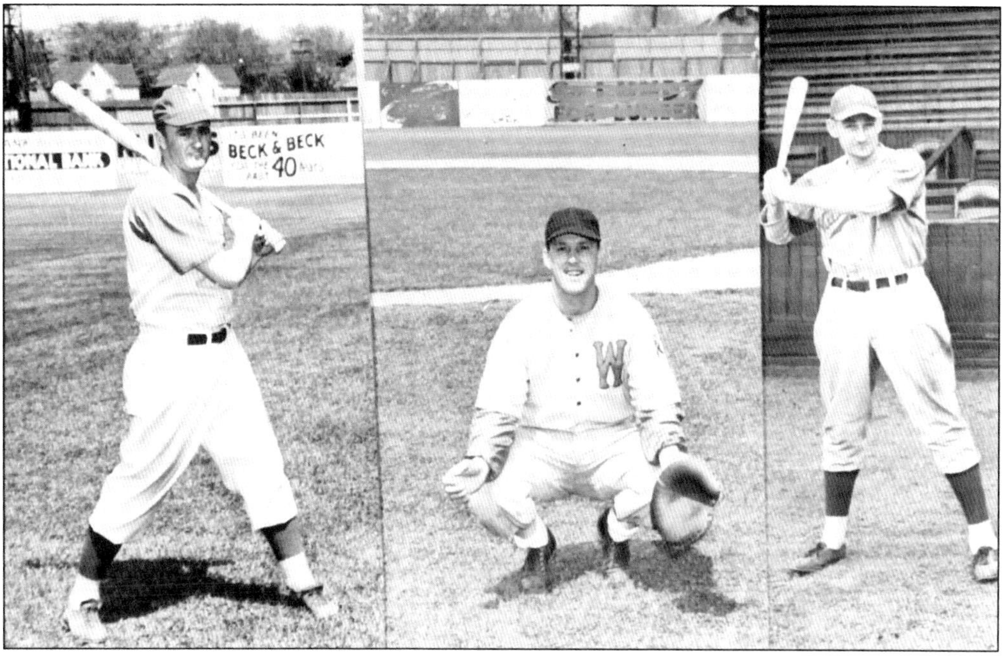

Williamsport Grays' Players (1940). John McCarthy(left), Gus Hixon(center), and John Mueller (right) were representative position players of the Grays' teams of the 1940s. They were durable, scrappy, and hungry to reach the majors. Catcher Gus Hixon and ex-Gray Bernie Snyder (playing for Albany in 1942) were involved in a memorable fight following a close play at home plate during a game at Bowman Field on August 25, 1942. Snyder reacted angrily at the way Hixon had blocked the plate when he attempted to score a run. (*GRIT*.)

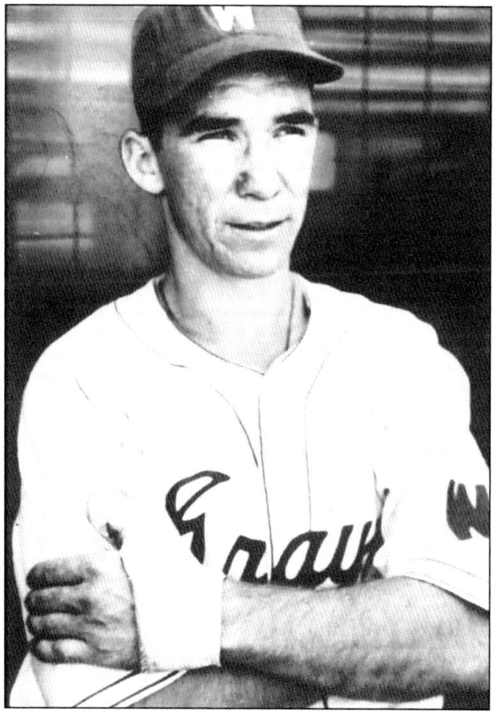

Bob Alberts, Williamsport Grays (July 23, 1944). Alberts, a member of the 1944 Grays, displays his wounds. During this era, players suited up and played through injuries for fear of being released by their clubs. (*GRIT*.)

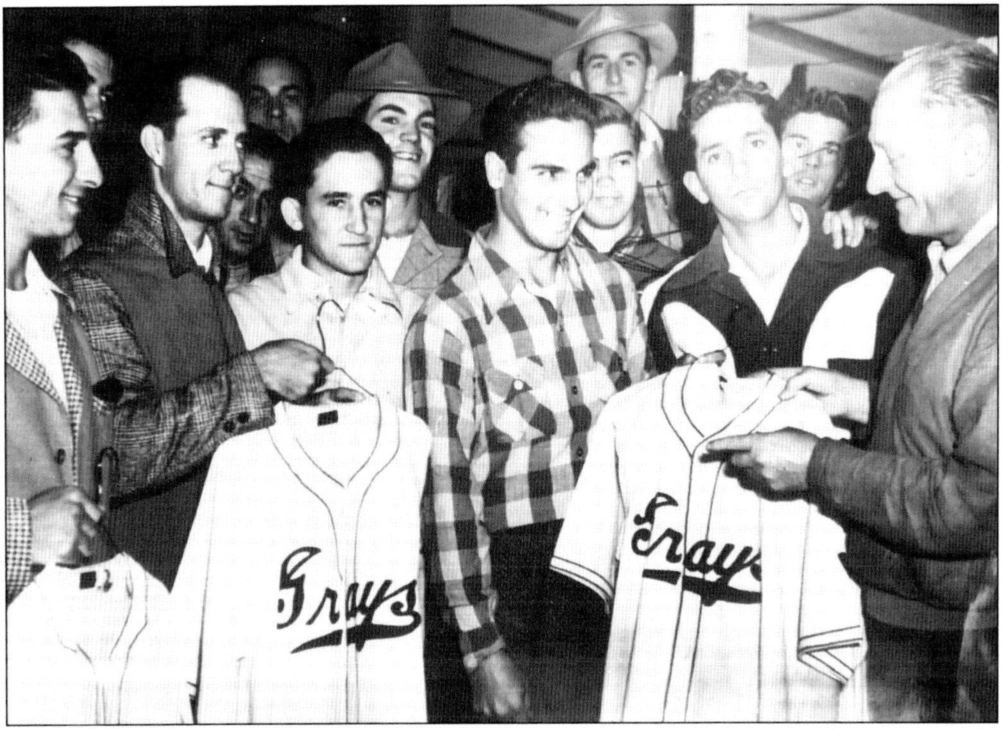

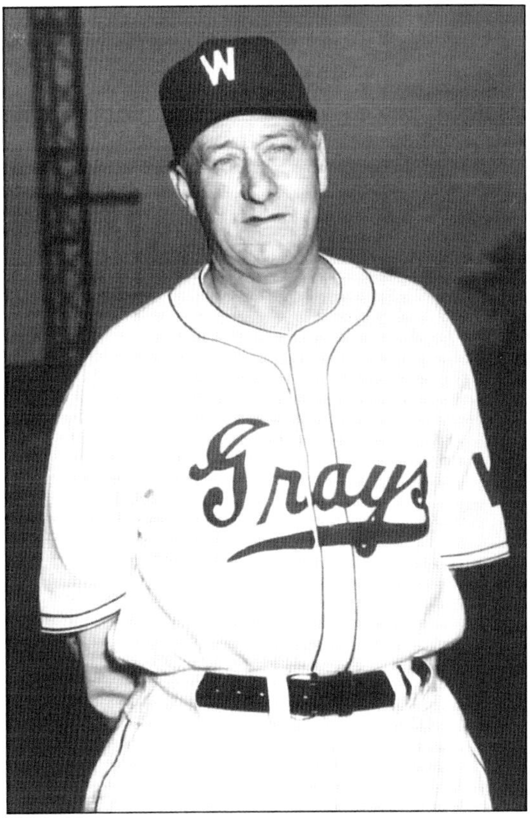

Cuban Players Arrive (May 9, 1945). Manager Ray Kolp presents Grays' uniforms to the new players. With the wartime manpower shortage, one of baseball's more unique experiments involved the signing of Latin American baseball talent to stock minor-league teams. Baseball historian Morris Beale noted that the Washington Senators (the Grays' major-league affiliate) and owner Clark Griffith signed so many Cuban players that they had to find a special farm for them in Williamsport, Pennsylvania. (*GRIT.*)

Manager Ray Kolp (1945). Veteran manager Ray Kolp guided the Grays during the "Cuban Seasons" of 1944 and 1945. Kolp had been a former major-league pitcher with the St. Louis Browns and Cincinnati, and served as the pitching coach for the Minneapolis Millers of the American Association. The hustling but erratic Cuban teams that played in Williamsport sorely tested his patience. (*GRIT.*)

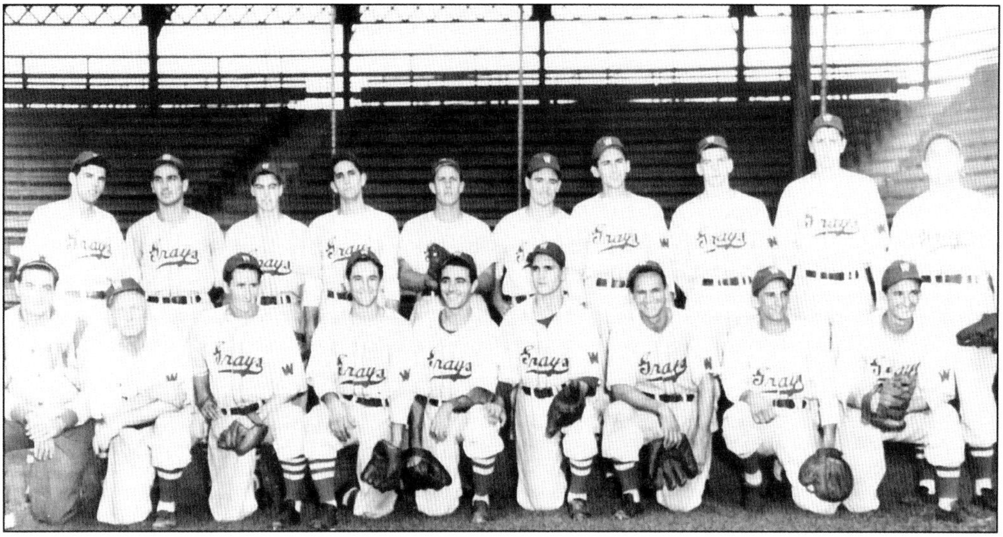

WILLIAMSPORT GRAYS. Dubbed the "Rhumba Rascals" by Eastern League sportswriters, Williamsport's largely-Cuban team became one of the top attractions of the circuit. The players' speed on the bases, coupled with their constant chatter and hustling ways, won the hearts of local fans. However, they encountered hostility on the road as opposing teams and fans engaged in race-baiting. The hapless Cubans finished near the bottom of the standings. (*GRIT*.)

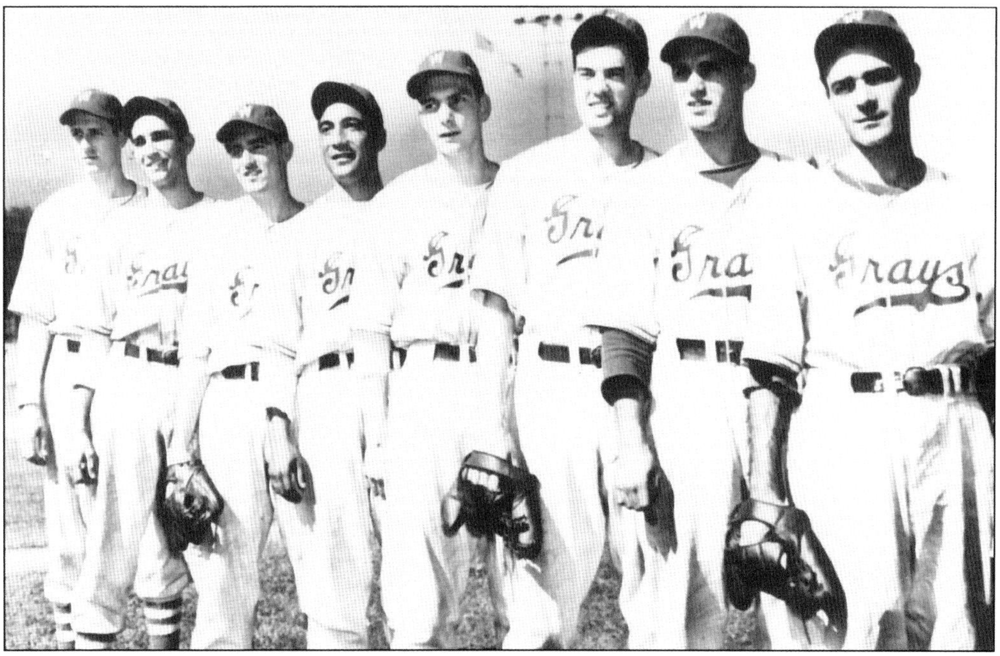

GRAYS' PITCHING STAFF (JUNE 24, 1945). These members of the 1945 Grays' pitching staff are, from left to right, Art Ecklund, Rodriquez, Leonard Goicochea, Jiminez, area sandlot sensation Dick Welteroth, Fred Guiliani, Armando Traspuesto, and Danny Parra. Welteroth, signed by the Senators at age 17, pitched three innings against the Philadelphia A's in an exhibition game played at Bowman Field before 3,708 fans in 1944. He later pitched for Washington in the big leagues. (*GRIT*.)

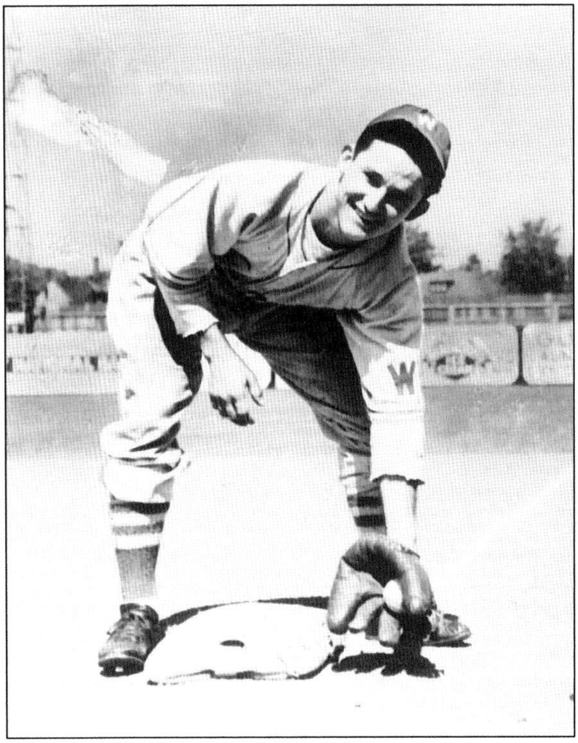

Frankie Gallardo, 1945 Grays (July 1, 1945). The colorful second baseman epitomized the dashing and entertaining style of play that defined the Grays during the Cuban seasons. Gallardo, one of the most popular players on the 1945 team, missed part of the season when he was injured in a water boiler explosion that rocked the Grays' clubhouse on May 27, 1945. (*GRIT*.)

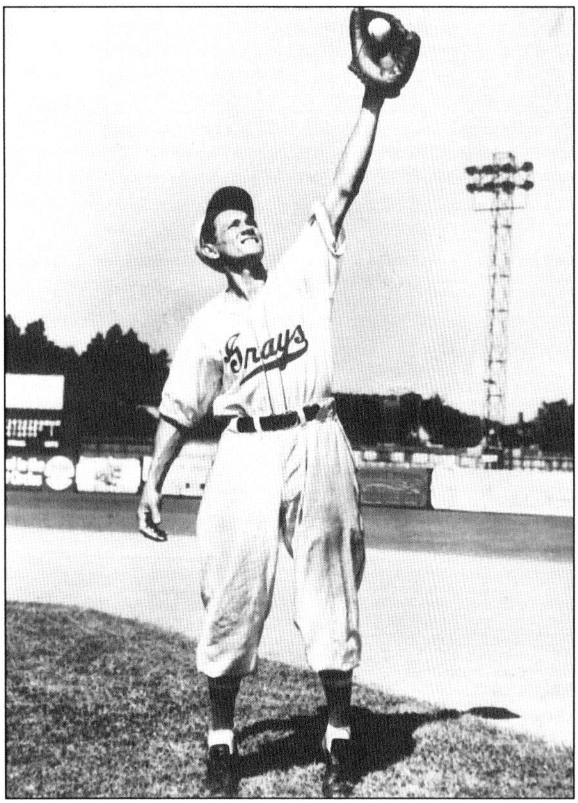

Chino Hildago, 1945 Grays (July 1, 1945). The second half of the Cuban keystone combination, Hildago thrilled local fans with his athleticism at shortstop and his speed on the base paths. Though small in stature, he was a fierce competitor. In the 1945 campaign Hildago batted .307. (*GRIT*.)

GRAYS' PITCHER JIMINEZ (1945). Grays' pitcher Jiminez displays his pitching form while tossing on the warm-up mound prior to the start of an Eastern League game at Bowman Field. (*GRIT*.)

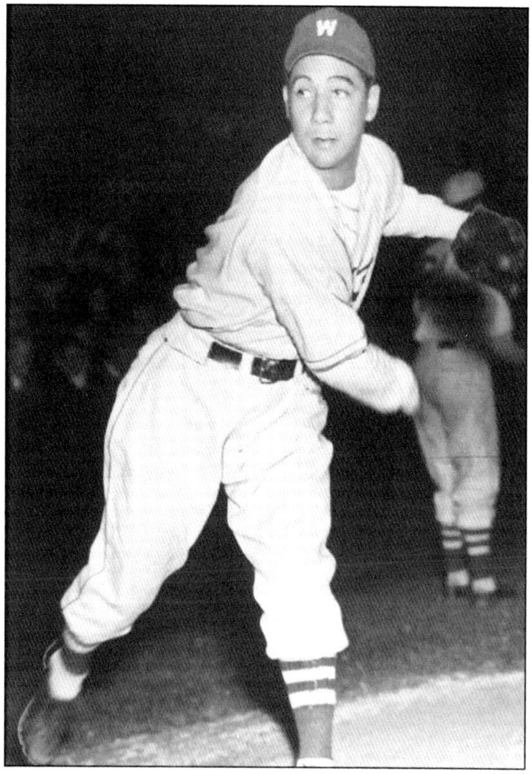

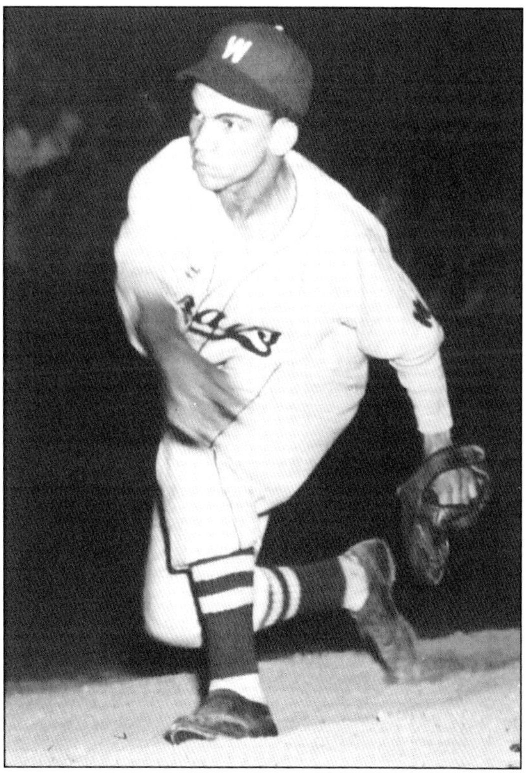

FASTBALL HIGH AND TIGHT (1945). Grays' pitcher Jose Napoles uncorks a pitch toward home plate during action at the uptown ballpark. (*GRIT*.)

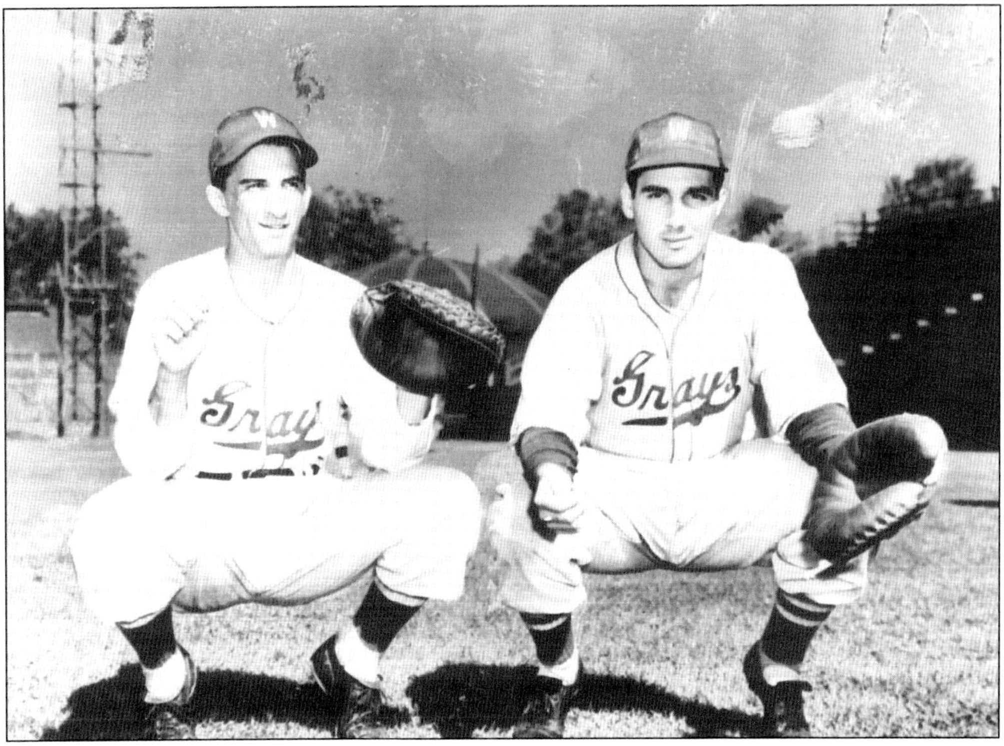

1945 GRAYS' RECEIVING CORPS (JULY 8, 1945). Grays' catchers Mario Diaz and Rogelio Valdes assume their familiar squat for the camera. Valdes had jumped the team the previous year after becoming homesick for his native Cuba. He returned in 1945 to play out the entire season. (*GRIT*.)

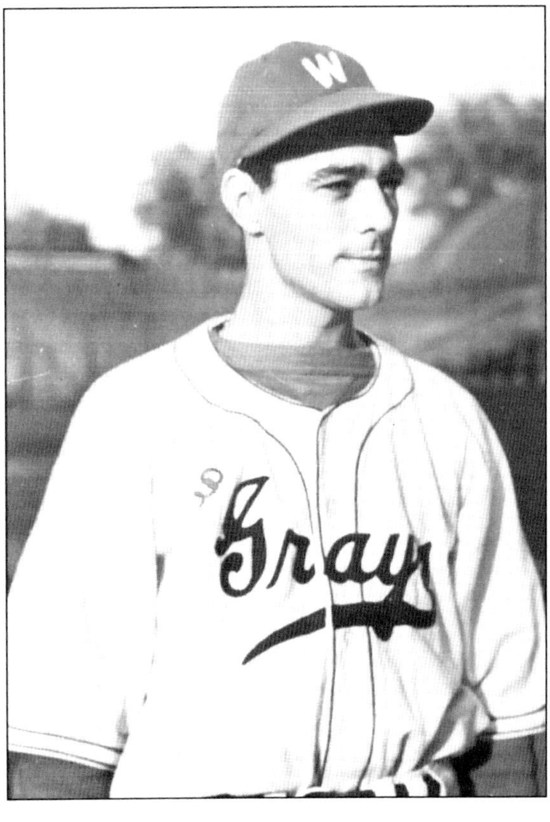

PITCHER DANNY PARRA (JUNE 25, 1944). One of few bright spots for the Grays' pitching staff was Danny Parra, who went 14-9 in 1944 and 16-14 in 1945. Parra spun consecutive shutouts against Albany (a two-hitter) and Utica (a one-hitter) in July 1945. He also fought Utica's race-baiting first baseman Cecil "Turkey" Tyson during a bitter brawl between the Grays and Blue Sox on July 16, 1945. (*GRIT*.)

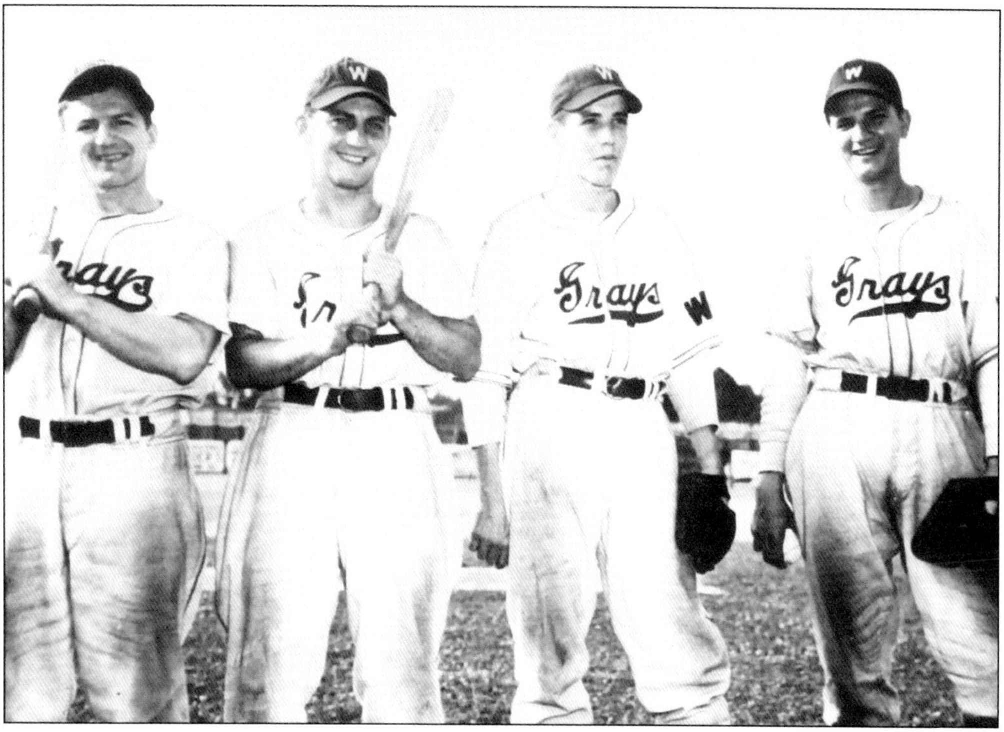

Grays' Players (July 29, 1945). Other members of the 1945 Grays were, from left to right, Sabrinsky, Yarnell, Gutierrez, and Del Monte. Joaquin Gutierrez, a 17-year-old pitching prospect, ended a Grays' ten-game losing streak by hurling an 8-1 win over the Scranton Red Sox on August 14, 1945. (*GRIT*.)

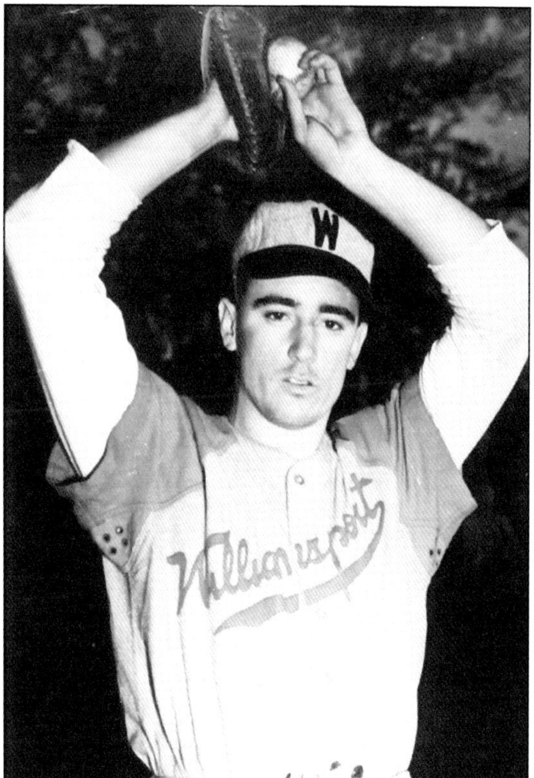

Pitcher Leo Goicochea (1945). Grays' pitcher Leo Goicochea compiled a 5-5 record in 1945 but won his teammates' admiration when he pitched high and tight against the hated Utica Blue Sox. In a game against Utica on July 8, 1945, "Turkey" Tyson took exception to an inside pitch and went after Goicochea with a baseball bat. The incident later sparked a bench-clearing brawl. (*GRIT*.)

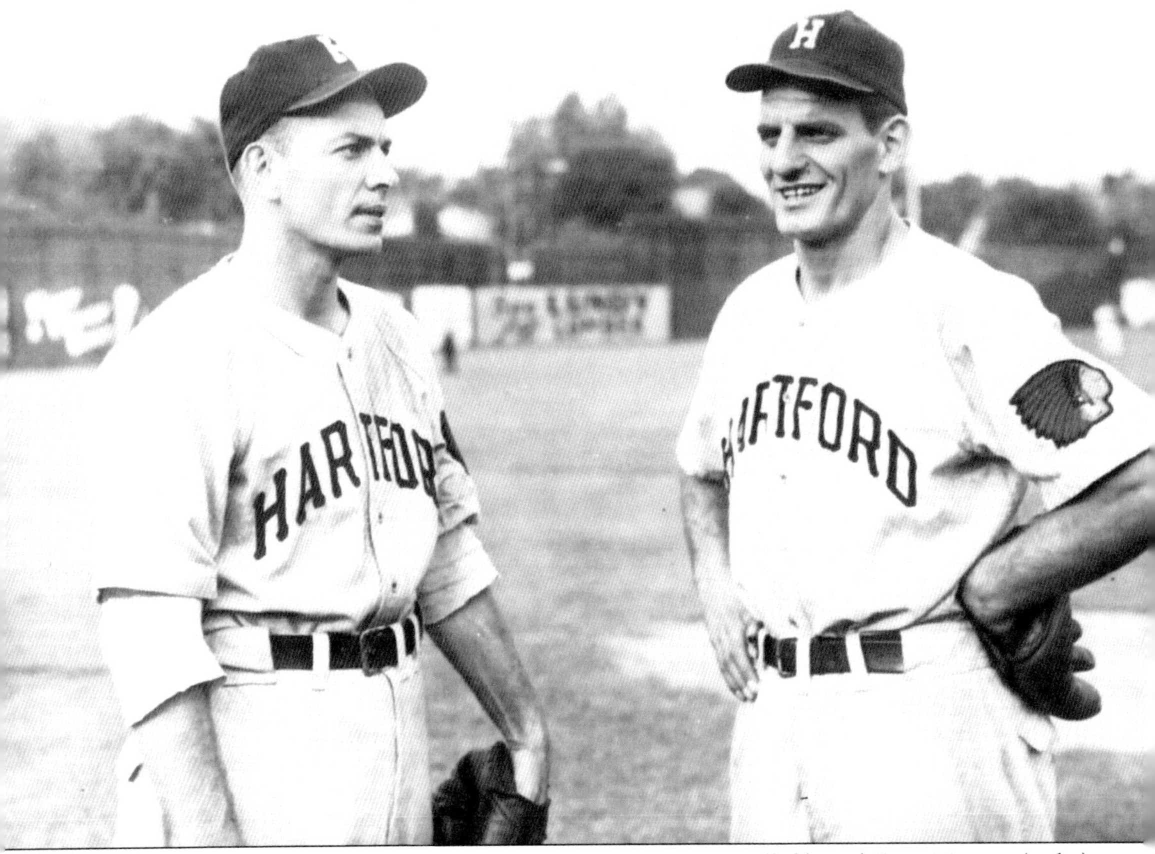

Return of the Natives (1946). City natives Ollie Byers (left) and Don Manno (right), wearing the visiting uniforms of the Hartford Chiefs, return home to take on the Grays. Manno began his professional baseball career while a senior in high school, appearing in an exhibition game with the Grays against York on August 29, 1933. He played under the assumed name of Don Dixon to preserve his amateur status before enrolling in college. Manno toiled in the Yankee farm system for several years before reaching the Major Leagues with the old Boston Bees. He hit a grand slam home run in his first major league at-bat with the Bees in 1940. Thereafter, he became a minor-league slugging star. In 1946 Manno led the Eastern League in home runs and RBIs. He finished out his playing career with the 1951 Williamsport Tigers. Byers, though never reaching the big leagues, carved out a successful minor-league career. His father, Jack "Bunion" Byers, had played on the very first Grays team in 1923. (*GRIT.*)

WILLIAMSPORT TIGERS' MANAGER GEORGE DETORE (APRIL 20, 1947). Manager Detore displays his fungo-hitting form during a pre-season practice session at Bowman Field. According to the press account accompanying this photograph, he could simultaneously hit three balls in different directions to three players. Detore had played briefly with the Cleveland Indians and later managed at Flint, Michigan, in the Michigan State League. (*GRIT*.)

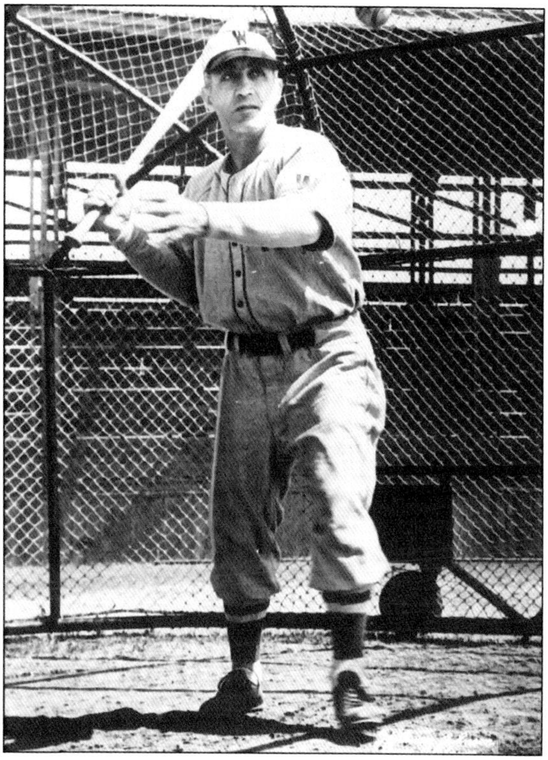

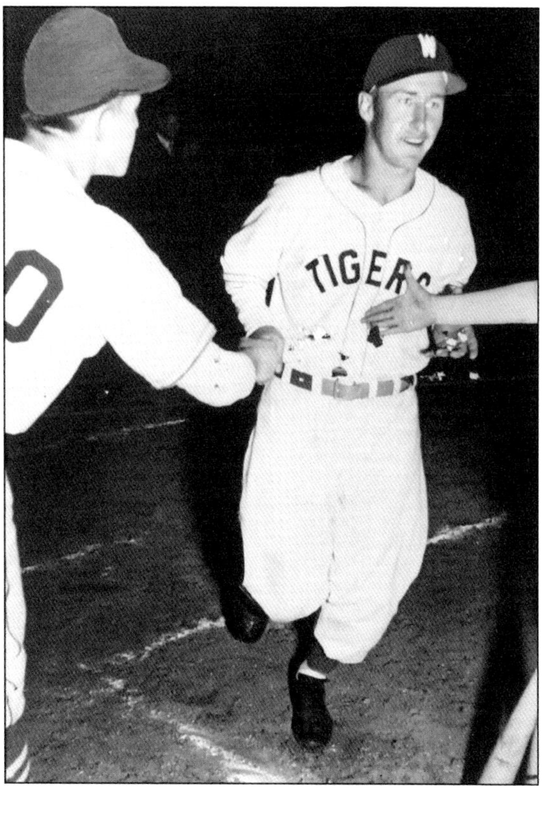

TOUCH 'EM ALL AMIL (JUNE 1, 1947). Tigers' outfielder Amil Brinsky crosses the plate with a wide grin after hitting a home run. Brinsky led Williamsport in home runs (10) and RBIs (80) in 1946. (*GRIT*.)

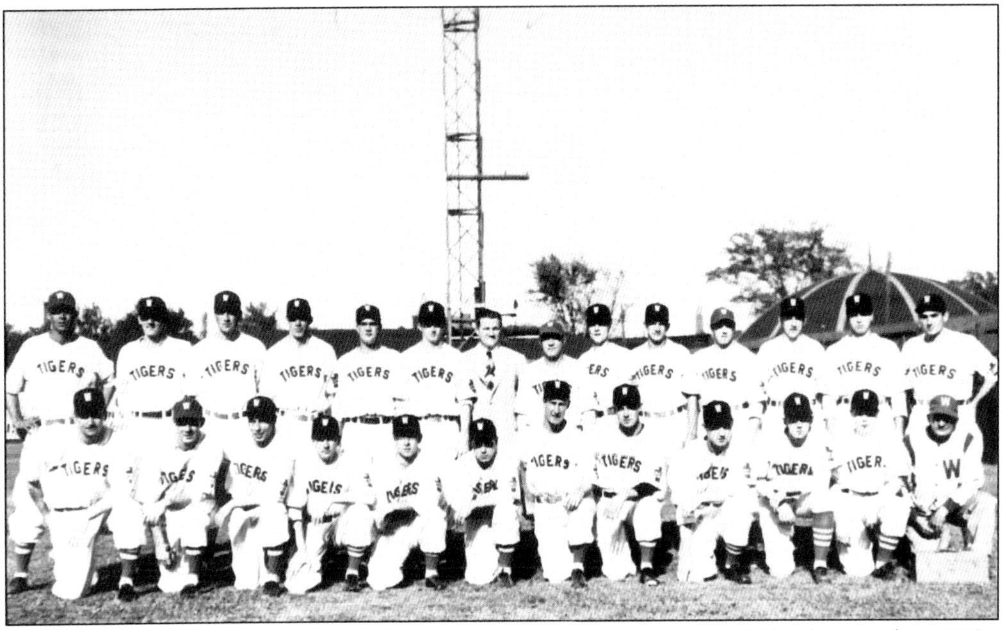

1947 Williamsport Tigers. The 1947 Tigers ended the season in fifth place with a 67-74 record. Members of the team included the following, from left to right: (front row) Dewey Waugh, George Lerchen, Myron "Joe" Ginsberg, William Heist, Bruce Blanchard, John "Clem" Koshorek, Amil Brinsky, Jerry Burke, an unknown player, batboy Phil Campbell, ballboy Dick Mott, and trainer Art Kepler; (back row) Rankin Johnson Jr., Charles Giddens, Herm Bishop, Norm Scott, Frank Heller, Jim Moran, Earle W. Halstead, George Detore, Dick Dressler, John Groth, William Wigle, Art McConnell, Elbie Flint, and an unidentified player. (PV-LCHS.)

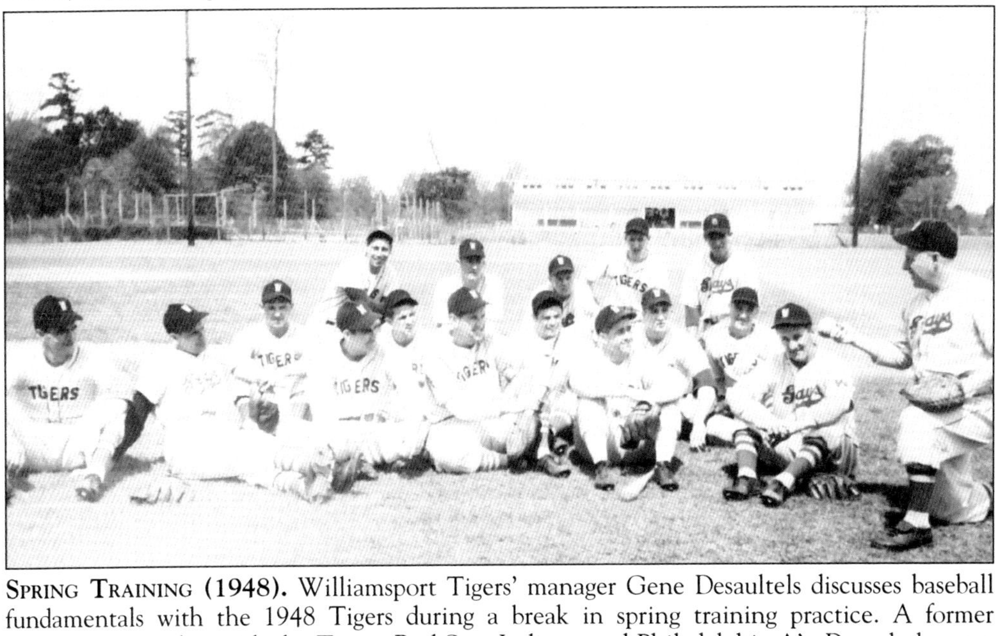

Spring Training (1948). Williamsport Tigers' manager Gene Desaultels discusses baseball fundamentals with the 1948 Tigers during a break in spring training practice. A former journeyman catcher with the Tigers, Red Sox, Indians, and Philadelphia A's, Desaultels was a well-respected minor-league manager. He was the only manager during Williamsport's affiliation with Detroit (1946–1952) to manage two full seasons. (*GRIT*.)

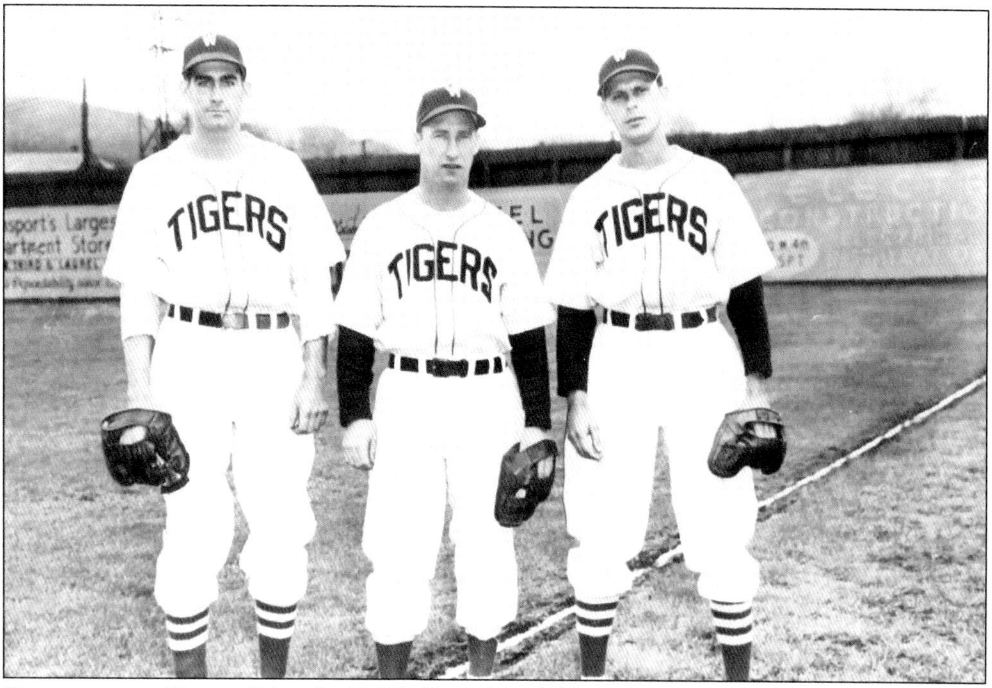

TIGERS ON THE PROWL (MAY 2, 1948). Tigers' outfielders Ken Humphreys, Amil Brinsky, and Walt Chipple pose along the right field foul line. Humphreys hit .287 and drove in 67 runs for Williamsport during the 1948 campaign. Brinsky contributed 73 RBIs and batted .273. (*GRIT*.)

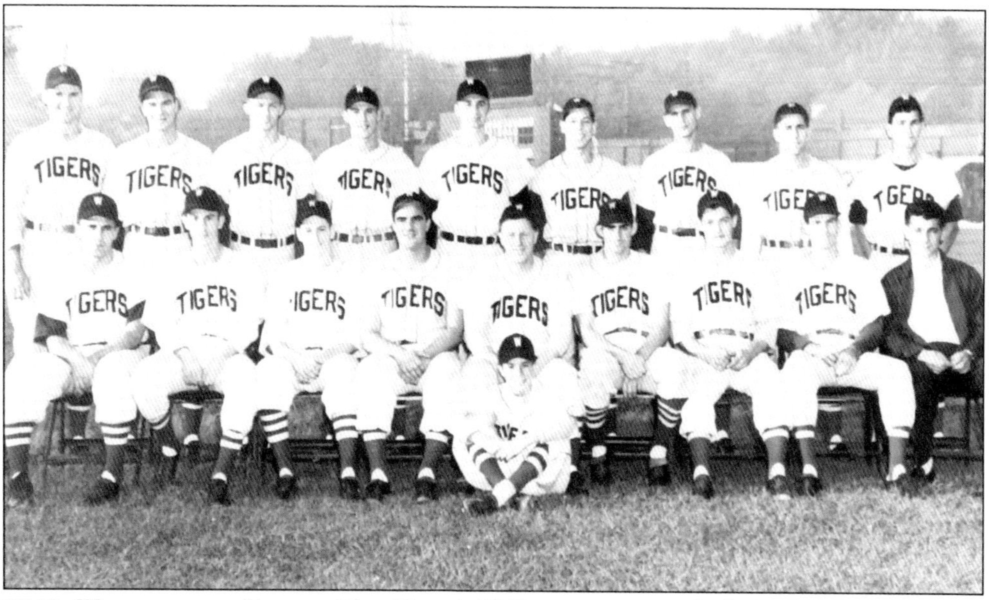

1948 WILLIAMSPORT TIGERS. The Tigers' 1948 campaign marked the best season for a Williamsport team since the Governor's Cup appearance of the 1941 team. Led by hurler Lou Kretlow (21-12, 219 strikeouts, and a no-hitter) and Eastern League batting champion Bruce Blanchard (.327), the Tigers just missed clinching a playoff berth. Kretlow (second row, fifth player), Blanchard (second row, eighth player), and catcher Joe Ginsburg (second row sixth player) earned berths on the 1948 Eastern League All-Star team. (*GRIT*.)

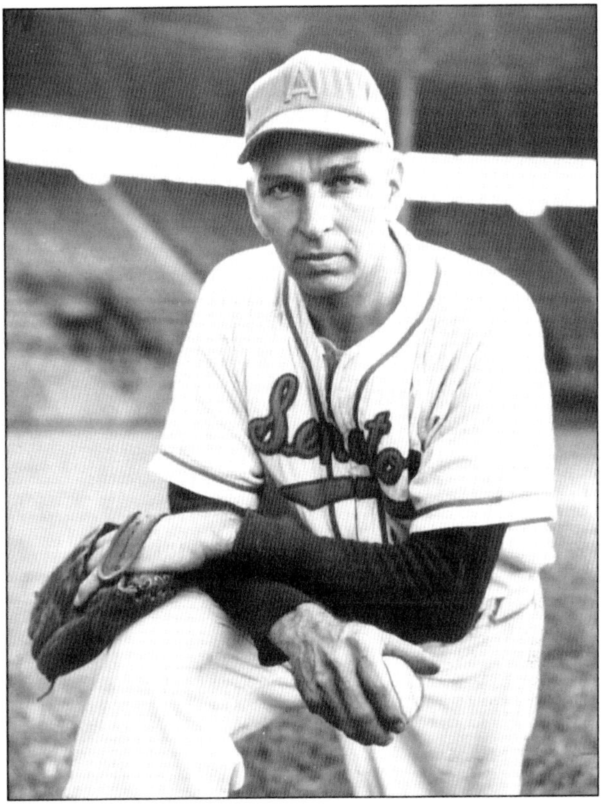

Grand Old Man of Pitching (1949). Pitcher Orrie Arntzen, formerly with the Williamsport Grays during the early 1940s, was a model of longevity. Shown here in the visiting uniform of the Eastern League Albany Senators, the 39-year-old veteran was a 20-game winner and the Minor League Player of the Year in 1949. (*GRIT*.)

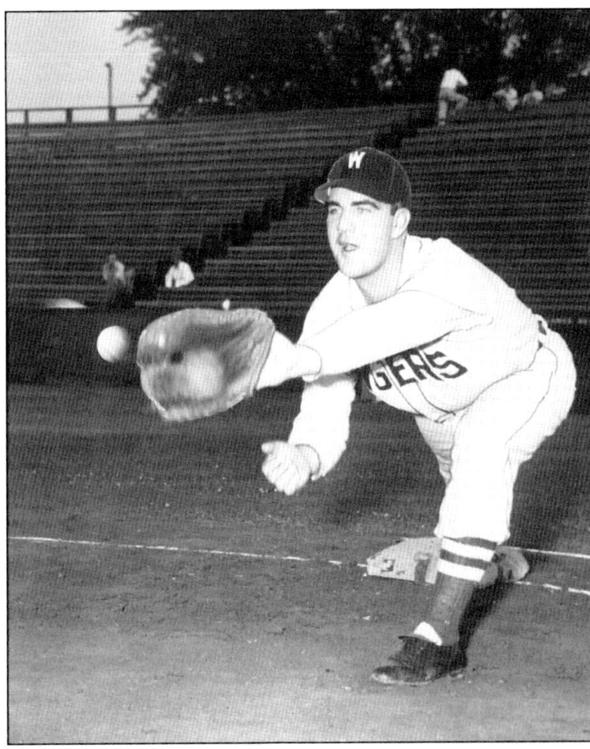

Tigers' First Baseman Frank Heller (1948). Heller shows his form as he stretches for a throw at first base. A favorite with local Tiger fans, Heller clouted 18 home runs and led the Eastern League in RBIs with 98 in 1947. He was Williamsport's lone representative on the Eastern League All Star team that year. Though his power statistics declined in 1948, Heller still managed to hit for a respectable average of .306. (*GRIT*.)

ELMER'S CORNER (1948). Big Elmer Swanson, bat in hand, holds court with the right field bleacher bums on a chilly April day. Tiger fans enjoyed Swanson's humor and loved to barb him from the cheap seats. (*GRIT.*)

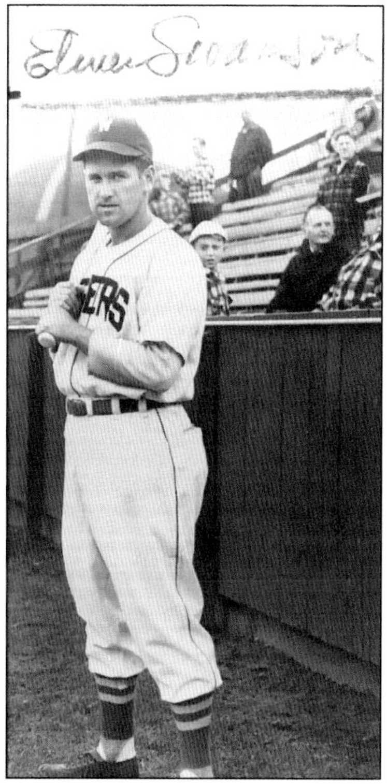

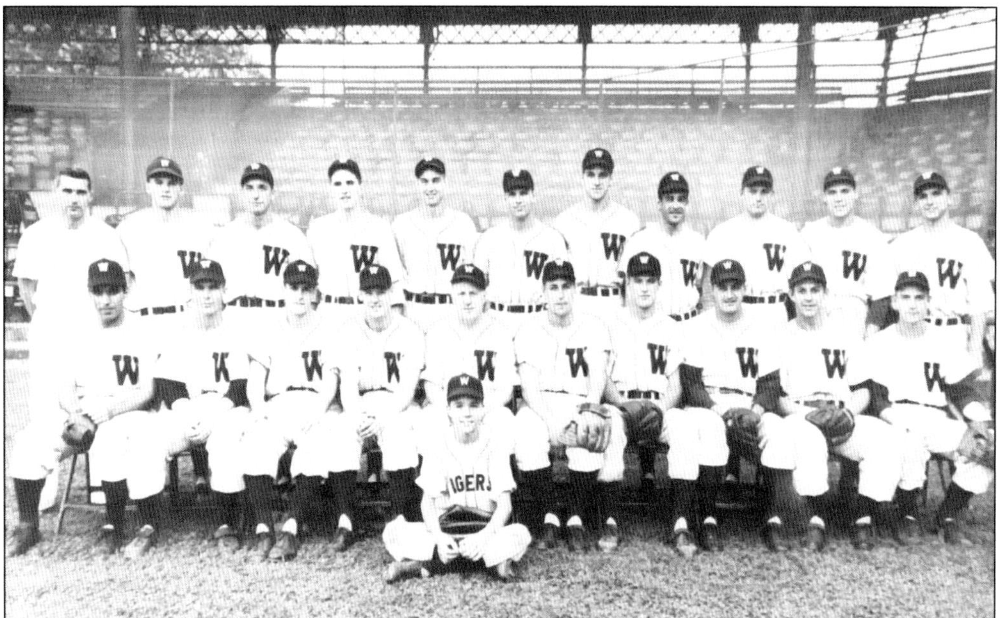

1949 WILLIAMSPORT TIGERS. A porous defense, coupled with a battered pitching staff, spelled disaster for manager Gene Desaultels and his charges. The Tigers finished in fifth place with a record of 66-74. One bright sport for Williamsport was the emergence of slugger Dale Long. Long, a future major leaguer with the Cubs, hit 11 home runs and drove in 81 runs for the Tigers in 1949. (*GRIT.*)

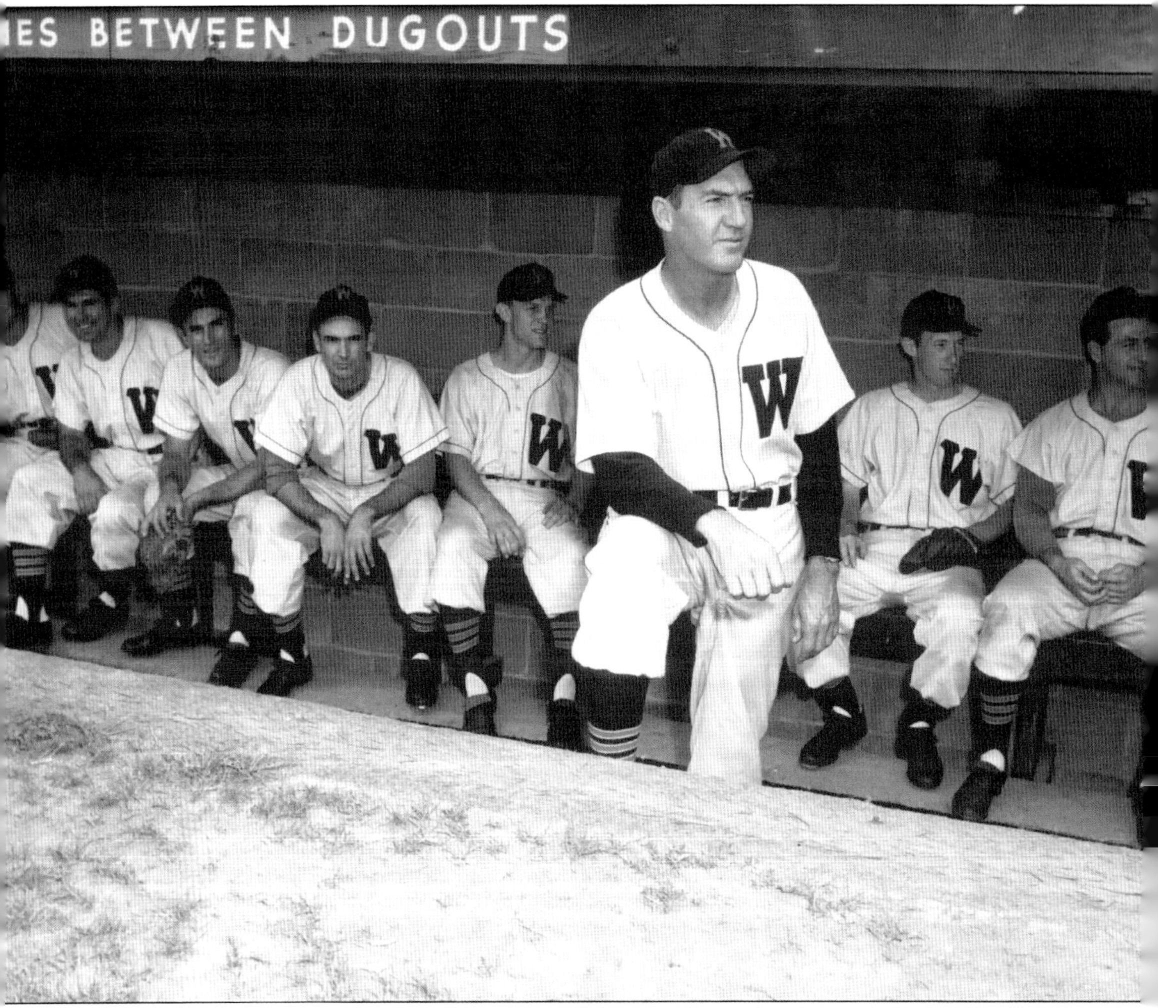

TIGERS' MANAGER LYNWOOD "SCHOOLBOY" ROWE (1951). Manager "Schoolboy" Rowe monitors the ballgame from the top steps of the home dugout. A former pitching ace of the Detroit Tigers, Rowe took the helm of the 1951 Williamsport Tigers and filled in as a spot starter for the team's depleted pitching staff. He earned a 6-3 mark during the 1951 season. Unfortunately, the Tigers' pitchers failed to learn from the master. With the exception of Alex McNeilance (11-9), no other Williamsport hurler achieved a winning record. In one game (May 3, 1951) against the Binghamton Triplets, the Tigers were shellacked by the score of 22-1. Rowe was very popular with Williamsport fans. On "Player Appreciation Night" he was presented with two hunting dogs to pursue his favorite pastime outside of baseball. (PV-LCHS.)

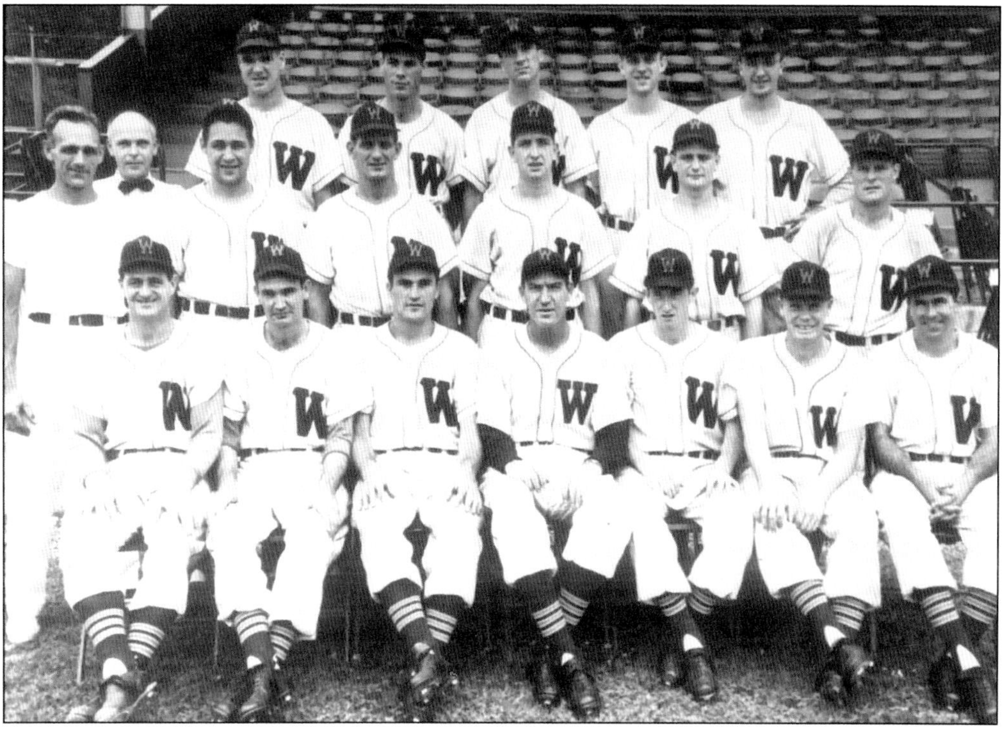

1951 Williamsport Tigers. The 1951 Tigers, a team composed of aging veterans and inexperienced younger players, finished next to last with a record of 55-84. Don Manno (second row, fourth person from left) concluded his stellar baseball career by being named to the 1951 Eastern League All Star team. Also in this picture is Williamsport's general manager, Robert Steinhilper (second row, second person from left), wearing his signature bow tie. (*GRIT.*)

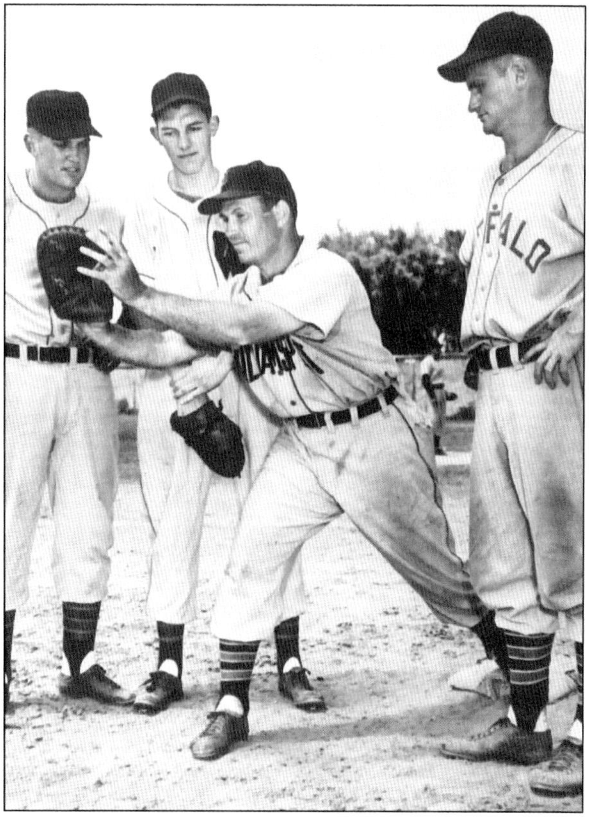

Manager Paul Campbell Instructs Tigers (April 20, 1952). Player-manager Paul Campbell shows prospective Tigers' first basemen Dick Giedlin (far left), Gordon "Digger" O'Dell (left center), and Tom Falk (far right) the proper way to hold a runner on first base. Campbell led the Tigers in hitting with a .318 average, second-best in the Eastern League in 1952. (*GRIT.*)

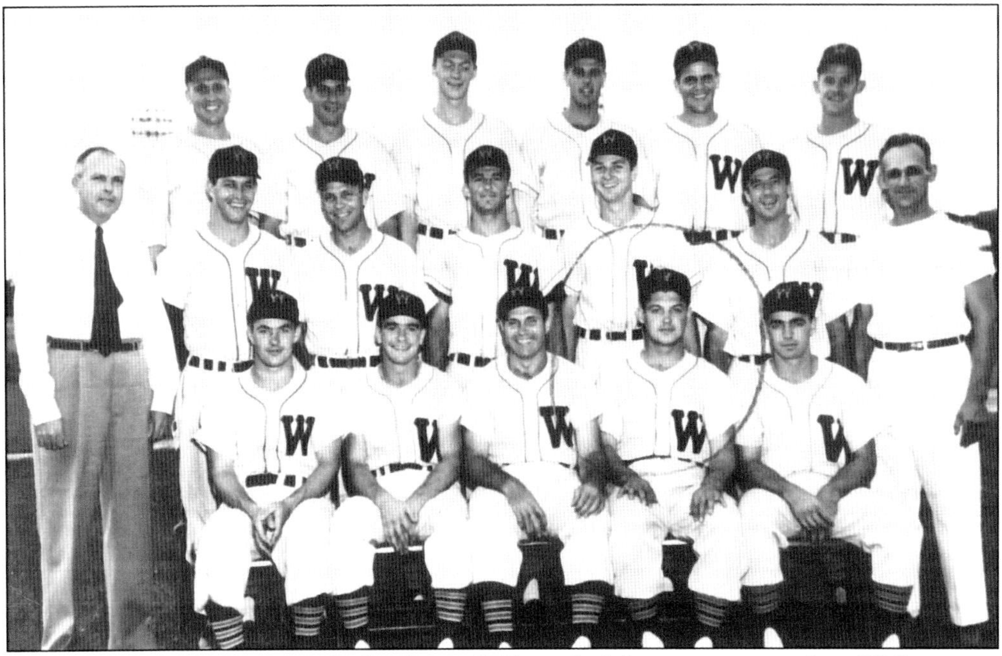

1952 WILLIAMSPORT TIGERS. The hapless 1952 Tigers had the worst season of any Williamsport franchise up to that point, finishing last with a record of 48-90, and the lowest attendance figure since the 1945 season. One notable member of the '52 squad was future Hall of Fame pitcher Jim Bunning, the lanky youngster in the back row (third person from left). Then 19, he suffered through his rookie professional season with a 5-9 record and 85 strikeouts. (*GRIT*.)

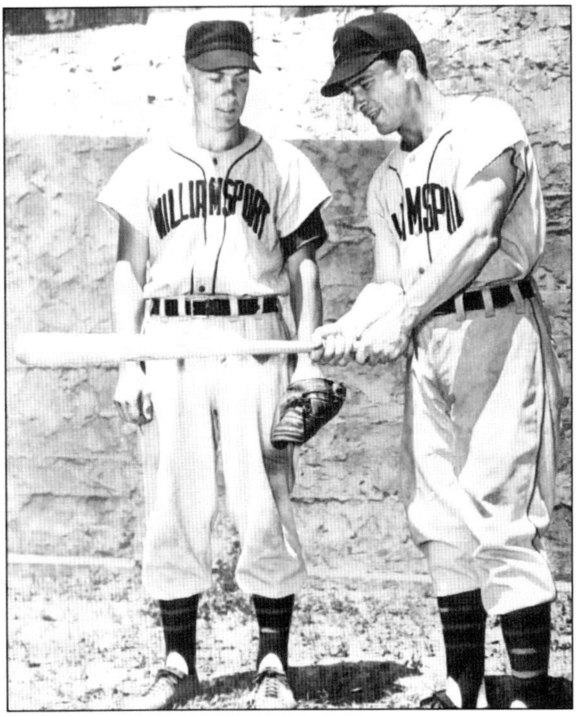

SPRING TRAINING (APRIL 20, 1952). Players Liesecki (left) and George Bullard compare hitting styles at the Williamsport Tigers' spring training complex before the start of the season. Bullard ended the season hitting at a .285 clip. (*GRIT*.)

Concentration on the Mound (April 27, 1952). Williamsport Tigers' pitcher Jim Martin gets ready to deliver a pitch during a pre-season workout at Bowman Field. (*GRIT*.)

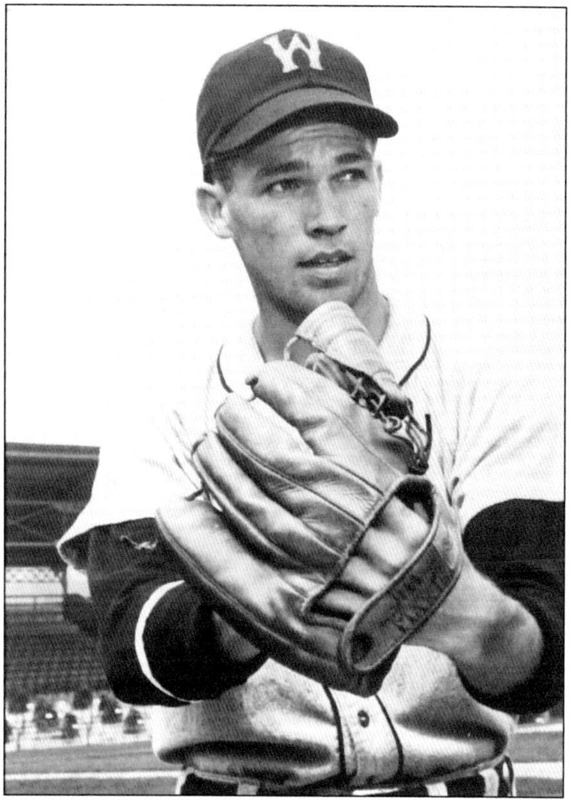

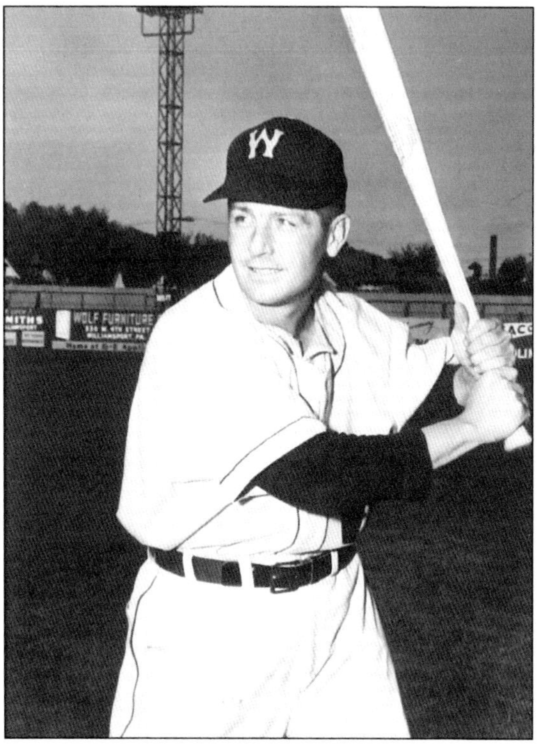

Fleet Flyhawk (1952). Williamsport Tigers' outfielder Bob Mavis displays his batting stance for the camera. Mavis split the 1952 season between Williamsport and Buffalo, and later played for the Detroit Tigers. He was one of five members of the 1952 Williamsport Tigers to eventually play in the Major Leagues. (*GRIT*.)

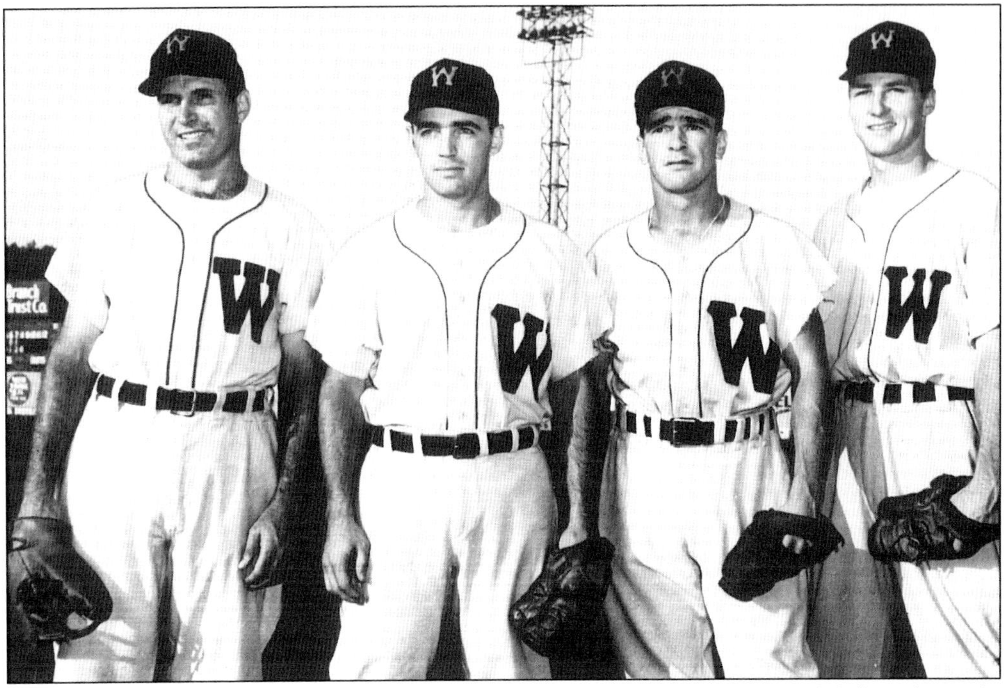

TIGERS' INFIELDERS (JULY 20, 1952). Williamsport's starting infield—Cumbdell, Bob Cook, George Bullard, and Frank Bolling—prepares to flash some leather at the opposition. (*GRIT*.)

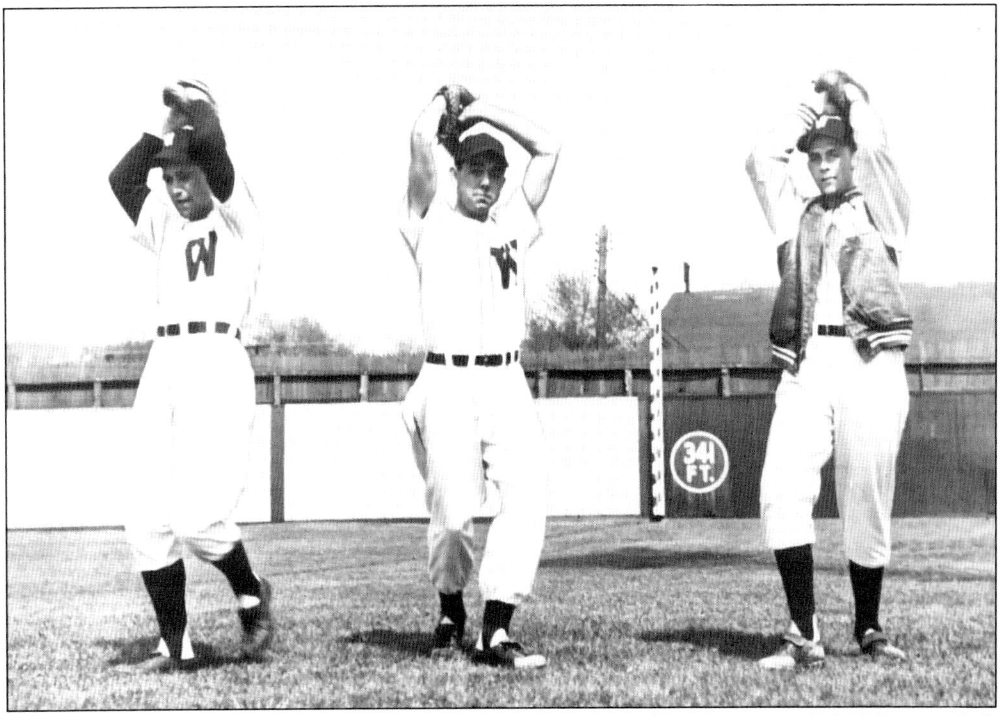

TIGERS' PITCHING TRIO (MAY 4, 1952). Williamsport pitchers Werner "Babe" Birrer, Bob Cruze, and Dick Marlow are shown in the middle of their respective windups as they loosen up during a Tigers' practice session. (*GRIT*.)

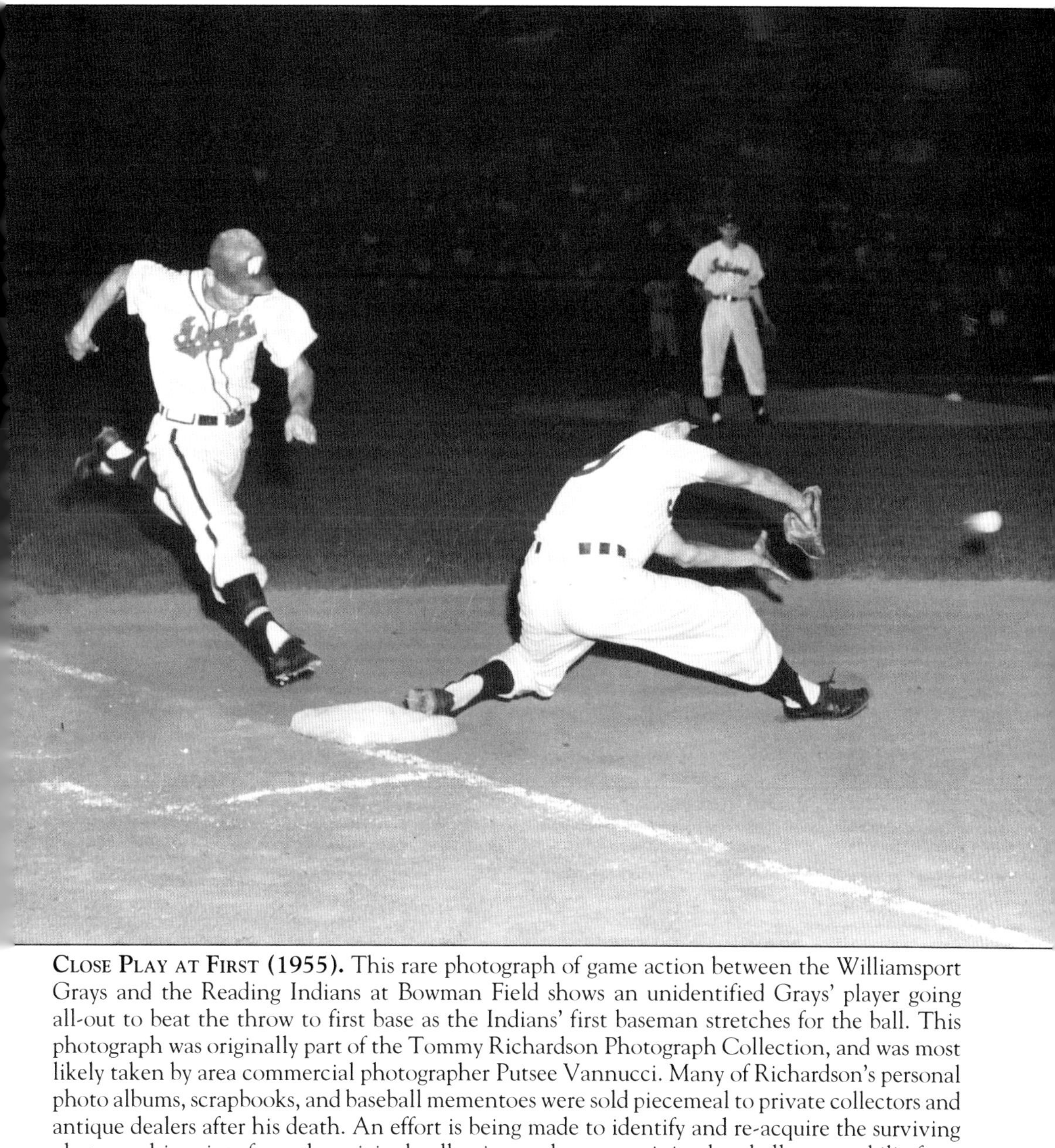

Close Play at First (1955). This rare photograph of game action between the Williamsport Grays and the Reading Indians at Bowman Field shows an unidentified Grays' player going all-out to beat the throw to first base as the Indians' first baseman stretches for the ball. This photograph was originally part of the Tommy Richardson Photograph Collection, and was most likely taken by area commercial photographer Putsee Vannucci. Many of Richardson's personal photo albums, scrapbooks, and baseball mementoes were sold piecemeal to private collectors and antique dealers after his death. An effort is being made to identify and re-acquire the surviving photographic prints from the original collection and any remaining baseball memorabilia from Richardson's collection. (TR.)

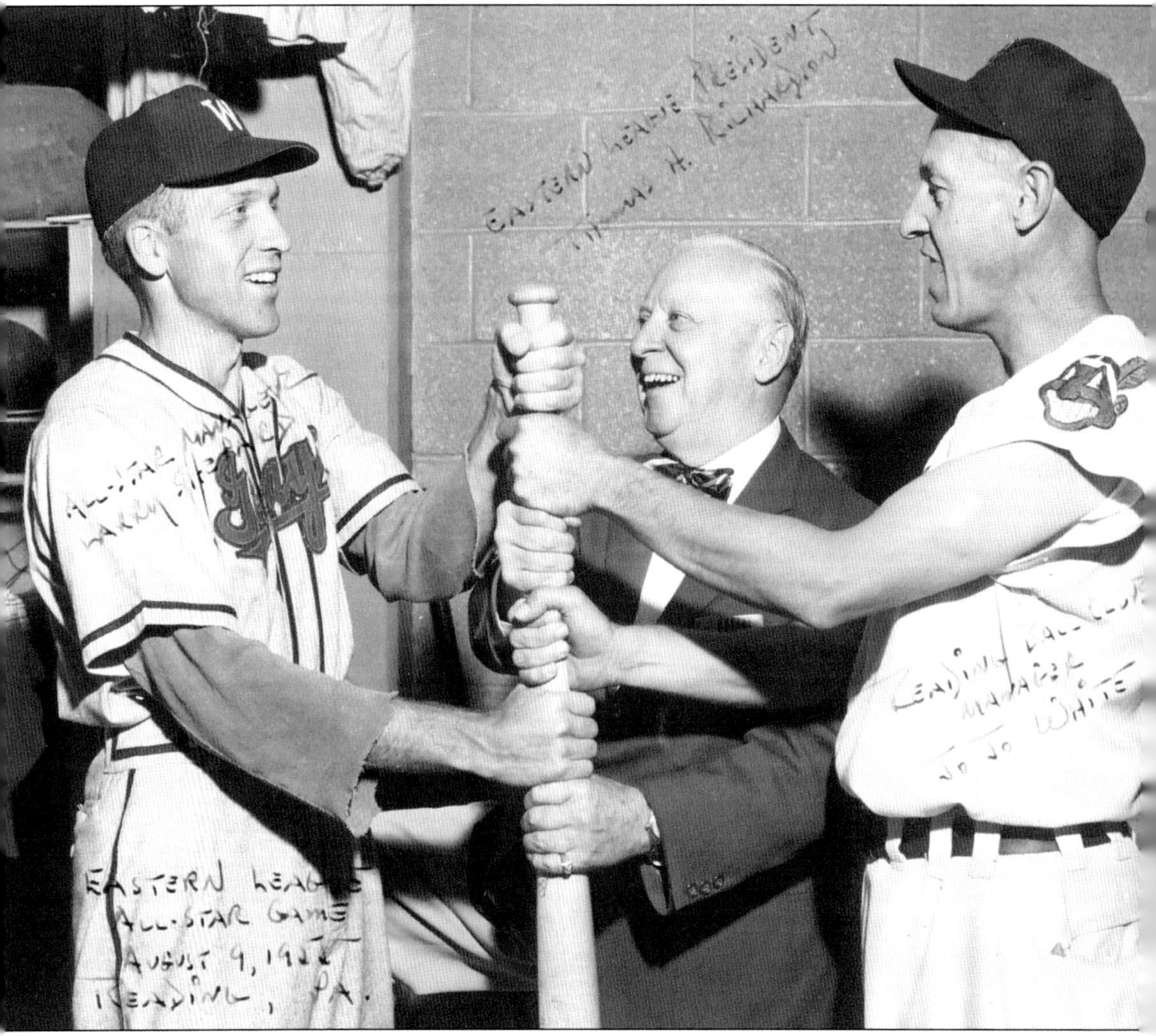

WHO'S UP FIRST (AUGUST 9, 1955)? Eastern League president Tommy Richardson (center) is flanked by Williamsport Grays' manager Larry Shepard (left), and Reading Indians' skipper Jo Jo White (right) as they engage in a friendly game of grip-the-bat prior to the start of the 1955 Eastern League All-Star game held at Reading in 1955. Shepard and White were tabbed as managers of the respective all-star teams. As a player-manager with the Grays in 1954 and 1955, Shepard was one of the oldest pitchers (36) in the Eastern League. At one point during the 1955 season he won 11 straight decisions, most of them coming in relief opportunities. He finished with a 16-9 record. Shepard later managed the Cincinnati Reds and Pittsburgh Pirates. (*GRIT*.)

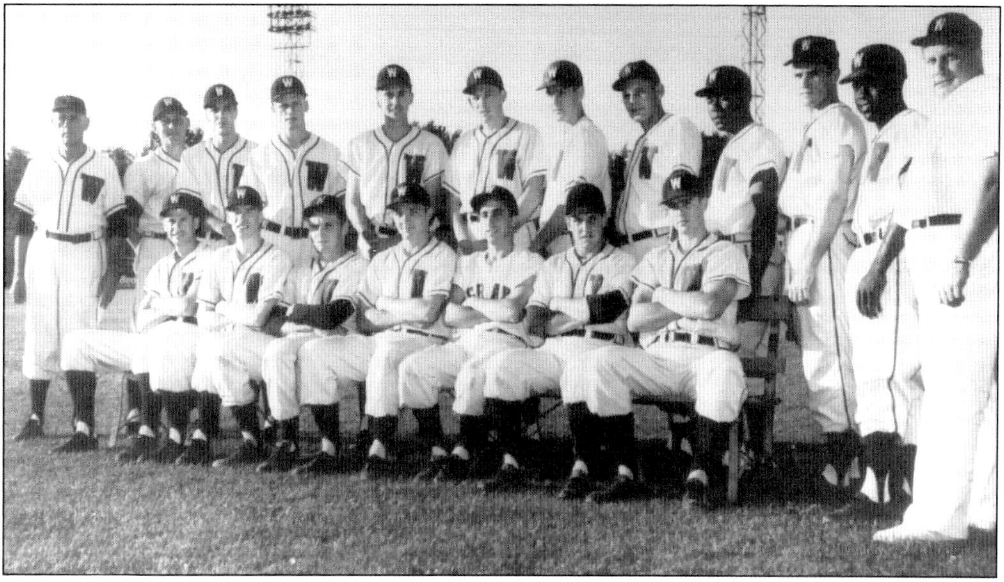

1955 Williamsport Grays. The 1955 Grays, an affiliate of the Pittsburgh Pirates, finished fifth in the Eastern League standings with a record of 71-66—just missing a playoff berth. It was the first year since 1948 that the local club sported a winning record. Williamsport's outstanding hitters were Milt Graff (.317), Emil Panko (24 home runs and 103 RBIs), and future Pirates' star Bill Mazeroski (pictured standing, second from left). (*GRIT*.)

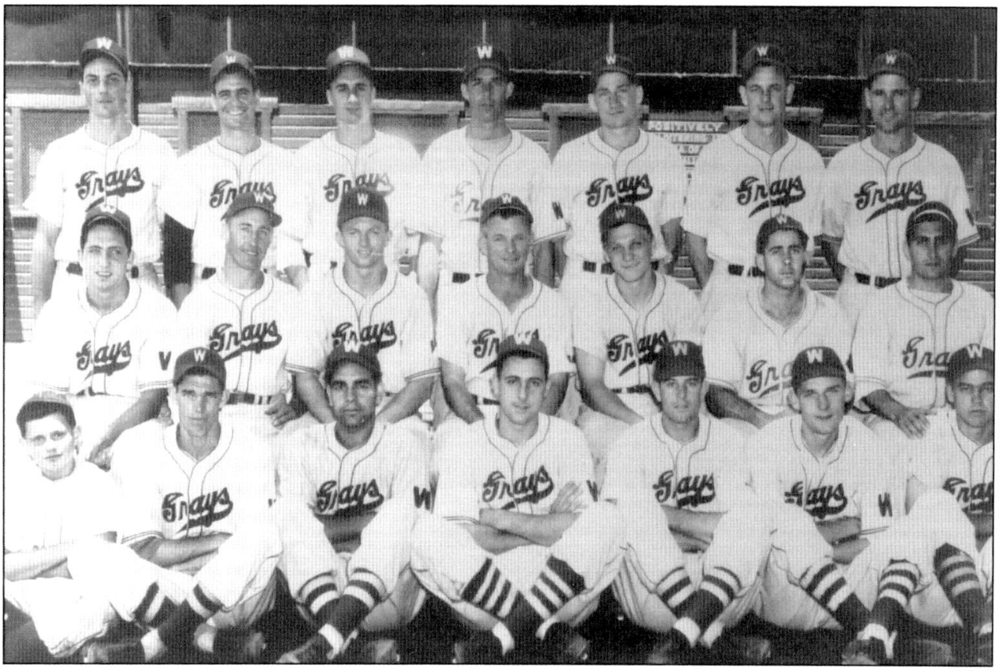

1956 Williamsport Grays. Plagued by anemic hitting, poor pitching, and financial problems in the front office, the 1956 Grays sputtered to a seventh-place finish with a record of 60-78. Tony Bartirome, Joe Christopher, and Charlie Buheller were the club's leading hitters that year. Bartirome went 4 for 4 the last game of the season to win the batting crown (.305) by a single point over his closest rival. (*GRIT*.)

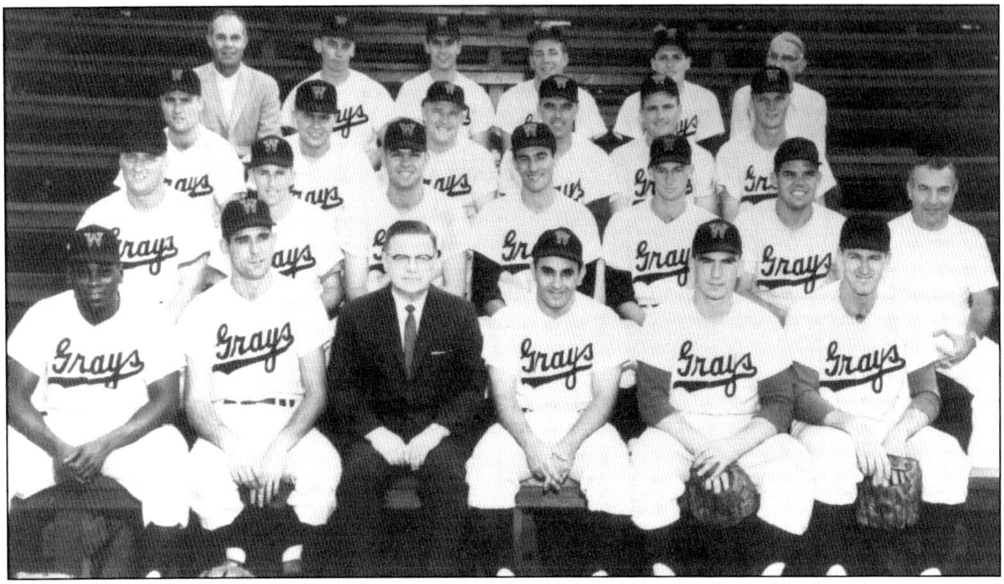

1959 WILLIAMSPORT GRAYS. Known as the "Blitz Kids," these Phillies' farmhands constituted one of the most power-laden teams in Williamsport baseball history. The 1959 Grays (81-60) swept Allentown in the first round of the Eastern League playoffs before bowing out to the powerful Springfield Giants. Managed by the irascible Frank Lucchesi, the team included veteran Phillies' pitcher Curt Simmons and such hitting stars as Fred Hopke, Jacke Davis, and Eastern League MVP Tony Curry. (*GRIT.*)

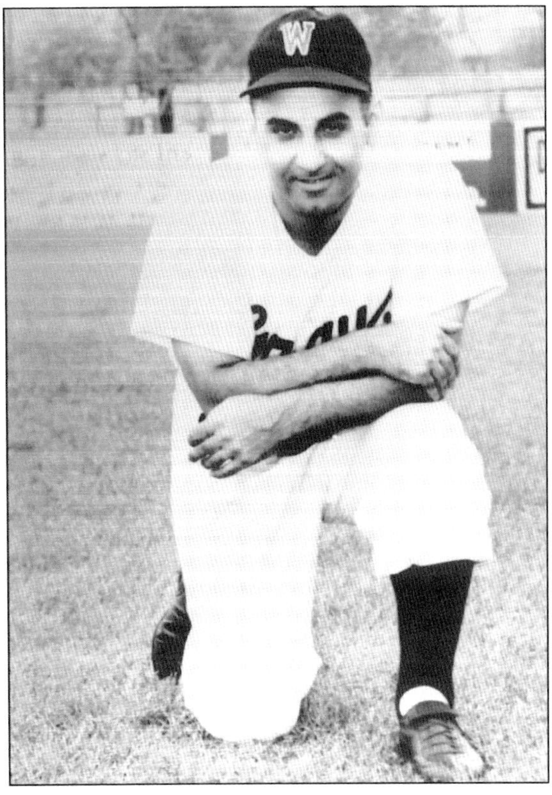

MANAGER FRANK LUCCHESI (1959). A crowd favorite at Bowman Field, particularly with Italians from Williamsport's "Little Hollywood" section, Lucchesi was famous for his antics and arguments with Eastern League umpires. During his three-year stint (1959–1960, 1962) with Williamsport, he compiled the second best managerial record in franchise history, second only to the Harry Hinchman. Lucchesi later managed the Phillies and Texas Rangers. (*GRIT.*)

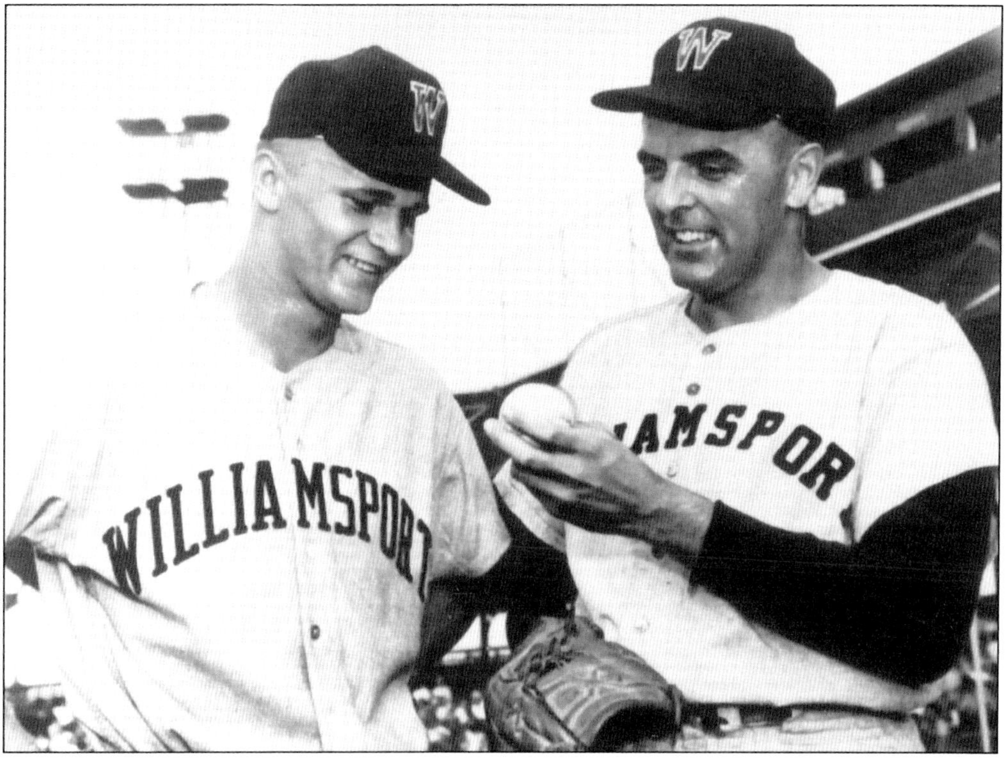

Curt Lends a Hand (1959). Veteran Philadelphia Phillies' pitcher Curt Simmons, on rehabilitation assignment from the parent club, shows Grays' pitcher Bob "Gunner" Gontkosky his grip for the two-seam fastball prior to a game at Bowman Field. Simmons' advice was well-heeded as "Gunner" hurled three one-hitters during the season, including a 15-strikeout performance on April 29, 1959. (*GRIT.*)

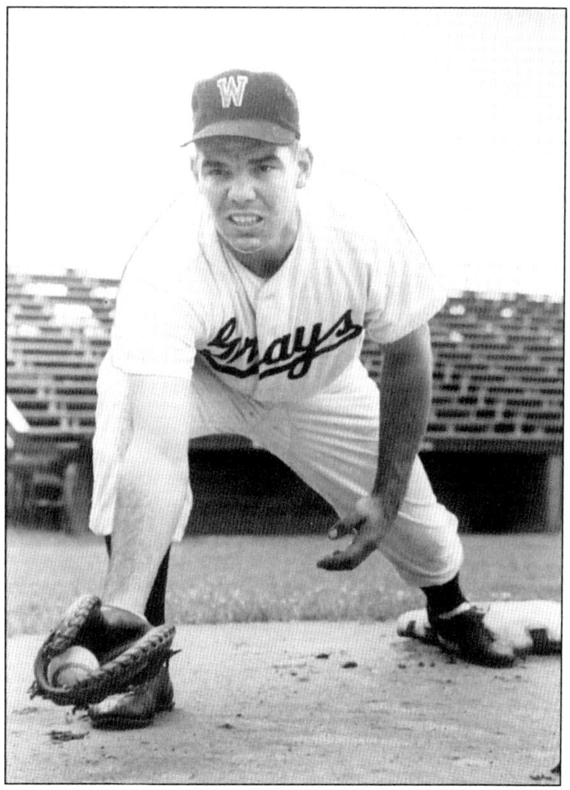

First Baseman Fred Hopke (1959). One of the main cogs of the 1959 "Blitz Kids," Hopke established Williamsport's all-time modern record for RBIs in a season with 130. He also clouted 30 home runs, batted .316, and earned Eastern League All-Star honors in 1959. Hopke displays his defensive form in this photograph. (*GRIT.*)

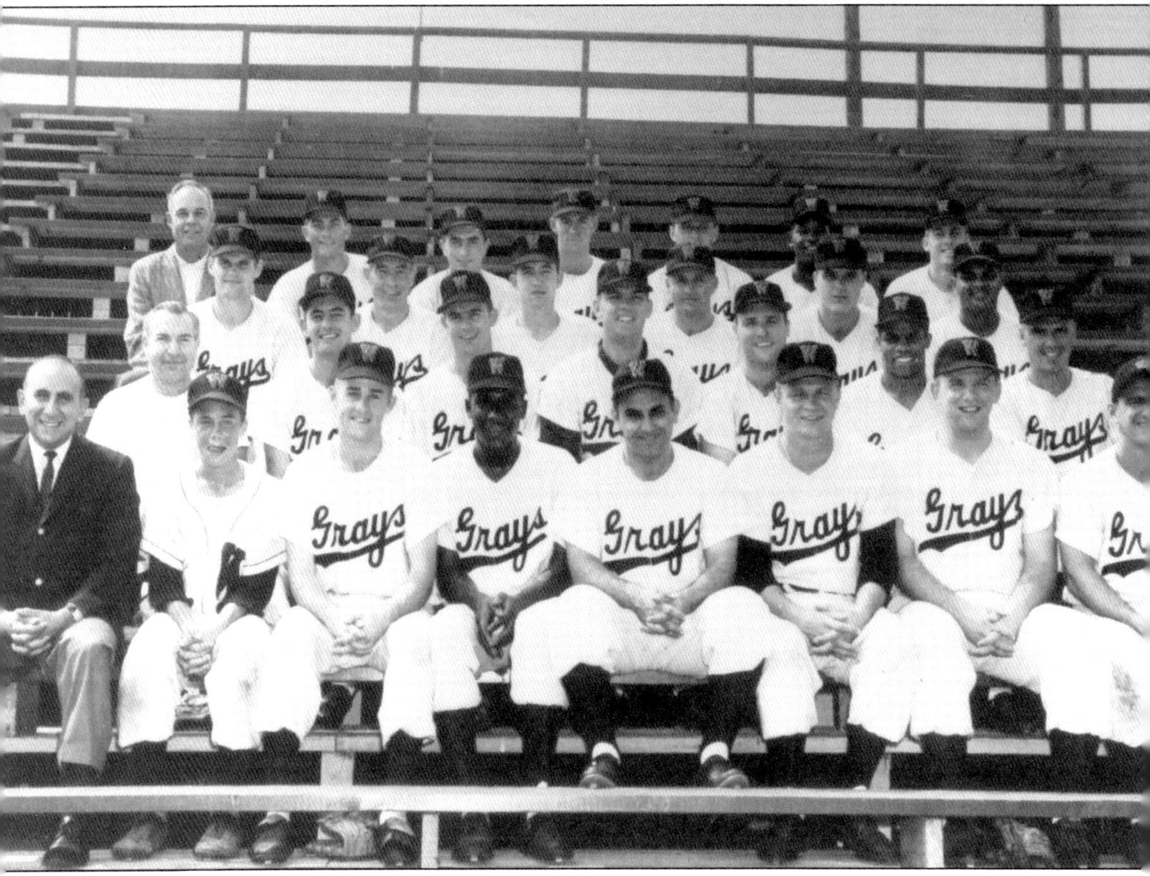

THE "GO-GO GRAYS" (1960). The Williamsport "Go-Go Grays" of 1960 were arguably one of the city's best baseball teams in a generation. Piloted by Frank Lucchesi, the spirited club included ten players destined for the Major Leagues. After knocking on the door for Eastern League championship honors the previous season, the Grays finally achieved their goal of winning the regular season pennant. Though Williamsport ultimately shared the title with the Springfield Giants (Hurricane Donna forced the cancellation of the championship series), the team's place in Williamsport's baseball history was forever etched. The 1960 Grays possessed a fine blend of hitting, speed, and pitching. Paced by speedster Ted Savage, the Eastern League leader in stolen bases, the team was very aggressive on the base paths. Other notable players on the Go-Go Grays were slugger John Hernstein, Danny Cater (later a member of the Oakland A's, New York Yankees, and Boston Red Sox), Lee Elia, and pitchers Norm Camp and Jerry Kettle. (WS-G.)

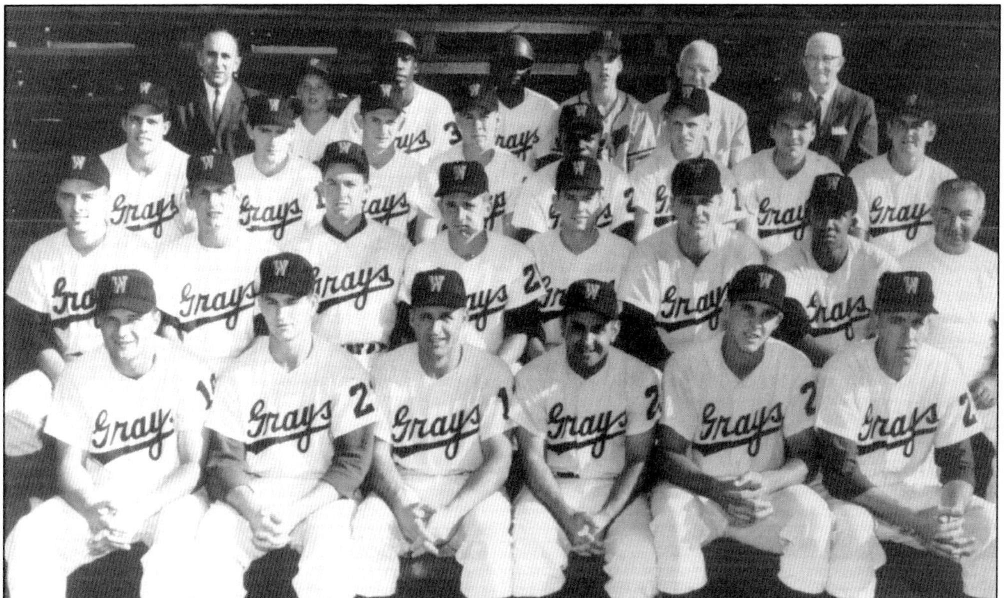

1962 Williamsport Grays. The 1962 pennant-winning Grays were led by future Phillies' slugger Richie "Dick" Allen (fourth row, fourth person from left), outfielder Bobby Sanders (fourth row, third person from left), and pitchers Ray Culp and "Gunner" Gontkosky. The team had a stellar record of 83-57 but fell to Elmira in the league championship series. Future Hall of Fame pitcher Ferguson Jenkins (second row, second person from right) joined the Grays in late August but did not appear in any games. (*WS-G*.)

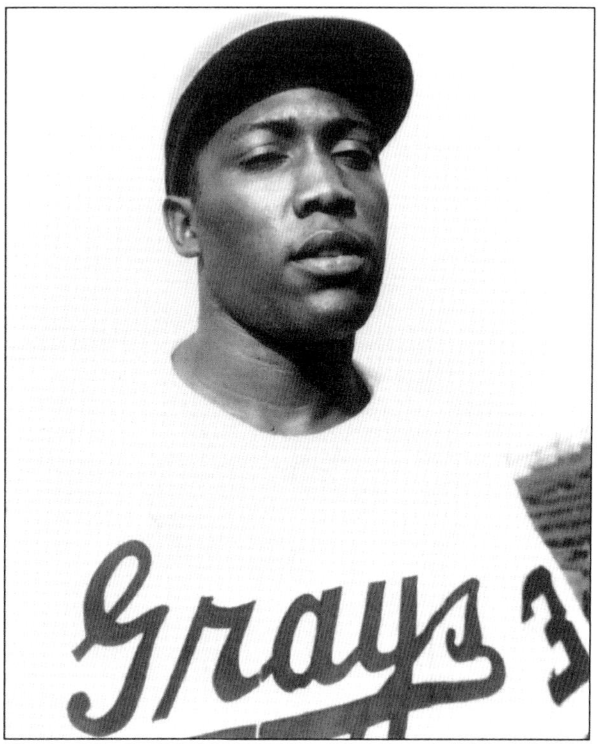

Outfielder Bobby Sanders (1962). One of the main pistons in Williamsport's drive for the 1962 Eastern League pennant was outfielder Bobby Sanders, pictured here wearing his batting helmet. Sanders, the Eastern League MVP in 1962, batted .310, smacked 20 home runs and 79 RBIs, and led the league in runs scored with 98. (*GRIT*.)

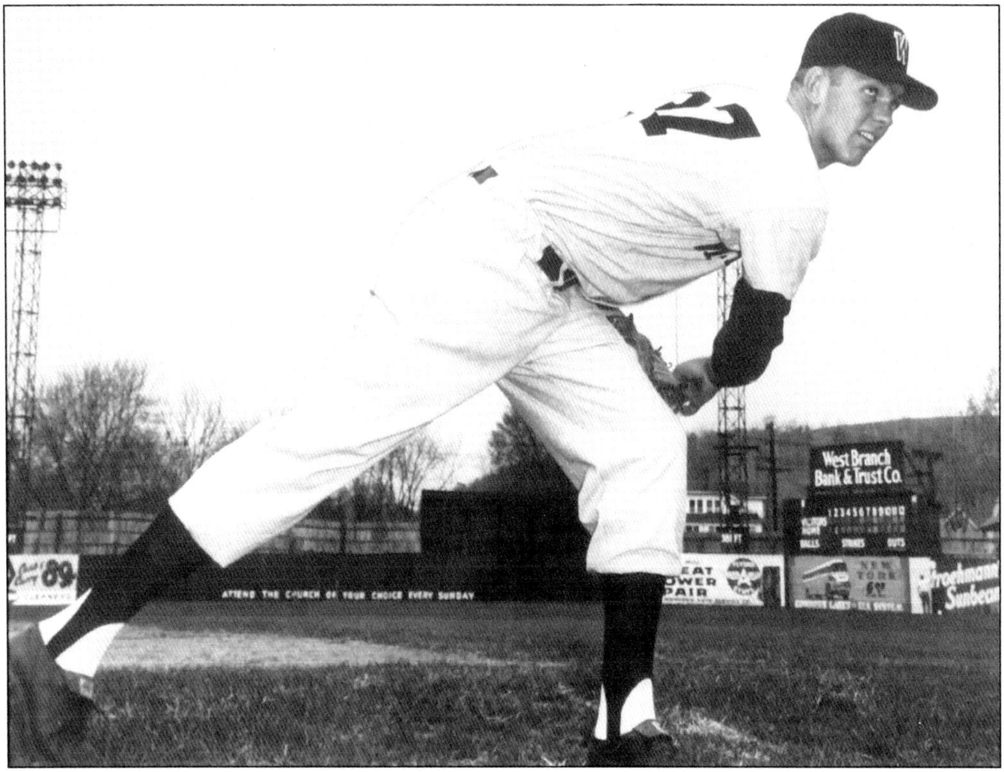

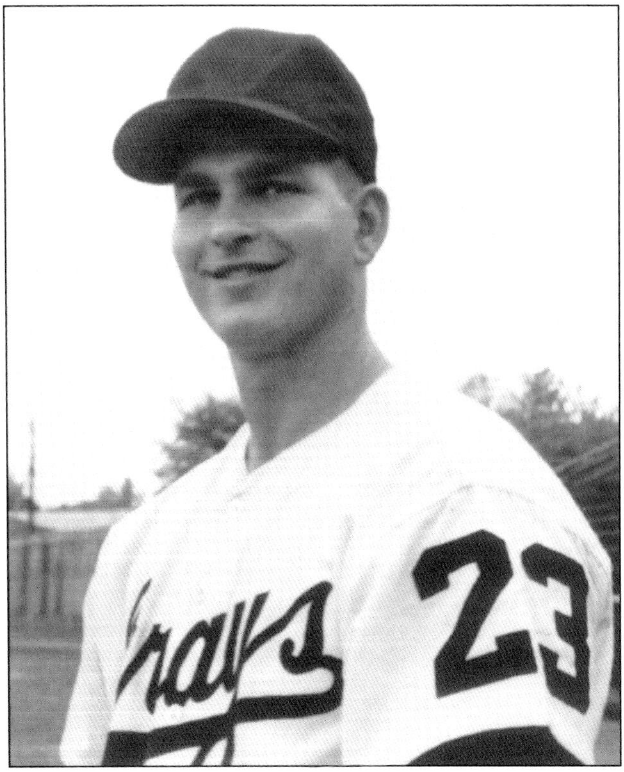

Pitcher George Horvath (1960). One of the unsung heroes of the Grays' pitching staff and bullpen was youngster George Horvath, shown here during a pre-season workout at Bowman Field. (*GRIT*.)

Pitcher Ray Culp (1962). Ray Culp's boyish grin belies the fiery competitiveness and intensity that propelled him to a lengthy major-league career. Culp anchored the 1962 Grays' pitching staff with a 13-8 record and 185 strikeouts. He beat the Philadelphia Phillies in an exhibition game that year, tossing a five-hitter. (*GRIT*.)

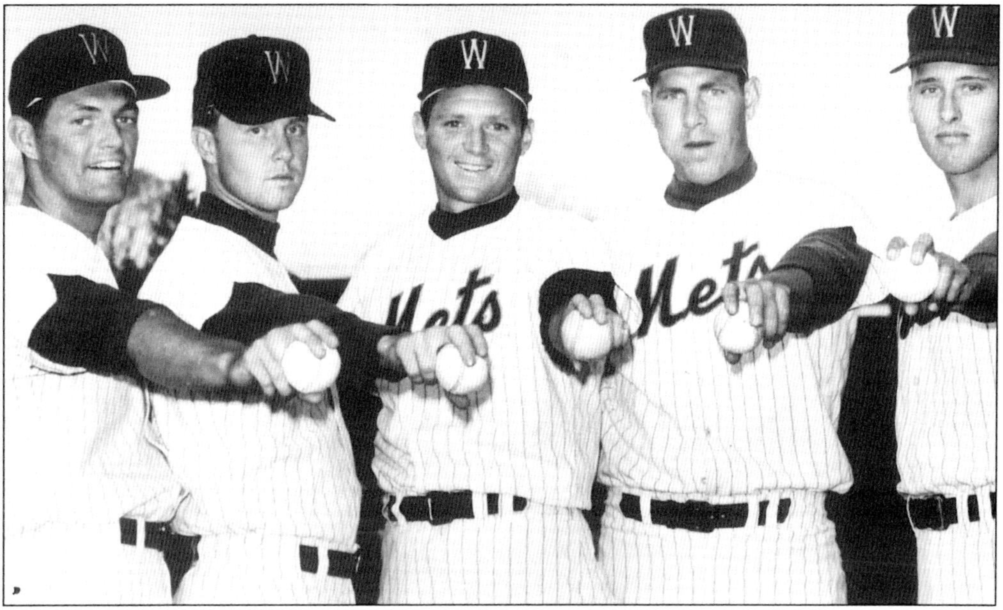

Meet the Mets (April 24, 1966). Williamsport gained a new parent club in 1964, the New York Mets, and the "lovable losers" were the darlings of the town during their period of affiliation with the local franchise from 1964 to 1967. From left to right, Mets' pitchers Bill Denehy, Jay Cardin, Terry Christman, Jerry Kraft, and "Bonus Baby" Les Rohr display their respective grips for the fastball. (*GRIT.*)

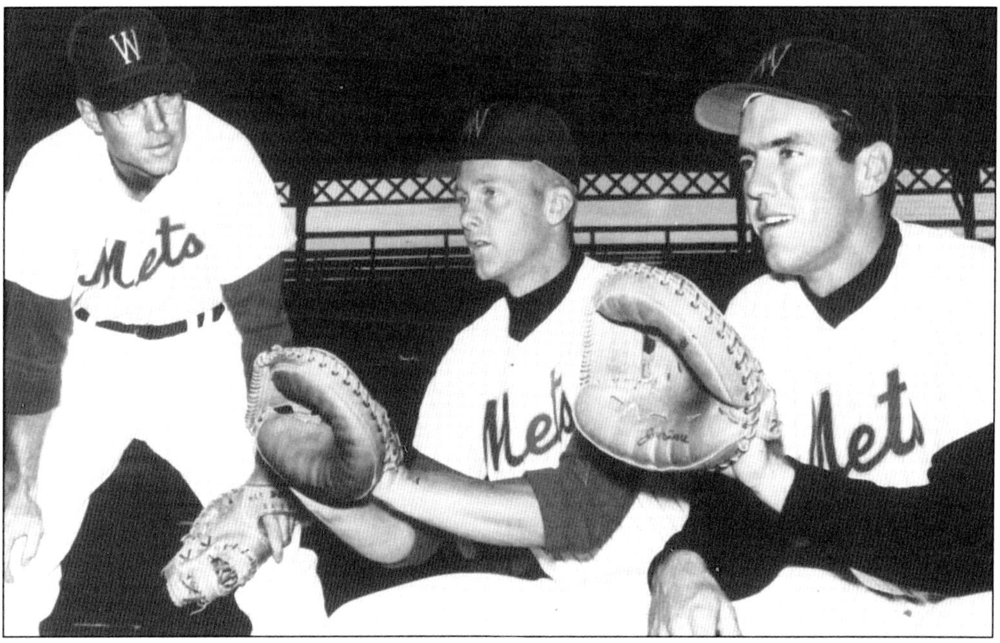

Williamsport Mets' Catching Corps (April 24, 1966). Manager Bill Virdon checks the form of his primary receivers Lloyd Flodin (center) and Hank McGraw (right). Traded to Elmira in mid-season, McGraw won the league home run title with 12. The free-spirited catcher was later suspended from one team for refusing to cut his long hair. Hank's brother, Frank "Tug" McGraw, was a "closer" for the champion 1969 Mets and 1980 Phillies. (*GRIT.*)

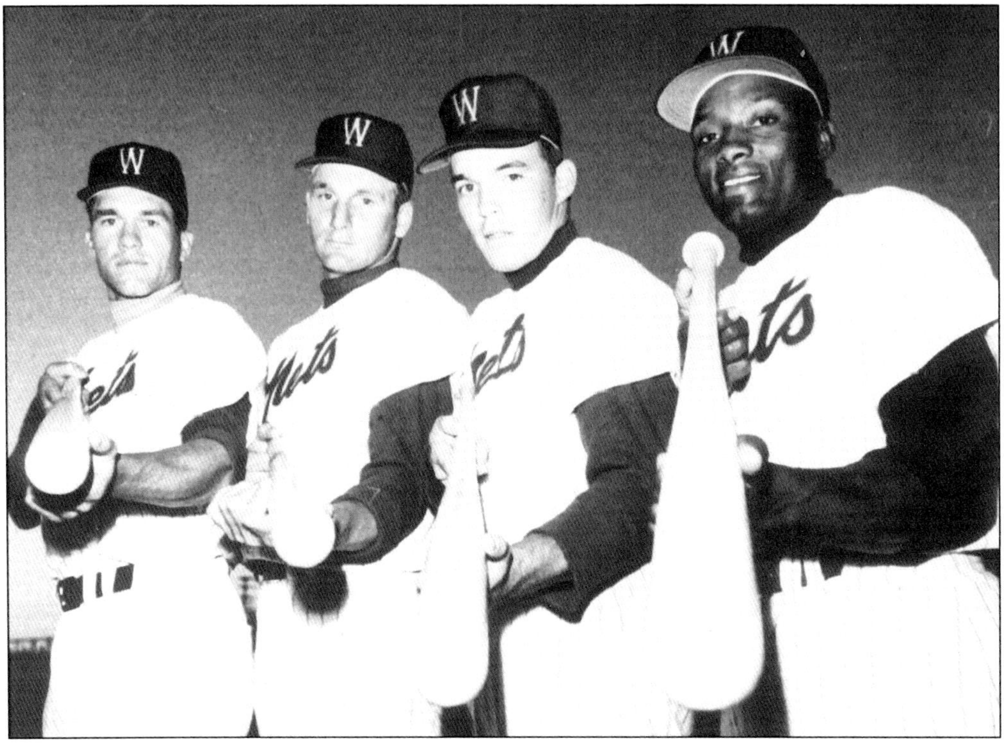

Mets' Outfielders and Their Lumber (April 24, 1966). From left to right, outfielders Jon O'Dell, Al Yates, Jim Lampe, and Bernie Smith provided a formidable line-up on opening day. Smith, the fleet-footed center fielder, was a crowd favorite at Bowman Field. In 1967 he took the batting crown (hitting .307) and was named Eastern League MVP for the season. (*GRIT*.)

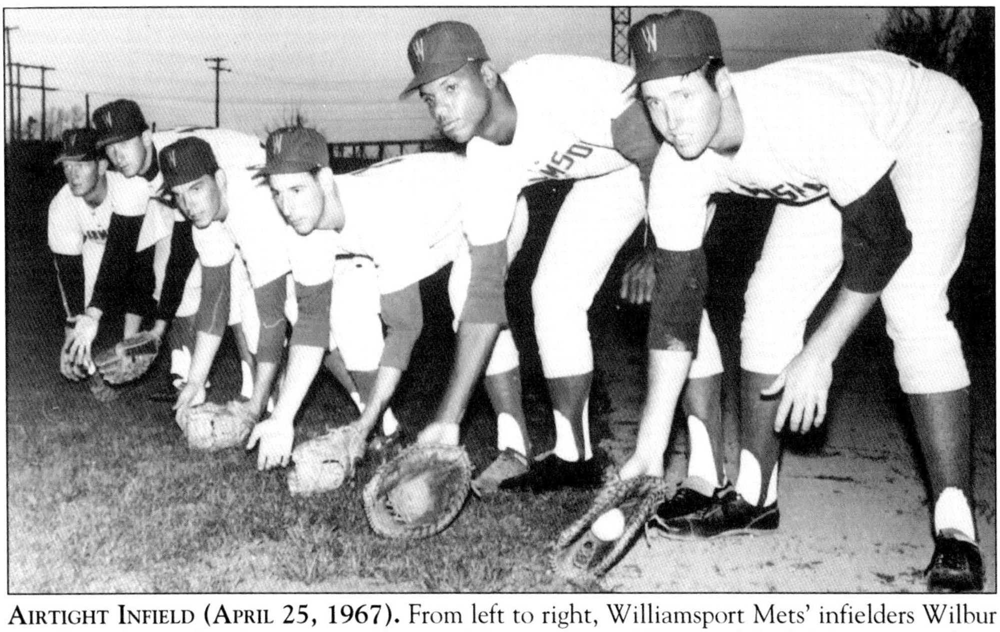

Airtight Infield (April 25, 1967). From left to right, Williamsport Mets' infielders Wilbur Huckle, John Pavlus, Jim Lampe, Sherwin Minster, Dave Allen, and Dick Martin pose for a *Grit* photographer after a pre-season workout under the Bowman Field lights. (*GRIT*.)

CARL "NELS" NELSON (1964). Williamsport Mets' pitcher Carl Nelson is a model of intensity in this portrait captured before the start of the 1964 season. Nelson produced one of the few highlights in the Mets' inaugural season in Williamsport by tossing a seven-inning no-hitter in the first game of a doubleheader against York on June 30, 1964. (*GRIT*.)

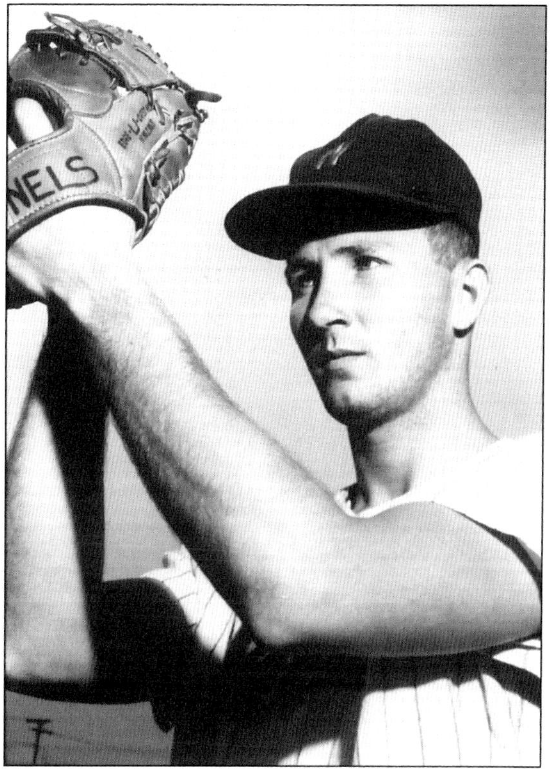

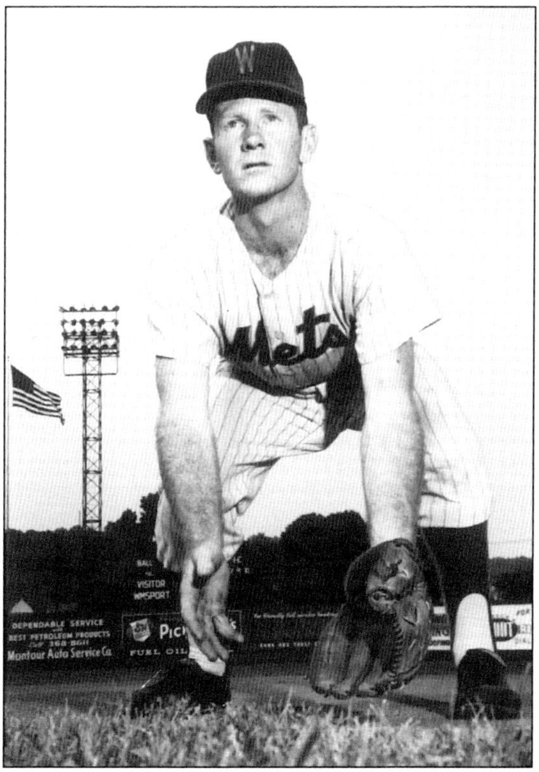

OLD RELIABLE (1965). Shortstop Wilbur Huckle had the surest hands of any Mets' infielder and delighted Bowman Field fans with his hustle and work ethic. Though small in stature, the affable red-head was a scrapper and one of the most popular players during the Mets' years in Williamsport. He often conducted impromptu fielding clinics for neighborhood kids outside his Cherry Street apartment before arriving at the ballpark for official duty. (*GRIT*.)

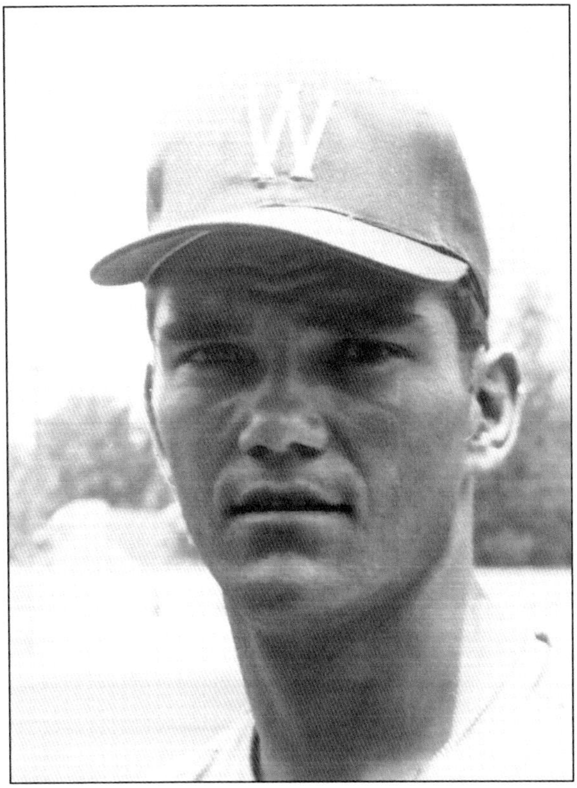

METS' CATCHER "DUFFY" DYER (1967). Mets' catcher Duffy Dyer, a name forever linked with New York's "Miracle Mets" of 1969, put together a solid year in Williamsport before advancing up the organizational chain. Local fans, however, might remember him as the rambunctious player who by-passed Jon O'Dell on the bases after hitting an apparent grand slam home run against York on June 22, 1967. He was ruled out and credited with a three-run triple. (*GRIT*.)

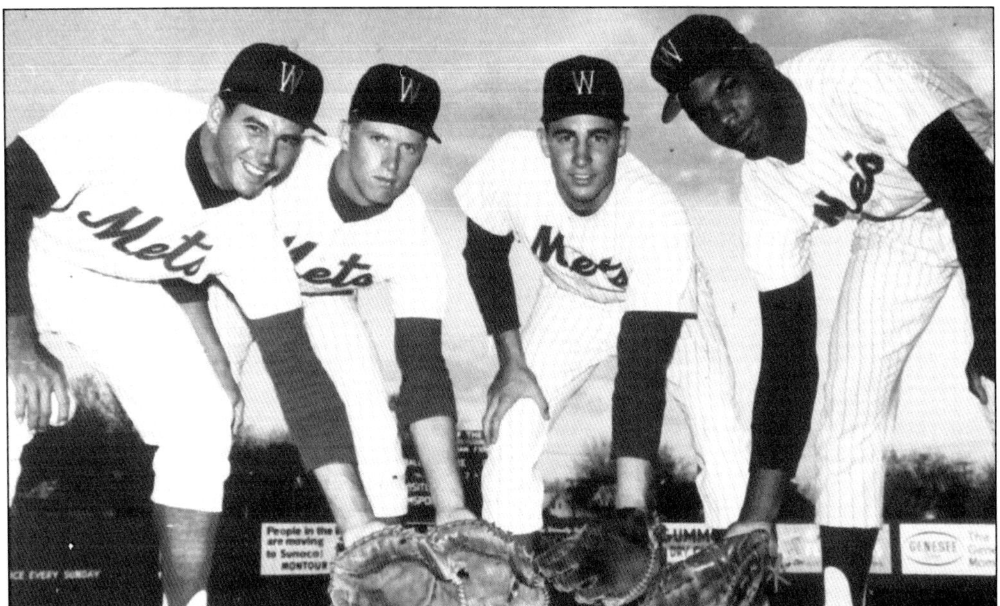

GOT THE SACK COVERED (APRIL 24, 1966). From left to right, Williamsport Mets' infielders Dave Smith, Kevin Collins, Ken Boswell, and Dave Allen pose in front of third base. Boswell later played on the 1969 New York Mets' World Series championship team and carved out a successful major-league career as a utility infielder and spot starter. (*GRIT*.)

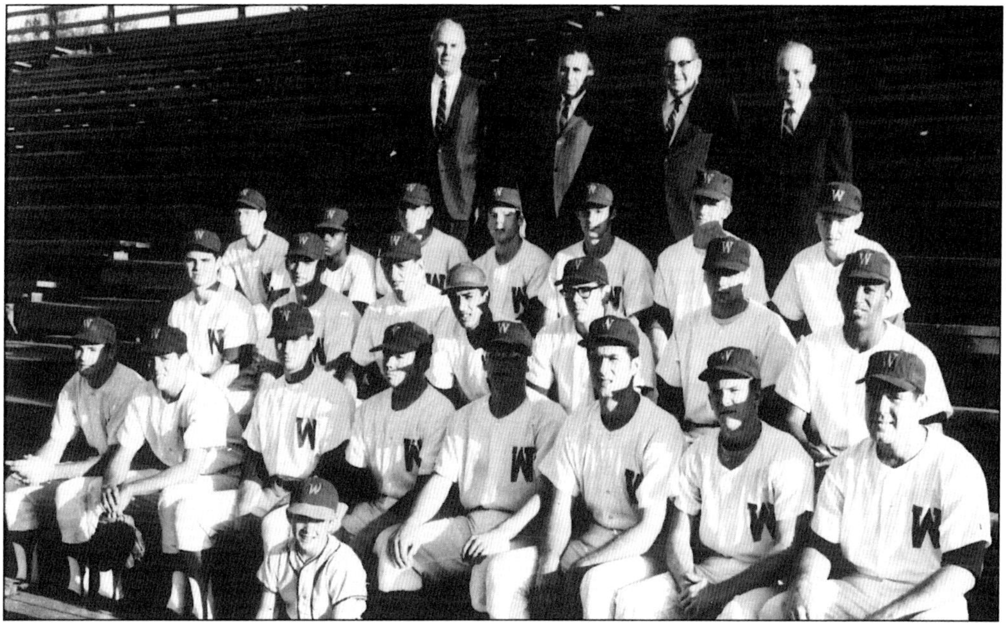

1968 WILLIAMSPORT ASTROS. The first Williamsport club to play in the short-season Class A New York-Penn League, the Astros finished third with a 40-35 record. The team qualified for a league playoff spot before losing to Auburn in the first round. From left to right in the back row of this team portrait are Rankin Johnson Jr., Bill Pickelner, Clair Bishop, and owner Joe Romano, the club's principal officers. Future Houston Astros' pitcher Ken Forsch pitched for Williamsport in 1968. (*GRIT.*)

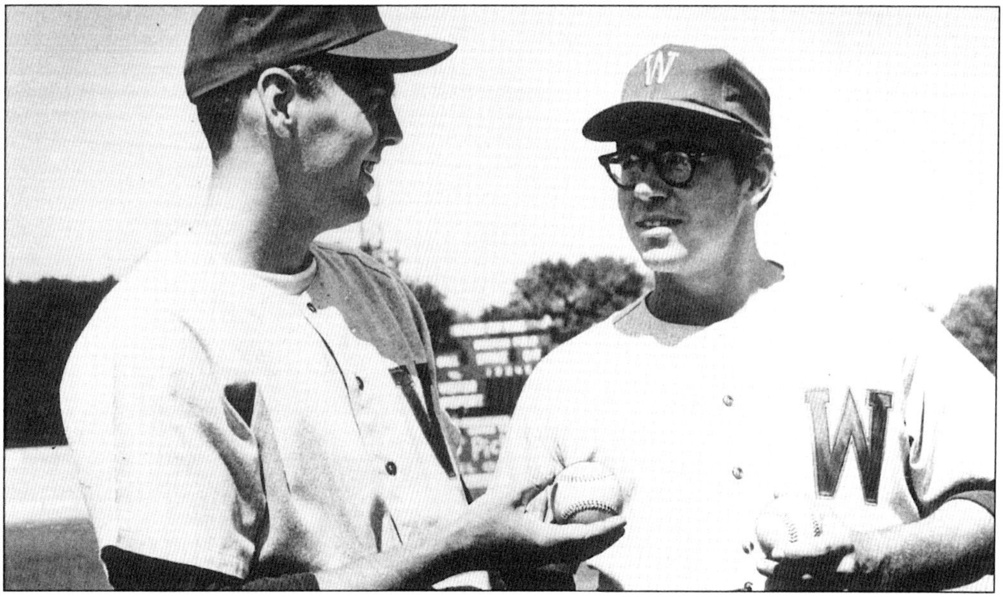

YOUNG MOUND HOPEFULS (JUNE 6, 1968). Williamsport Astros' pitchers Mike McFarland (left) and Mike Pierce (right) discuss pitching strategy during a pre-season tune-up under the broiling sun. McFarland was the ace of the 1968 staff, compiling a 9-5 record, with 90 strikeouts and a superb 2.27 earned run average. The Astros' pitching staff suffered that year due to the drafting of several players for service in the Vietnam War. (*GRIT.*)

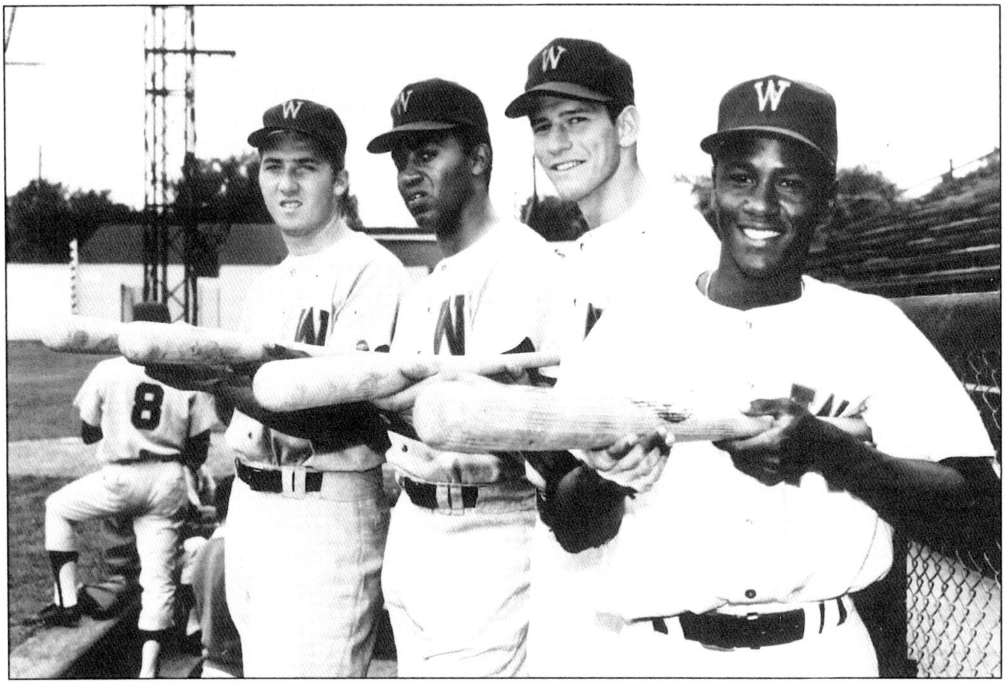

Williamsport Astros' Outfielders (June 23, 1968). From left to right, Astros' outfielders Steve Lohrer, Oscar Brown, Rick Hartzog, and Miquel Hernandez proudly display their bats near the home dugout before a game. Brown was Williamsport's leading home run hitter in 1968 with five and earned New York-Penn League All-Star honors. Hartzog hit a respectable .277 for season. (*GRIT.*)

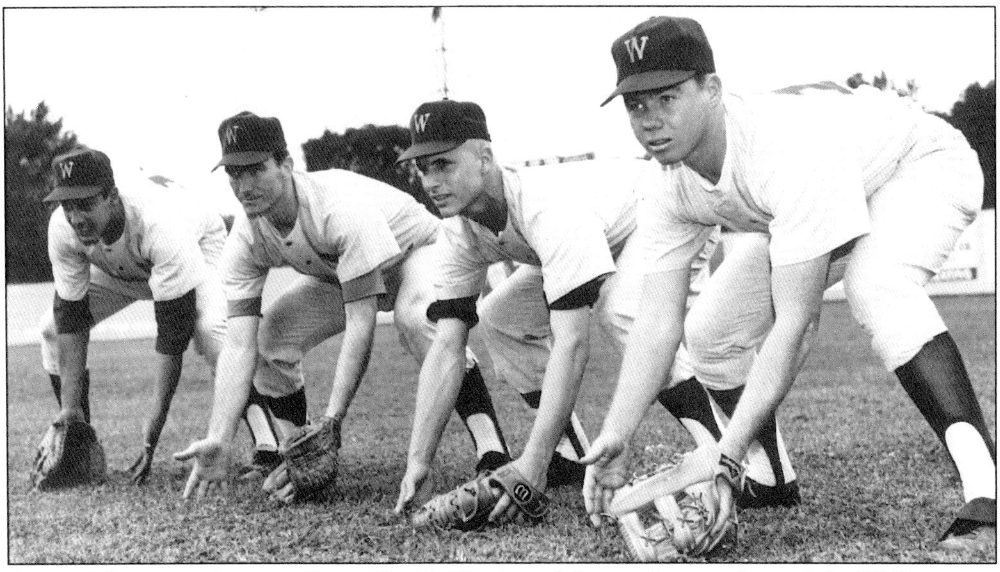

Astros' Starting Infield (June 23, 1968). From left to right, members of the Williamsport Astros' infield—first baseman Butch Marceno, shortstop Dick Davis, third baseman Bruce Davis, and second baseman Bud Cunningham—strike a customary pose. Marceno was the Astros' RBI leader in 1968 with 44. Cunningham singled home the winning run in a dramatic 1-0 win over the Corning Royals on August 2, 1968. (*GRIT.*)

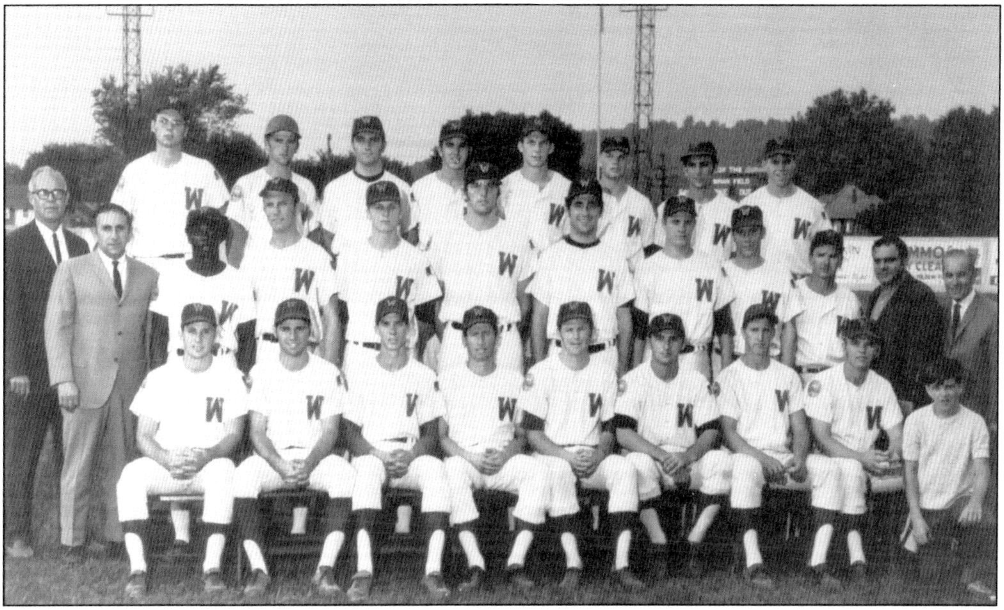

1969 Williamsport Astros. The 1969 Williamsport Astros finished fourth in the standings with a record of 39-36. They were paced by slugger Larry Mansfield (back row, first player on left) and speedster Lambert Ford (middle row, first player from left). Mansfield, "The Gentle Giant," hit a short-season franchise record of 21 homers and captured the 1969 New York-Penn Rookie of the Year Award. Ford, the Astros' lead-off man, hit .292 and played center field. (*GRIT.*)

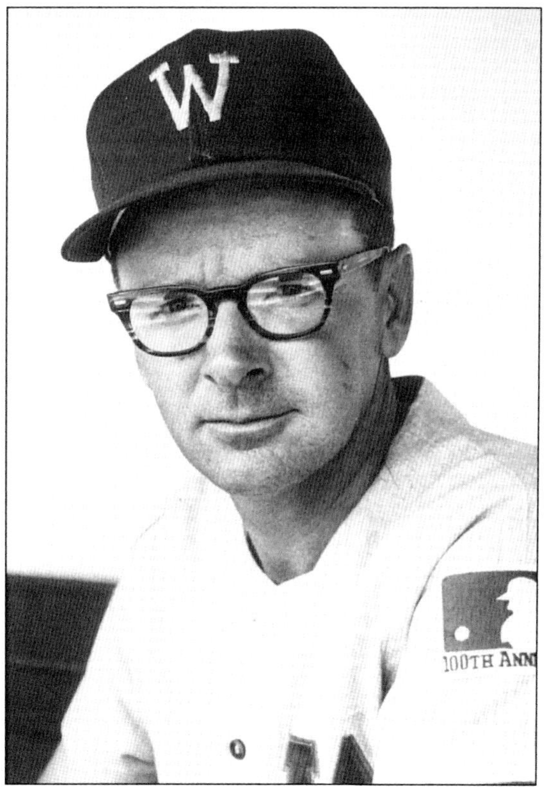

Manager Billy Smith (June 22, 1969). The Williamsport Astros' bespectacled manager strikes a pensive pose for his opening day portrait. A veteran coach with the Houston Astros' organization, Smith placed a premium on patience and developing young baseball talent. Note the major league baseball centennial patch adorning the left sleeve of Smith's uniform. (*GRIT.*)

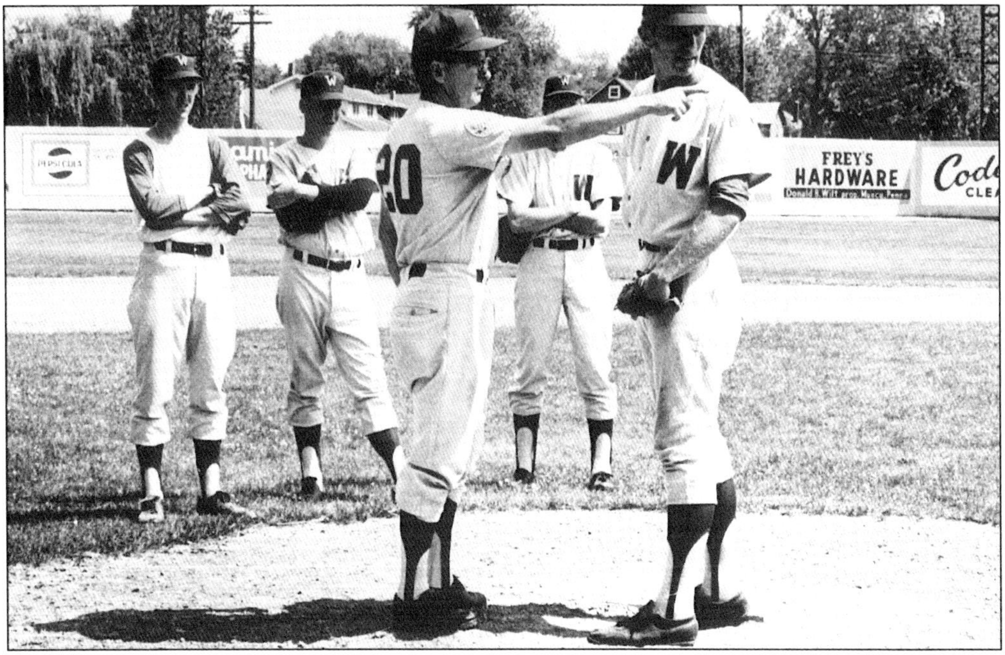

PITCHING CLINIC IN SESSION (JUNE 15, 1969). Manager Billy Smith gives mound instruction to Eric Bendenkop (on the mound) regarding the holding of runners. Astros' pitchers John Grant, Ken Barnes, and Kim Hillstrom observe in the background. (*GRIT*.)

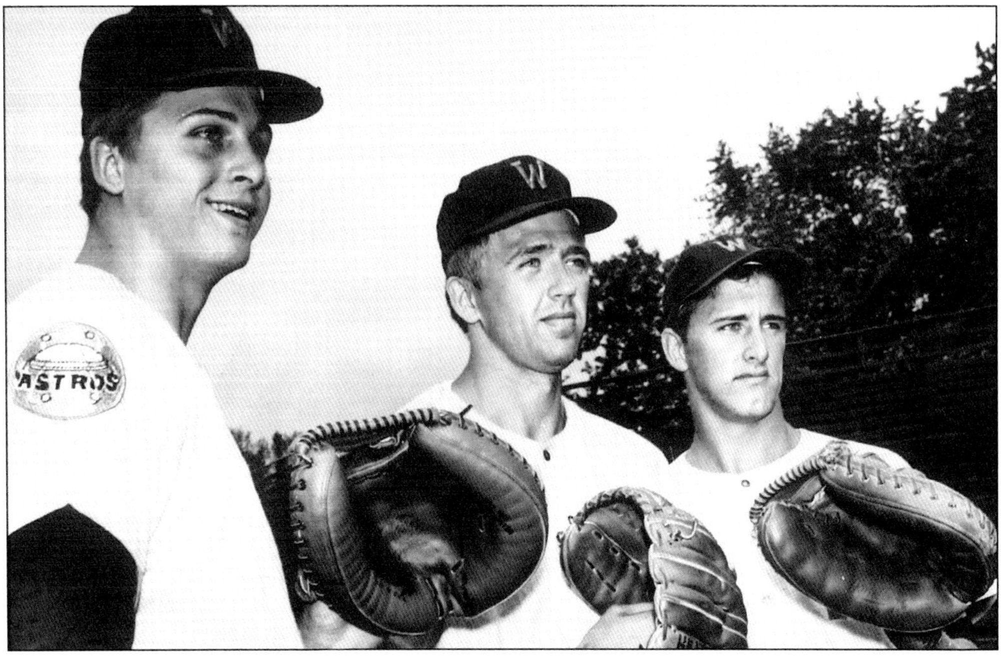

HILLSTOM GETTING THE NOD (JUNE 22, 1969). Pitcher Kim Hillstrom (center) was designated the Astros' opening day starter in 1969 by manager Billy Smith. He is flanked by catchers Marty Cott (left) and Shane Hummell (right). Though he did not lead the team in wins that year, Hillstrom pitched several gems for the Billtown nine, including a 1-0 three-hit shutout over the Batavia Trojans on July 14, 1969. (*GRIT*.)

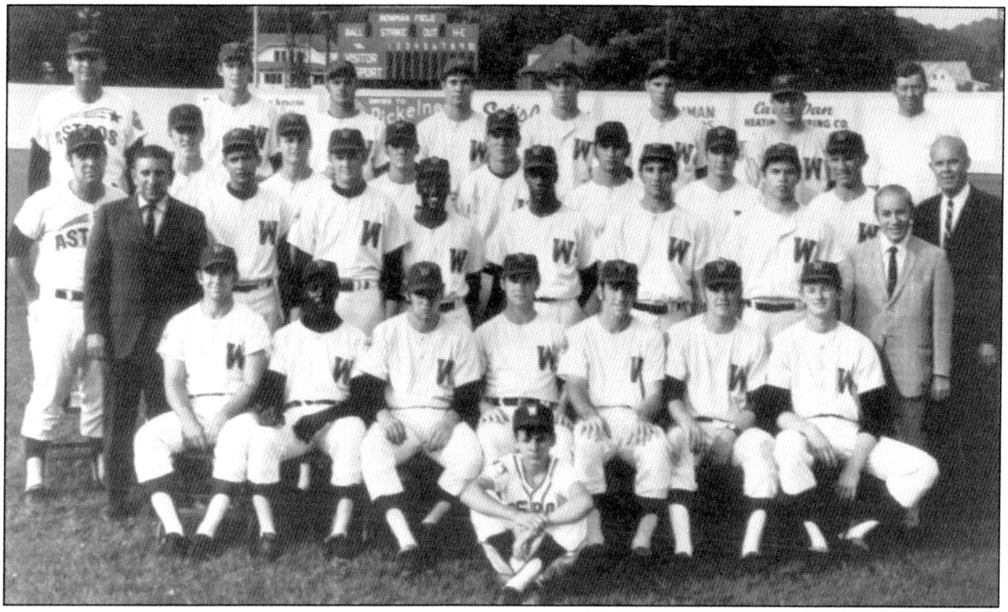

1970 Williamsport Astros. Managed by Dick Bogard, the 1970 Astros finished in the basement of the New York-Penn League standings with a mark of 28-42. The highlight of the season was Williamsport's Lambert Ford winning the league batting crown with a .368 average. Marty Cott led the team in home runs with eight. Larry Sheansburg was the Astros' best pitcher in 1970, posting a 6-3 record with an ERA of 2.63. (*GRIT.*)

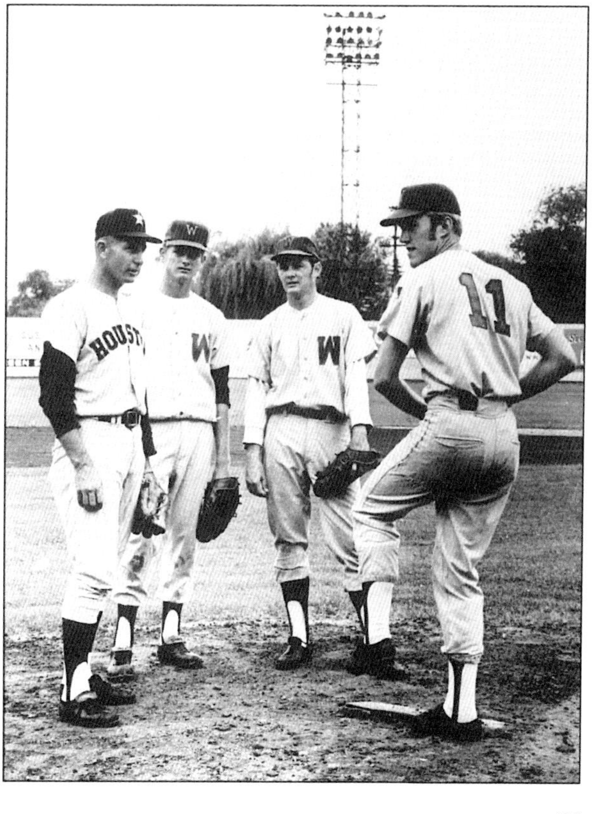

Mound Tips (June 21, 1970). Pitcher Pat Darcy pushes off the pitching rubber while Astros' pitching coach Jim Walton checks his form. Behind them are pitchers Dick Hicks (left) and Harold Boggs (right). Darcy later became a footnote in one of baseball's enduring moments as he surrendered Carlton Fisk's game-winning home run in the epic sixth game of the 1975 World Series. (*GRIT.*)

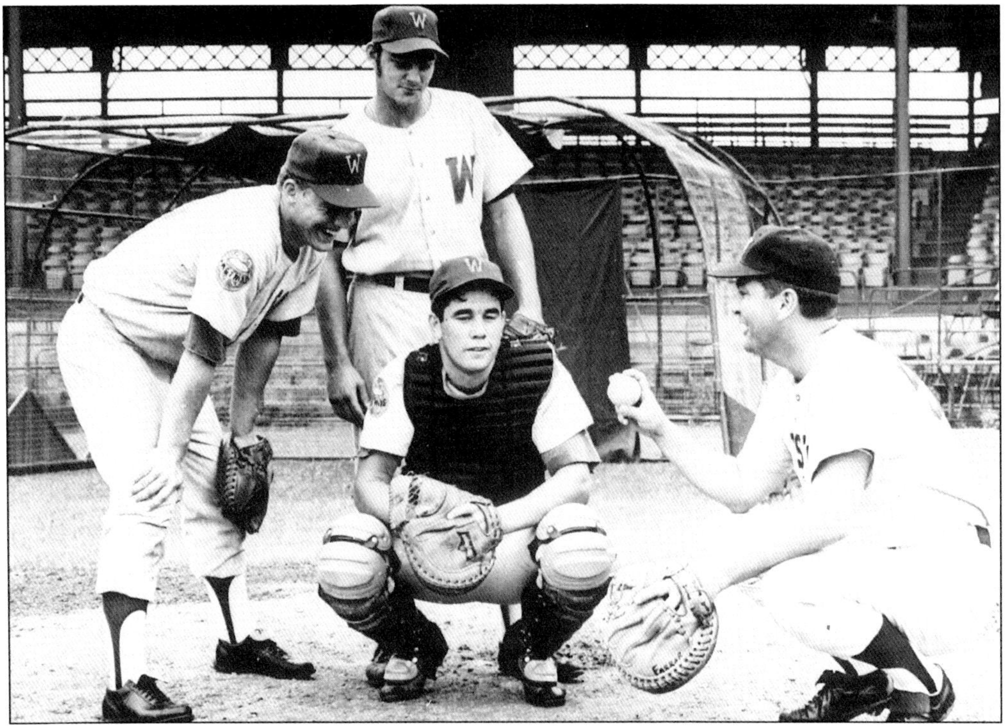

ASTROS' RECEIVERS (JUNE 21, 1970). From left to right, Williamsport's catchers Harlan Keller, Ray Hoellwarth, and George Vasquez (squatting in catcher's gear) receive instruction on blocking balls in the dirt from coach Jim Farrar. (*GRIT*.)

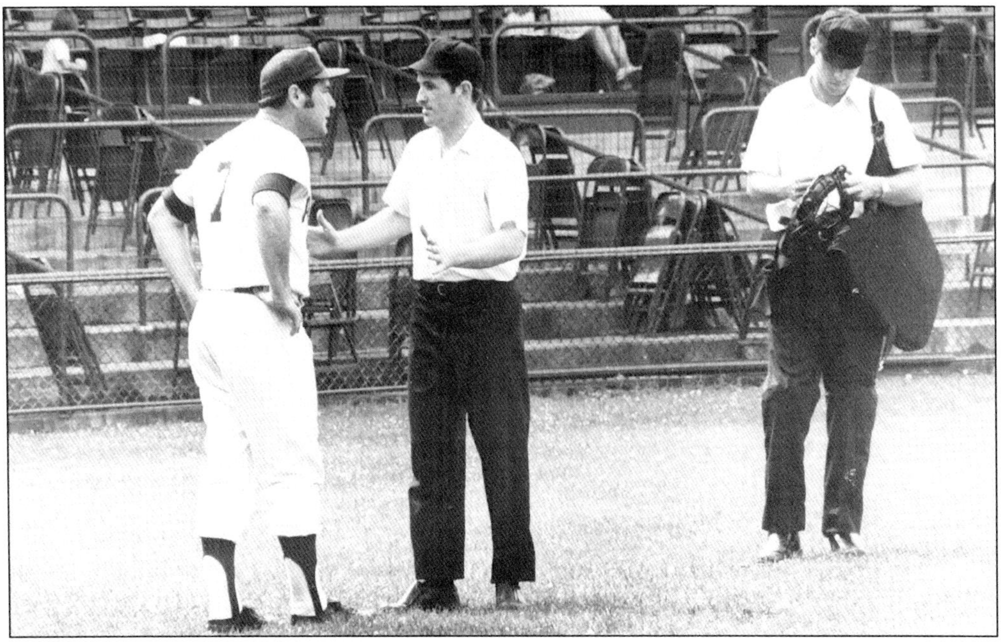

SAFE! (JULY 5, 1970). Williamsport Astros' manager Dick Bogard states his case to the umpires prior to his ejection from the game. Bogard, who skippered the Astros in 1968 and 1970, had previously coached in the Astros' minor-league chain. (*GRIT*.)

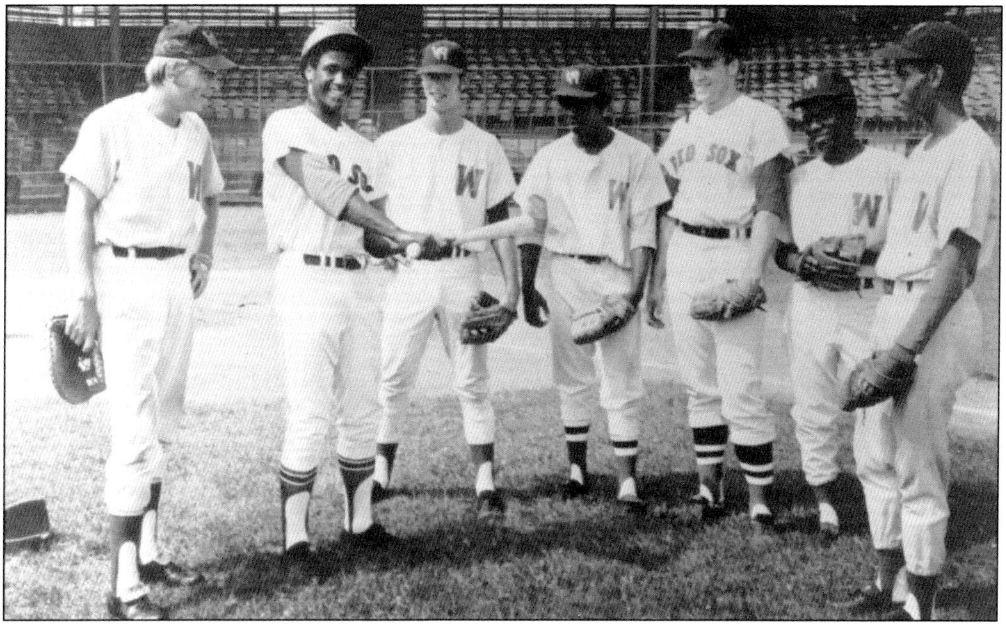

1971 Williamsport "Billsox." Members of the Williamsport Red Sox, dubbed the "Billsox" by the local press, line up for a pre-season publicity photo shoot. Included in this image was a young Jim Rice (second from left, with bat), future slugging sensation of the Boston Red Sox. *GRIT* sports editor Al Decker observed that Rice was so undeveloped as a talent that "he looked like he was in his first pair of baseball shoes." (*GRIT*.)

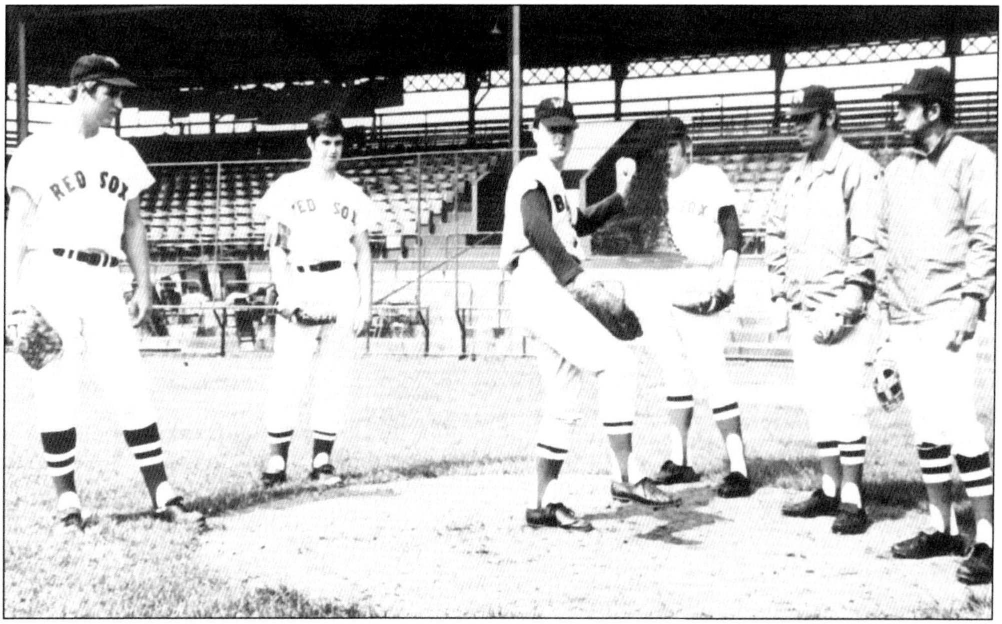

A New Season for the Billsox Hurlers (June 21, 1971). Fresh from Winter Haven, Florida, and extended spring training, these young mound hopefuls prepare for the start of the 1971 season in their new home. From left to right are Earl Nance, Mike Steelman, Steve Foran (with baseball), Jimmy Peets, Karl King, and Jesus Reyes. Foran paced all Billsox pitchers with a nifty 10-4 record and 2.38 ERA during the 1971 campaign. (*GRIT*.)

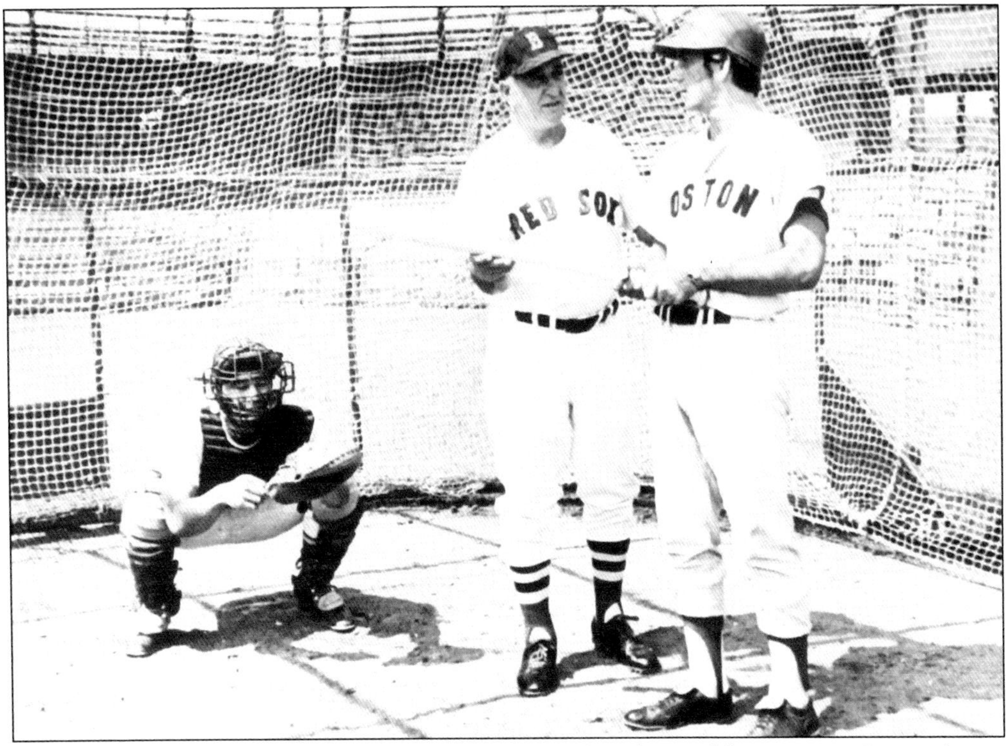

In the Cage (June 18, 1972). Even first round draft picks need hitting tips. Boston bonus baby Joel Bishop listens intently as Bosox scout Sam Mele imparts his baseball wisdom. Mele was no stranger to Bowman Field. Older fans will remember him as a pitcher with the old Scranton Redsox during the mid-1940s, and he was the manager of the 1965 pennant winning Minnesota Twins. (*GRIT*.)

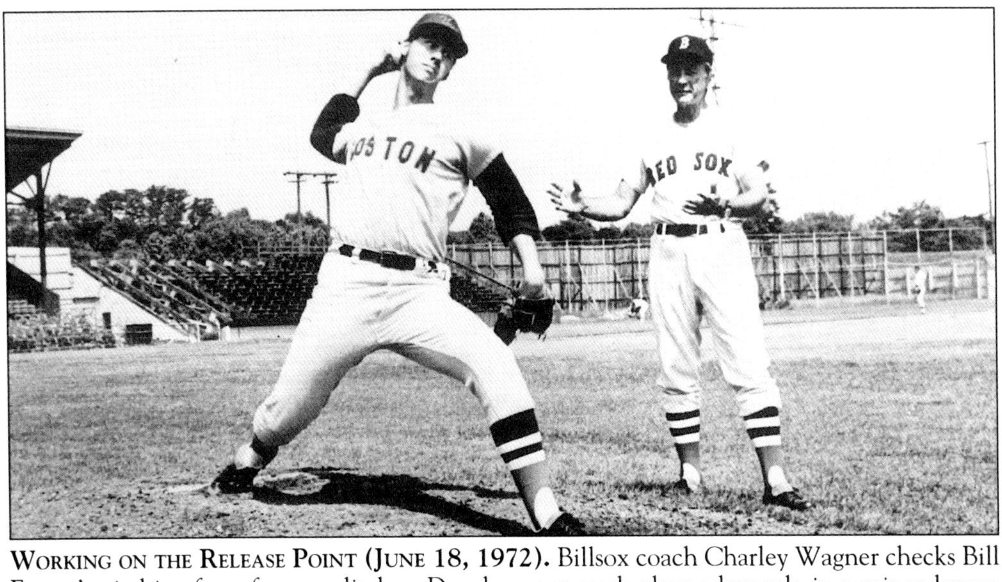

Working on the Release Point (June 18, 1972). Billsox coach Charley Wagner checks Bill Fewox's pitching form for any glitches. Development work plays a key role in a minor-league player's advancement through the ranks of the farm system. Much of this work goes on inside an empty stadium beyond the glare of the press and fans. (*GRIT*.)

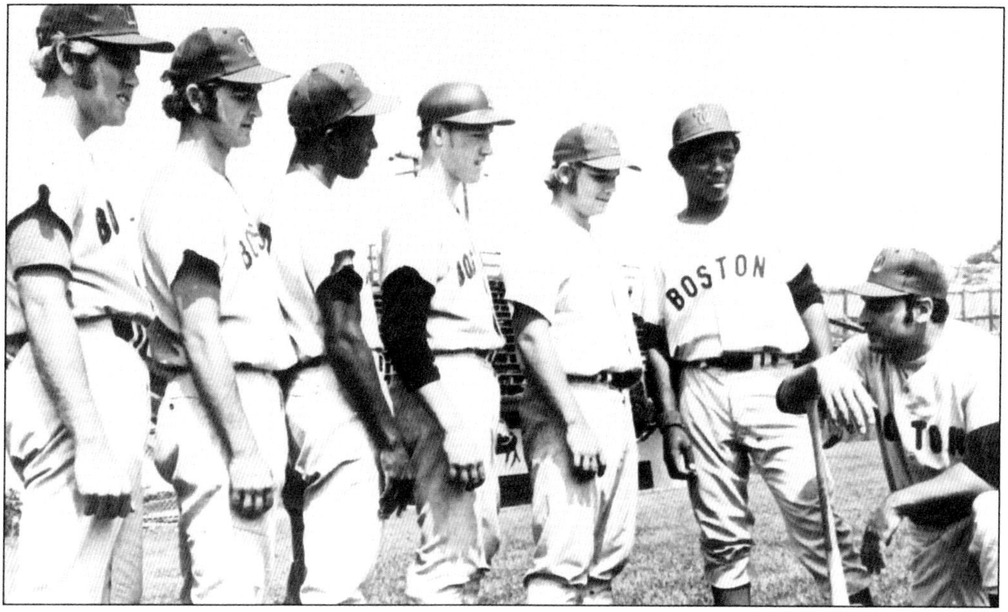

Welcome Back (June 18, 1972). Manager Dick Beradino (kneeling with bat) greets returning veterans from last year's squad. Among the returnees, from left to right, are pitcher Jimmy Peets, outfielders Mike Auerick and Chet Lucas, catchers Mike Mooney and Ken Nicar, and third baseman Milt Jefferson. The 1972 Billsox were a disappointment to fans, finishing last with a record of 22-47. Chet Lucas was Williamsport's MVP that year, batting .285 and swatting 12 home runs. (*GRIT*.)

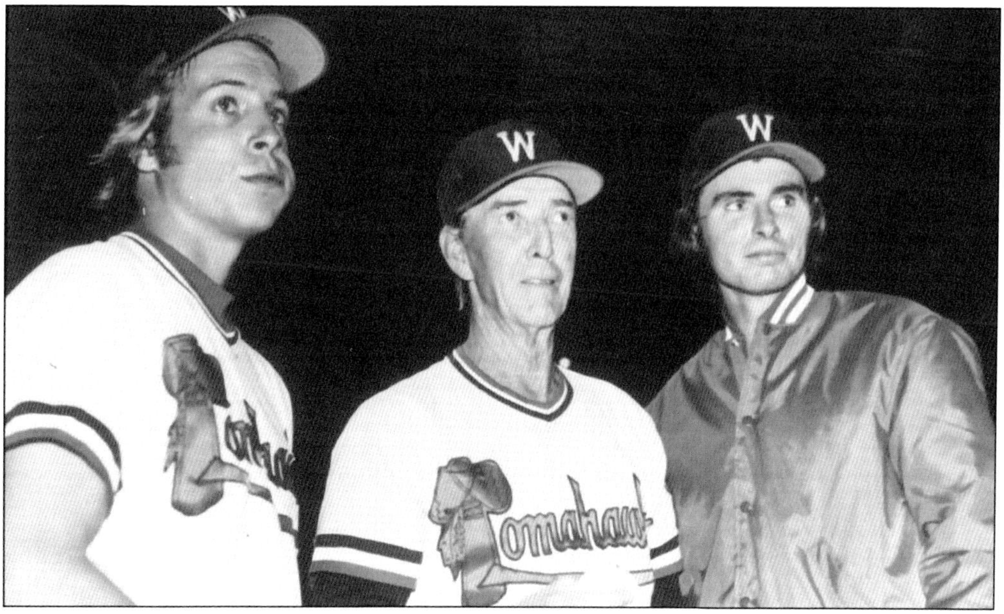

1976 Williamsport Tomahawks' Battery (April 18, 1976). After a ten-year hiatus, Class AA Eastern League baseball returned to Billtown in the form of the Williamsport Tomahawks, farmhands of the Cleveland Indians. Here, Tomahawks' manager John "Red" Davis (center) is flanked by his opening day battery, catcher Kris Yoder (left) and pitcher Tom Brennan (right). Davis once played for the 1941 New York Giants. (*GRIT*.)

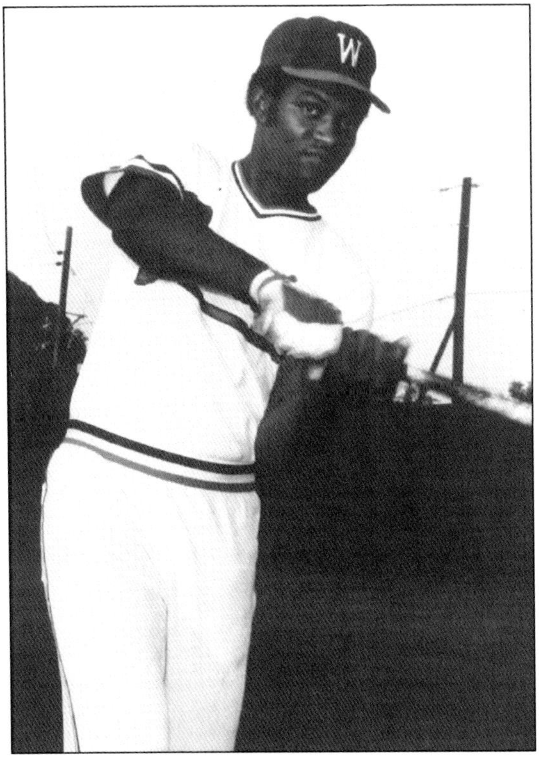

TOMMIES' SLUGGER WAYNE CAGE (APRIL 1976). Though the Williamsport Tomahawks were the worst team in the history of Williamsport baseball (48-91), the team managed to develop several major-league players, among them pitcher Larry Anderson and shortstop Alfredo Griffin. However, Williamsport's most popular player that year was the slugging first baseman Wayne Cage. Cage hit .286 and led the team in home runs (10) despite missing part of the season. (*GRIT*.)

TOMAHAWKS' OUTFIELDERS (APRIL 18, 1976). From left to right, outfielders Rich Guerra, Gary Cleverly, Bob Servoss, and Keith Bridges cross their bats for good luck prior to the start of the 1976 season. Center fielder Rich Guerra had a solid year for the Tommies, batting .285. (*GRIT*.)

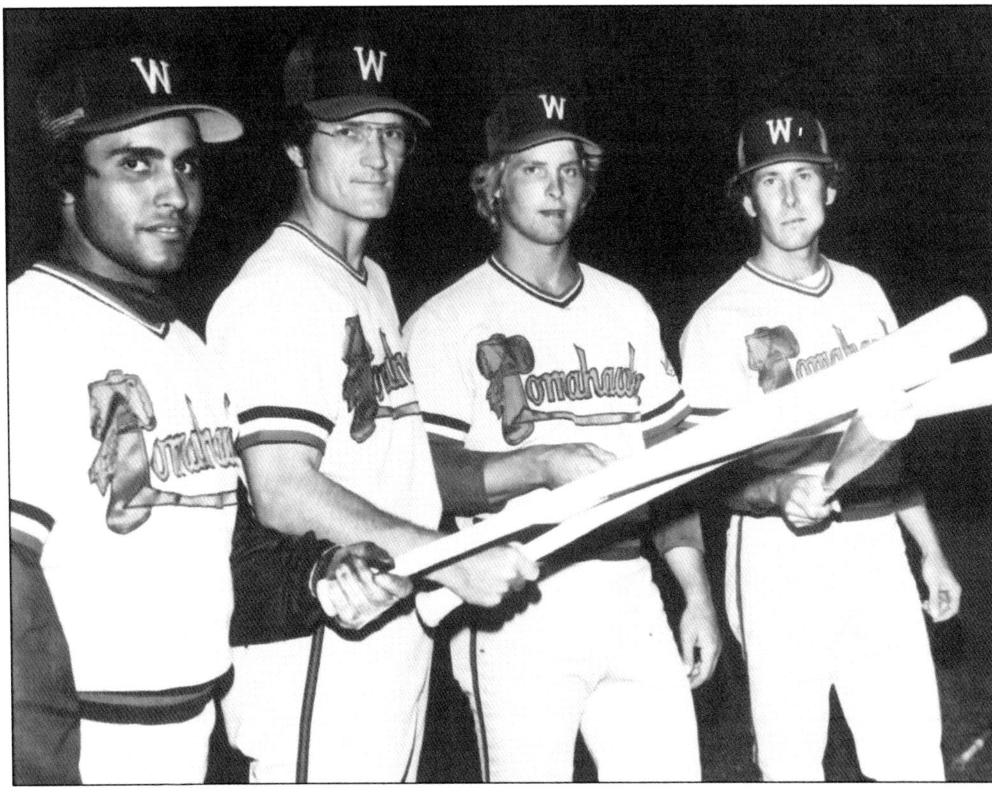

Three

Boosters, Promotions, and Events

Professional baseball in Williamsport evolved as a by-product of the "Gospel of Wealth." In addition to building lavish mansions and opera houses as testaments to their wealth and influence in the late 19th century, the city's lumber and tannery barons invested in local baseball as a civic and philanthropic endeavor. From the late 19th century and well into the 1940s, the Williamsport millionaires donated land and material for the construction of ballparks, financed stadium operations, paid players' salaries, and absorbed losses at the turnstiles. Among the city's leading industrialists, bankers, businessmen, and civic figures who promoted the game were J. Walton Bowman, Frank Bowman, Irvin W. and James B. Gleason, Nathaniel Burrows Bubb, Thomas Gray, Max Jaffe, Joseph Mosser, and Tommy Richardson.

Despite such largess, club investors realized the necessity of recruiting knowledgeable baseball administrators from the community to guide the day-to-day operations of the club and promote the game in general. An equally dedicated group of club directors, business managers, and team boosters—J. Roy Clunk, Robert Steinhilper, William Pickelner, and A. Rankin Johnson Jr.—charted the course of the Williamsport baseball franchise from the post-war era to the 1970s. Their efforts enabled Williamsport to support and sustain professional minor-league baseball at a high classification level (Class AA) when other larger cities affiliated with the minor leagues lost their teams. From 1923 to the present, with the exception of a ten-year hiatus and an odd year or two, Bowman Field has been occupied by a minor-league tenant.

Historically, minor-league baseball has always been a tough sell for owners and operators, notwithstanding the current economic boom. Team business managers operated on shoestring budgets during the Depression and lean war years, and weathered subsequent changes (televised baseball, parsimonious major league clubs, and absentee owners) in the 1950s and 1960s that threatened the survival of the game. Responding to the ebb and flow of baseball's popularity, Williamsport's baseball boosters devised novel marketing and season ticket sales plans; garnered the support of area merchants in sponsoring special giveaway nights; arranged exhibition games with major-league teams; assisted the fund-raising efforts of local community service organizations; and made Bowman Field a venue for special community-oriented celebrations and entertainment events. Their collective efforts, along with fan support, allowed minor-league baseball to flourish in Williamsport.

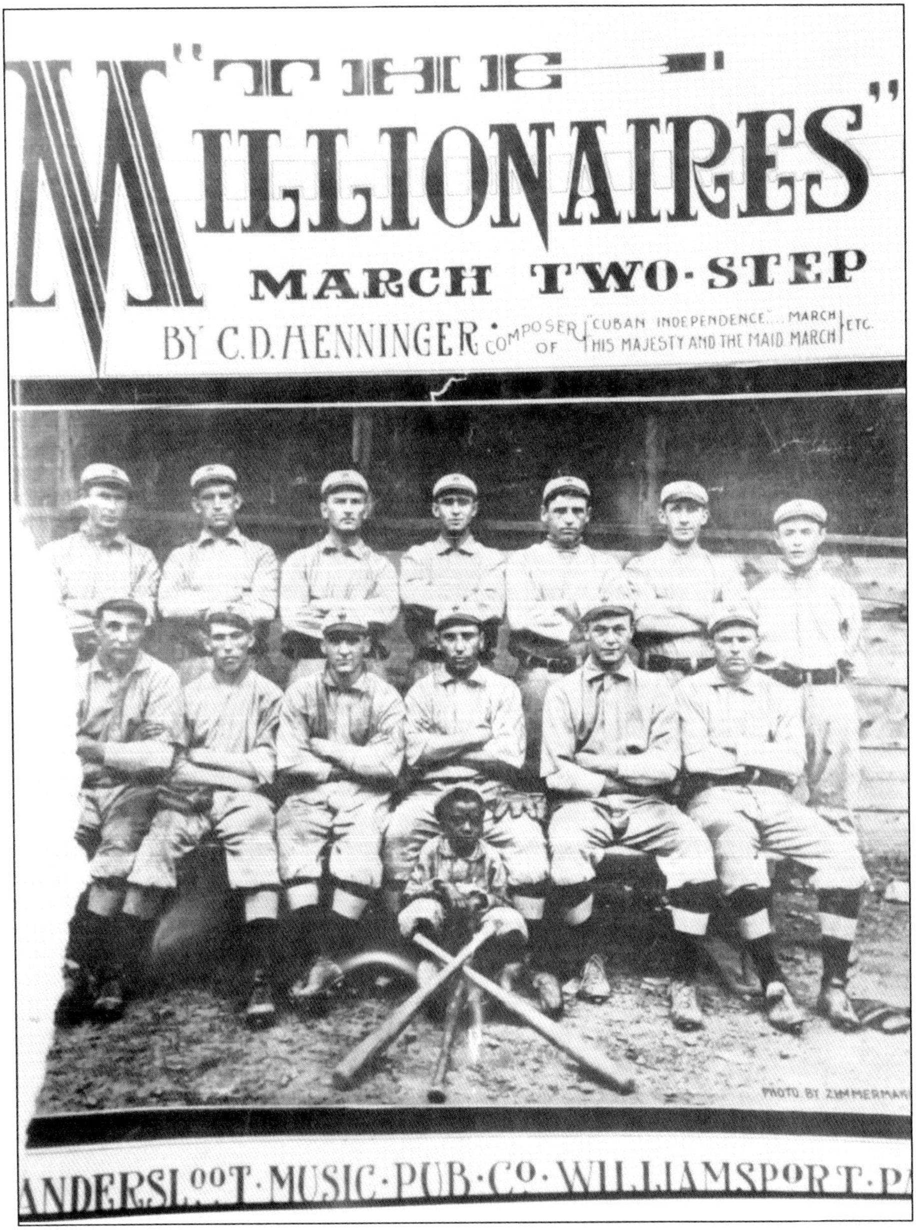

SHEET MUSIC COVER, "THE MILLIONAIRES MARCH TWO-STEP" (1910). One of the earliest promotions tied to Williamsport baseball entailed the commissioning of a music composition to celebrate the Williamsport Millionaires' 1908 Tri-State League championship season. C.D. Henninger composed "The Millionaires' March Two-Step" and approached the Vandersloot Music Publishing Company of Williamsport to produce and sell the sheet music. The cover is important, not only for its novelty, but for the fact that it contains the only surviving image of the 1908 team. Williamsport, in addition to lumber and its fine baseball teams, was also a center for the production of musical instruments and renowned for its community bands, particularly the Repasz Band and Imperial Teteques. These bands performed at many of the parades and civic celebrations honoring Williamsport's championship teams during the Tri-State League era. (JVB.)

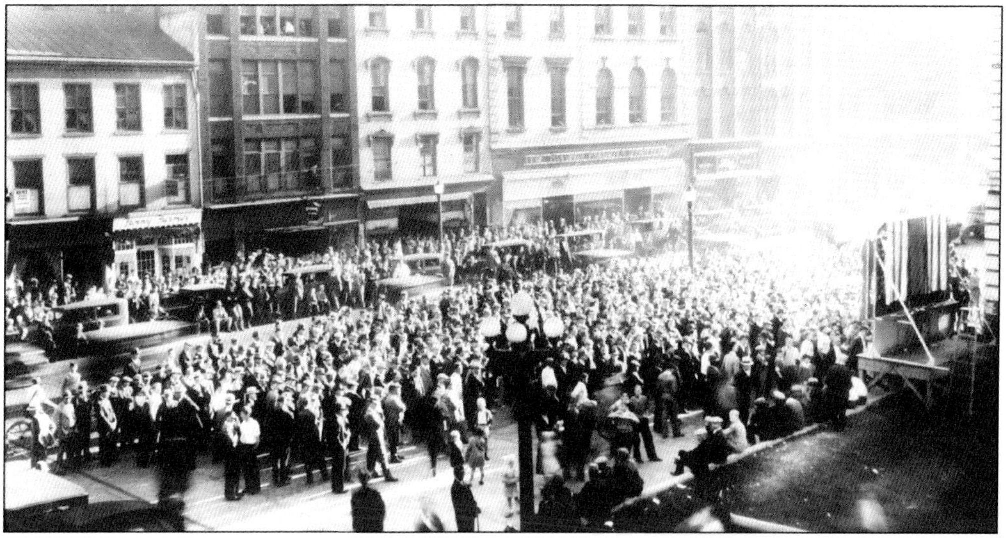

PLAY-O-GRAM BOARD (OCTOBER 10, 1931). Williamsport baseball fans gather on Third Street across from the courthouse to view the play-o-gram board monitoring the progress of the 1931 World Series. Information concerning the game was relayed from ticker-tape and wire to the board, allowing spectators to follow the World Series play-by-play. The board was also used for important Eastern League games involving the Grays. (DVS-LCHS.)

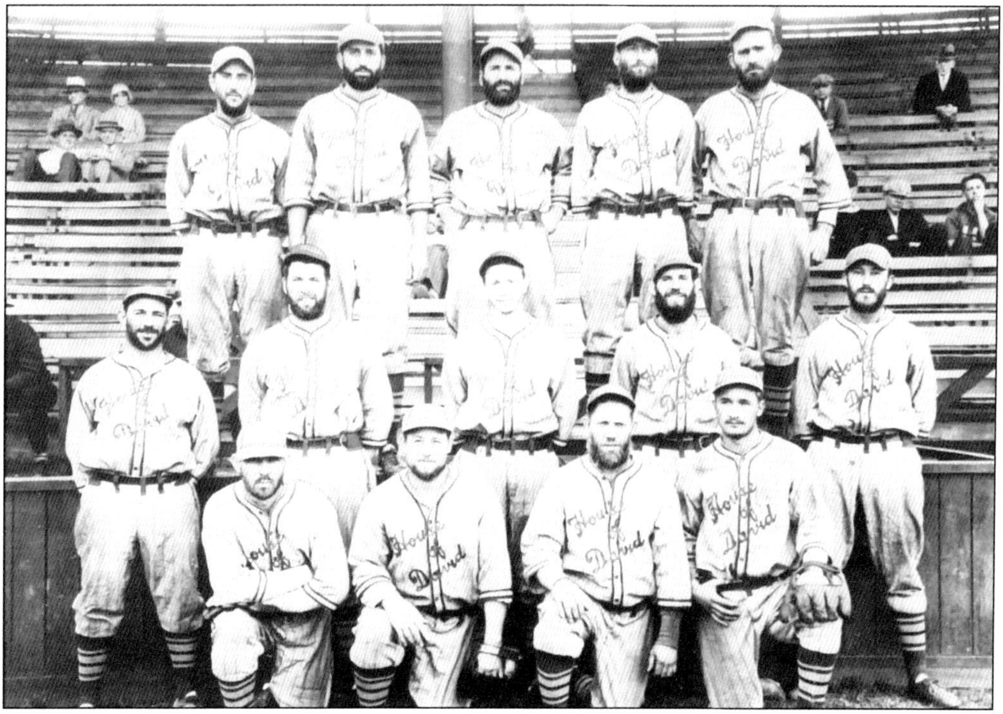

HOUSE OF DAVID TEAM (MAY 1, 1932). The barnstorming House of David team was a popular attraction in minor-league ballparks across the country. Their exhibition games with the local Grays always packed the park. Though claiming ties to the Davidian Church, the team was mostly composed of bearded semi-pro and ex-minor-league players trying to earn a steady paycheck during the Depression. (PV-LCHS.)

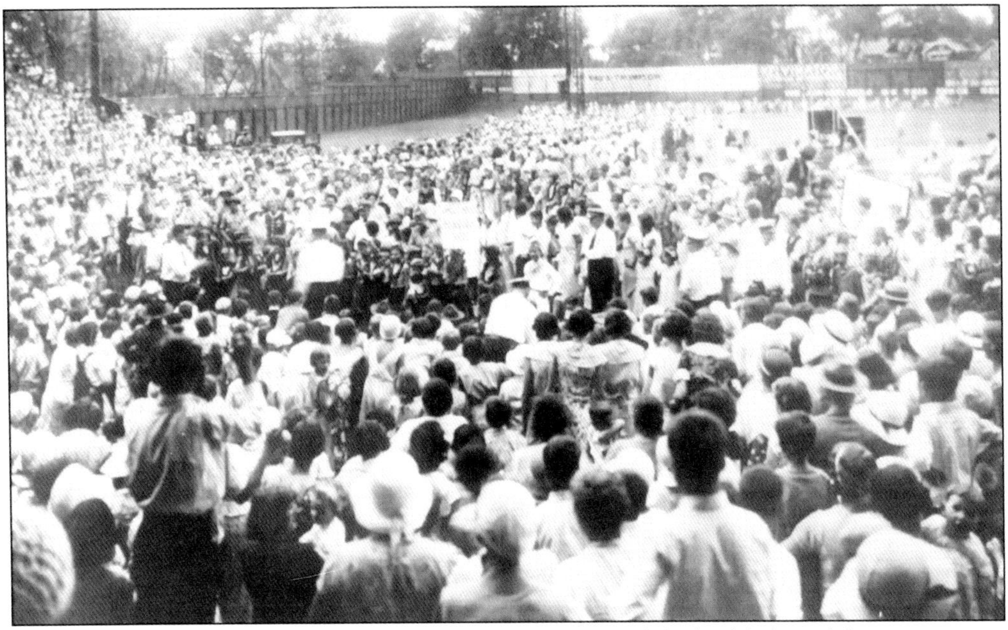

KIDDIES' DAY, BOWMAN FIELD (AUGUST 10, 1932). One of the highlights of the summer was the annual Kiddies' Day celebration at Bowman Field. The event featured games, contests, music, and performances involving area children as their proud parents looked on from the stands. Leo C. Williamson, Williamsport's popular mayor, often served as Master of Ceremonies. (PV-LCHS.)

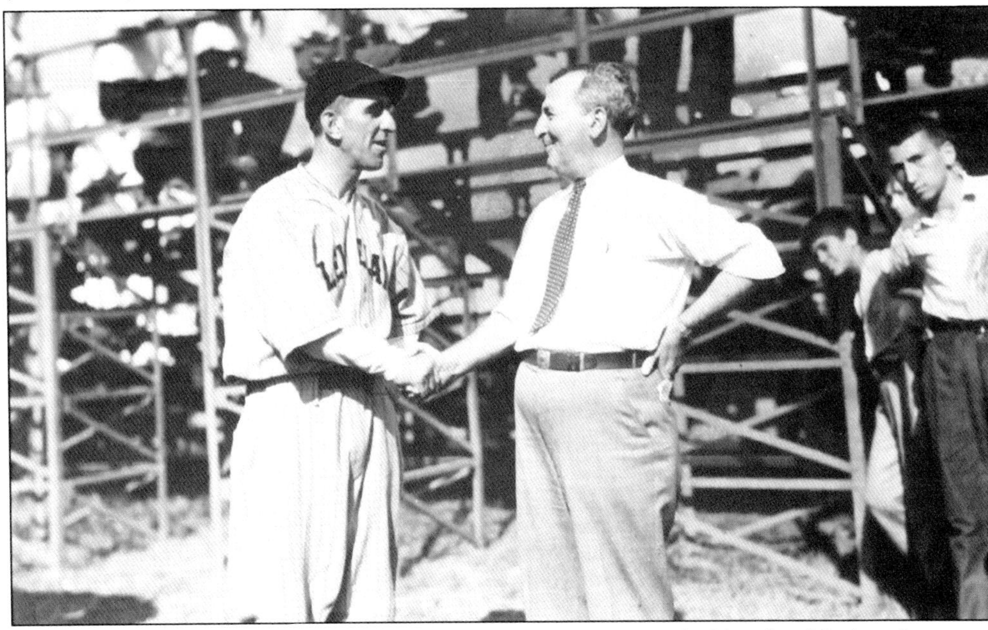

CLEVELAND INDIANS VISIT BOWMAN FIELD (SEPTEMBER 4, 1932). Cleveland Indians' manager Roger Peckinpaugh shakes hands with Max Jaffe, Williamsport Grays' business manager and chairman of the "Cleveland Day Committee." The Indians were just one of many major-league teams to play exhibition games at Bowman Field over the decades. Revenue generated by these games allowed the Grays to remain financially solvent during lean years. (*GRIT*.)

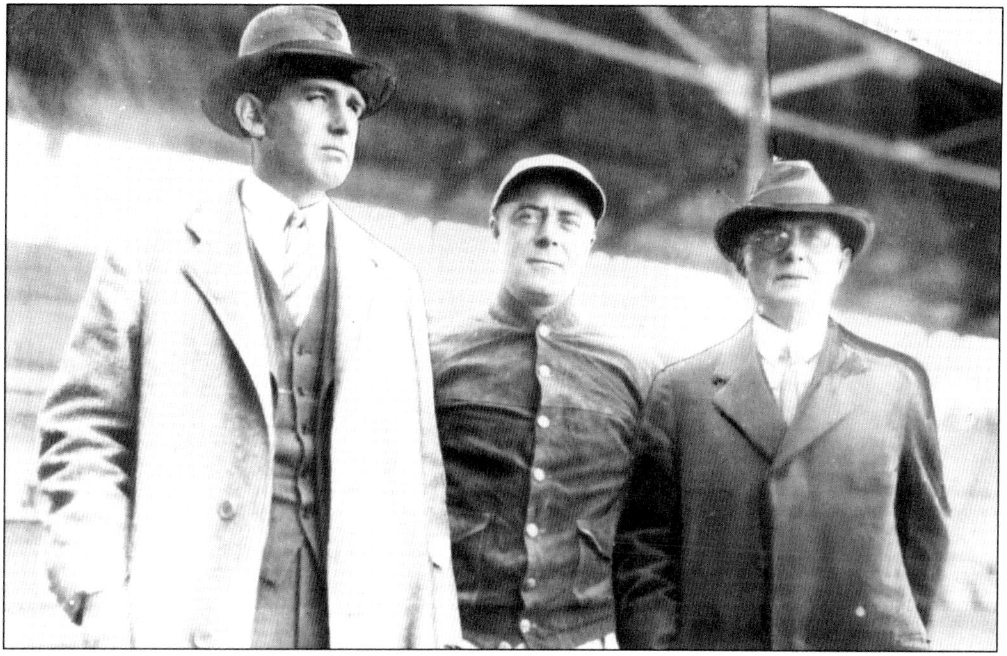

Top Brass Meeting (April 29, 1930). Williamsport Grays' business manager J. Roy Clunk, manager George Burns, and club president J. Walton Bowman survey the field in anticipation of opening day of the New York-Penn League season. Clunk served in the Grays' front office until 1961. Bowman was Williamsport's most influential booster of professional minor-league baseball during the 1920s and 1930s. (*GRIT.*)

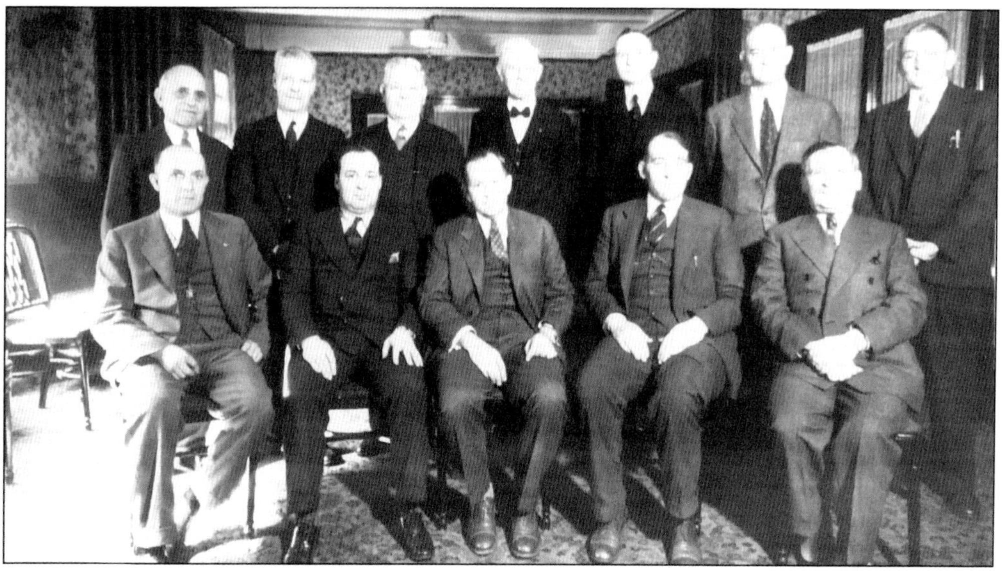

Williamsport Grays' Club Directors (March 26, 1933). This unique group portrait captures the Grays' principal shareholders. From left to right they are as follows: (front row) Edward Bullock, Tommy Richardson, Pat Thorne, J. Roy Clunk, and Max Jaffe; (back row) Max Lindheimer, Dan Kline, Henry Knarr, Elmer Schuyler, Tom Redmond, Rube Bressler, and Edgar Maitland. Shortly after this photograph was taken, the club directors voted to keep the Grays in Williamsport despite the financial losses suffered the previous year. (*GRIT.*)

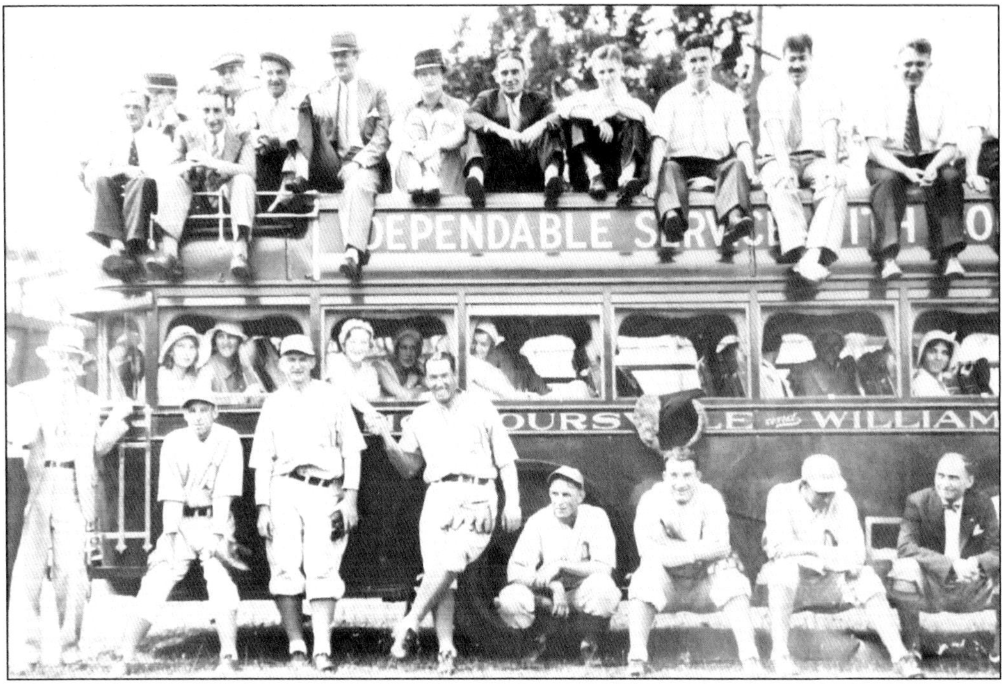

PHILADELPHIA A'S EXHIBITION GAME (AUGUST 2, 1931). Members of the Philadelphia A's baseball team pose with fans and the Camp Davitt bus outside Bowman Field prior to an exhibition game with the Grays. During the 1930s the Grays and A's played several games before overflowing crowds at the uptown ballpark. These games allowed local fans easy access to their major-league heroes. (*GRIT*.)

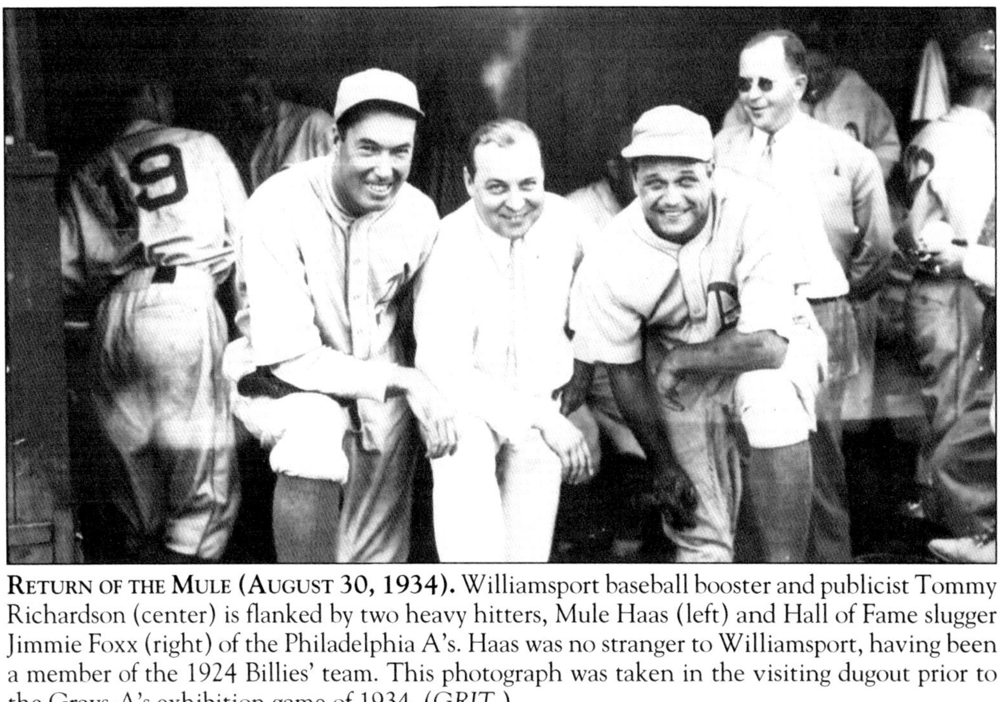

RETURN OF THE MULE (AUGUST 30, 1934). Williamsport baseball booster and publicist Tommy Richardson (center) is flanked by two heavy hitters, Mule Haas (left) and Hall of Fame slugger Jimmie Foxx (right) of the Philadelphia A's. Haas was no stranger to Williamsport, having been a member of the 1924 Billies' team. This photograph was taken in the visiting dugout prior to the Grays-A's exhibition game of 1934. (*GRIT*.)

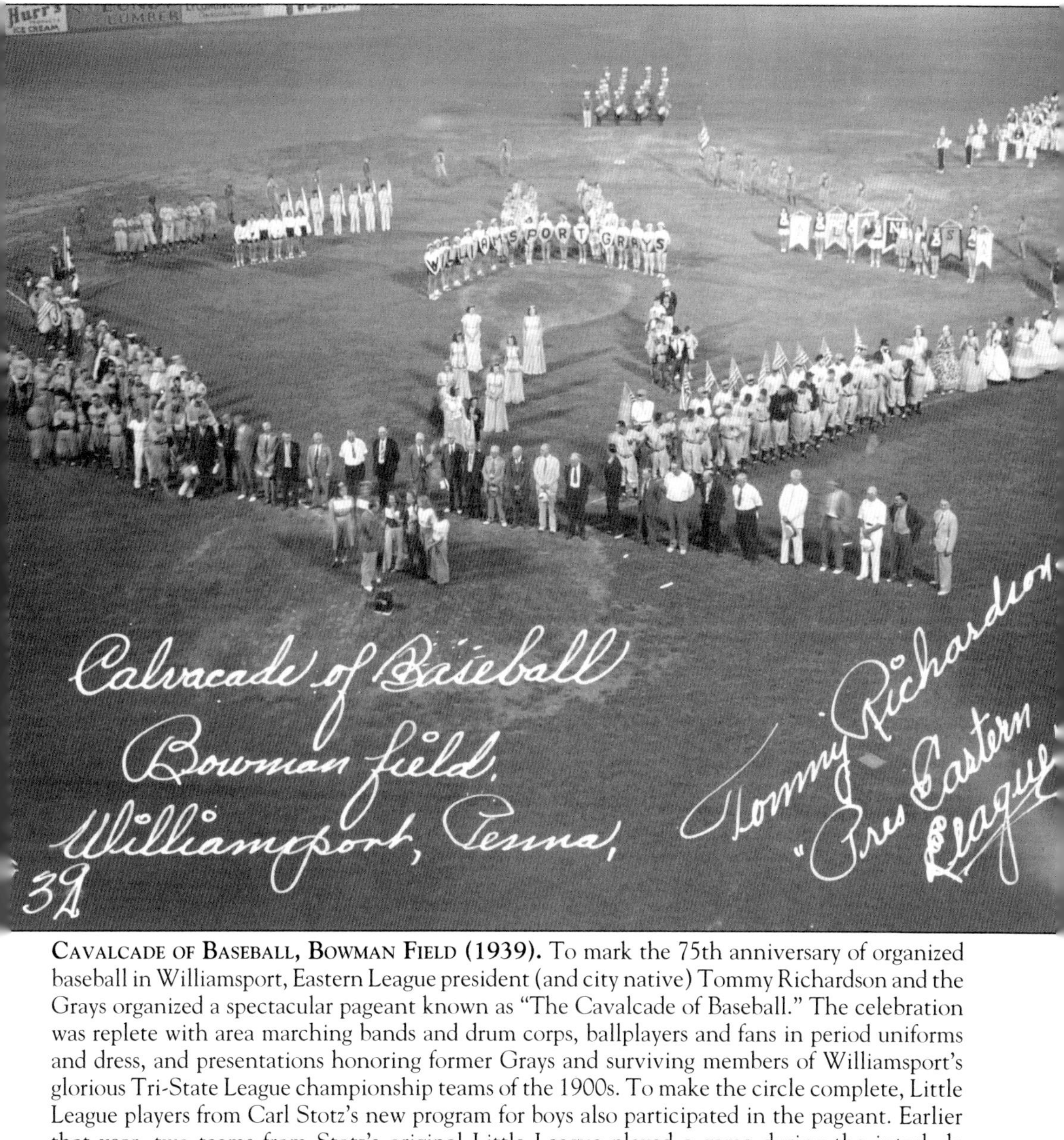

Cavalcade of Baseball, Bowman Field (1939). To mark the 75th anniversary of organized baseball in Williamsport, Eastern League president (and city native) Tommy Richardson and the Grays organized a spectacular pageant known as "The Cavalcade of Baseball." The celebration was replete with area marching bands and drum corps, ballplayers and fans in period uniforms and dress, and presentations honoring former Grays and surviving members of Williamsport's glorious Tri-State League championship teams of the 1900s. To make the circle complete, Little League players from Carl Stotz's new program for boys also participated in the pageant. Earlier that year, two teams from Stotz's original Little League played a game during the interlude between a Grays' doubleheader on "Community and Suburban Night." (TR.)

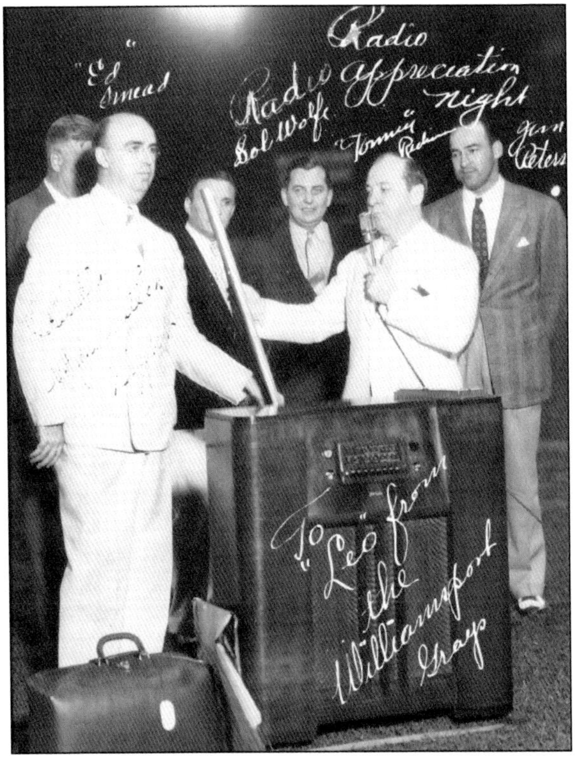

RADIO APPRECIATION NIGHT (1938). Tommy Richardson reads a plaque honoring Sol "Woody" Wolf (third person from left), the radio voice of the Williamsport Grays. Though Wolf gained notoriety as a football coach at Williamsport High School, he delighted local fans with his colorful radio play-by-play broadcast of Grays' baseball games. Wolf was also a master of recreating (away) games off the wire for radio broadcast. (TR.)

BOWMAN FIELD USHERS (1939). Bowman Field's award-winning ushers, voted the Eastern League's best, pose for a group photo. Older area baseball fans fondly recall the pre-war years of Williamsport baseball and the courteous and efficient service at the ballpark they received from Bobby Metzger, Jack McKee, and the Maynard twins, Charles and Laurence. (TR.)

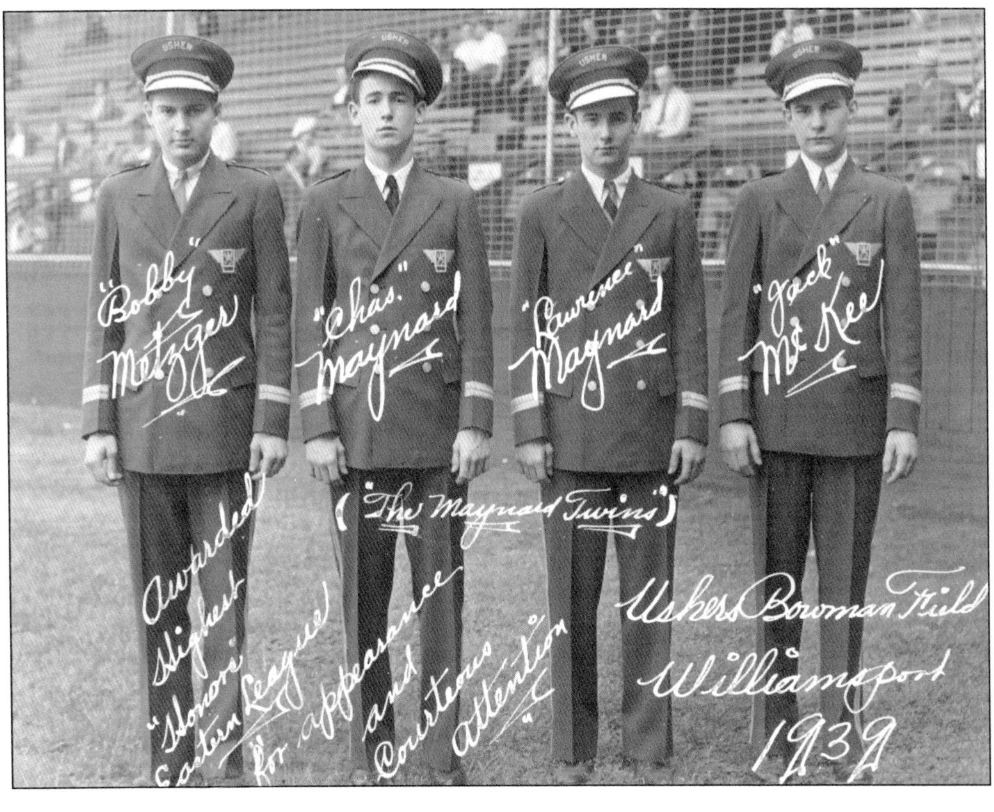

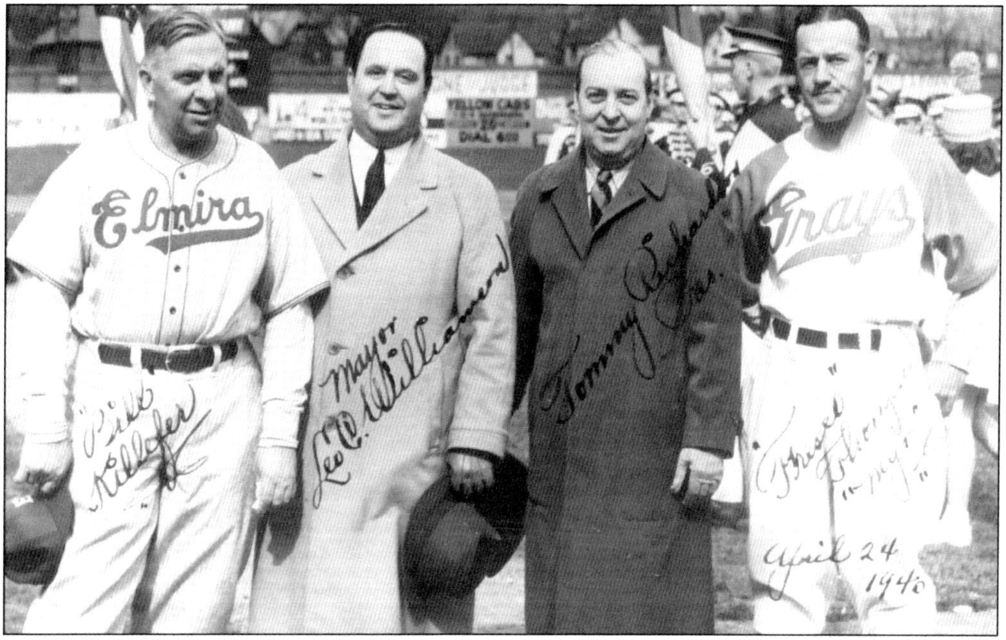

Opening Day, Elmira vs. Williamsport (April 24, 1940). The opening day of another Eastern League season at Bowman Field was always cause for celebration. Here, visiting Elmira manager Bill Killefer, Leo C. Williamson (mayor of Williamsport), Tommy Richardson, and Fresco Thompson (Grays' manager) gather near home plate during the opening day ceremonies. (TR.)

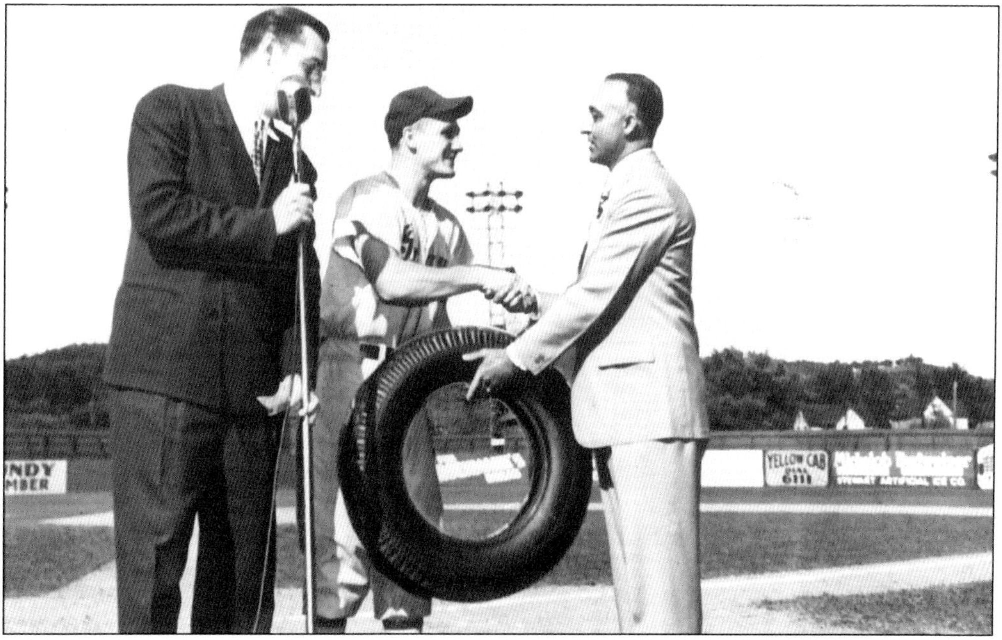

Thanks to Mr. Frey (1946). Eddie Modarski, voted the Grays' Most Valuable Player in 1946, receives four car tires courtesy of Frey's Tire Shop. This was not an insignificant gift as tires, like many consumer goods in the immediate post-war era, were in short supply. Modarski was Williamsport's leading hitter (.317) that year. (*GRIT*.)

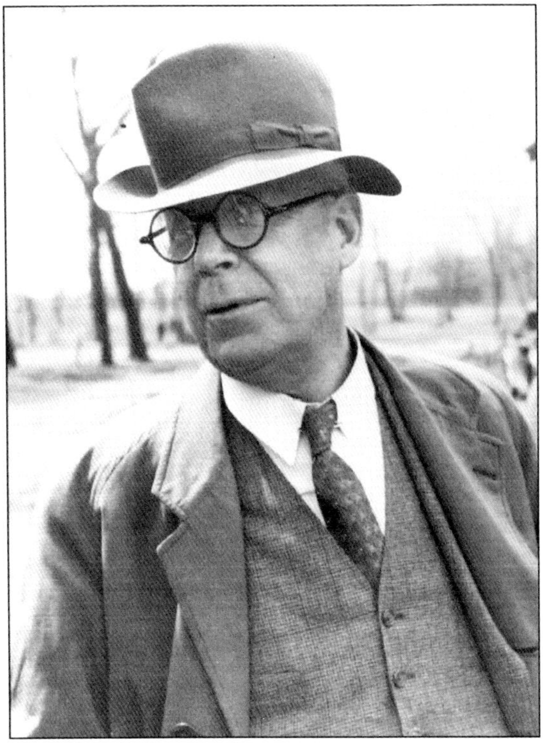

James B. Gleason and Irvin W. Gleason (early 1940s). The Gleason brothers, James and Irvin, were both early prominent boosters and financial backers of professional minor-league baseball in Williamsport. Owners of a lucrative tannery business—later sold to the Armour Leather Company—the Gleason family took an active role in community affairs. During the Depression James and Irvin Gleason took a particular interest in the administration of the Grays' front office and periodically tapped the family coffers to support Williamsport's baseball team. They were chiefly responsible for providing the funds for the erection of Bowman Field's first light towers in 1932, paving the way for night baseball in Williamsport. (*GRIT*.)

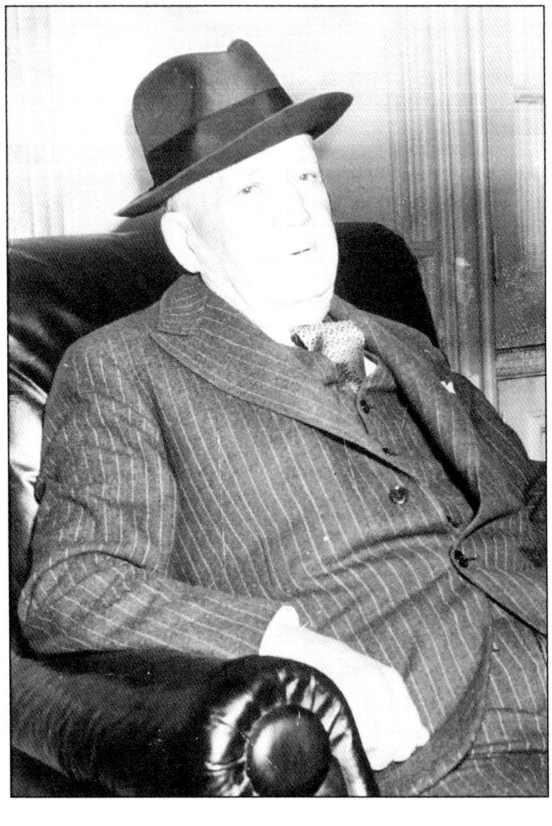

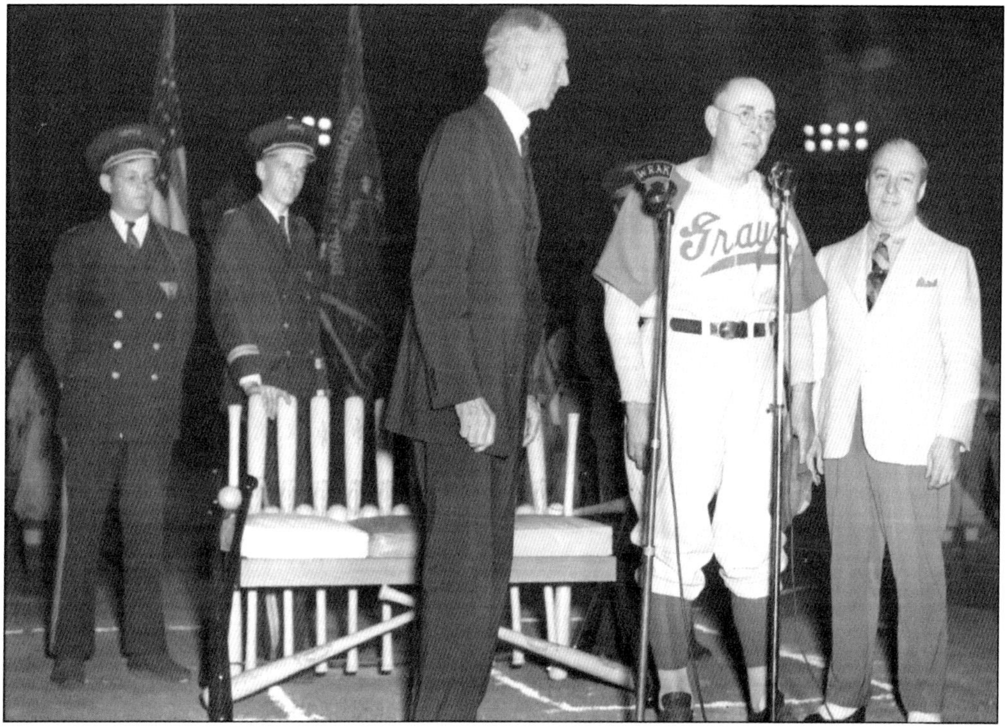

Connie Mack (1941). The grand old man of baseball, Connie Mack, is honored before a game at Bowman Field. In the foreground, from left to right, are Mack, Grays' manager Spence Abbott, and Eastern League president Tommy Richardson. Richardson and Mack enjoyed a long friendship. In the background is the bench made from baseball bats that Mack received that night as a gift from the Williamsport Grays. (TR.)

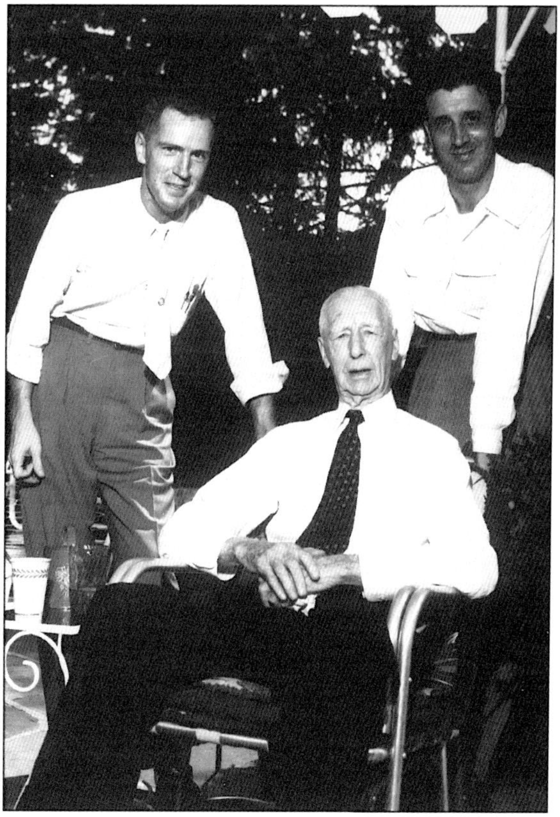

Sportswriters Meet the Man (1951). The Philadelphia A's leading emissary, Connie Mack, was a frequent visitor to Williamsport—whether to call on his friend Tommy Richardson or to evaluate talent for his A's. During the 1930s and early 1940s Williamsport was a de facto farm club of the A's. In this photograph Mack (sitting) is flanked by local sportswriters Mike Bernardi (left) and Ray Keyes (right). This photograph was taken at Richardson's backyard patio. (PV-LCHS.)

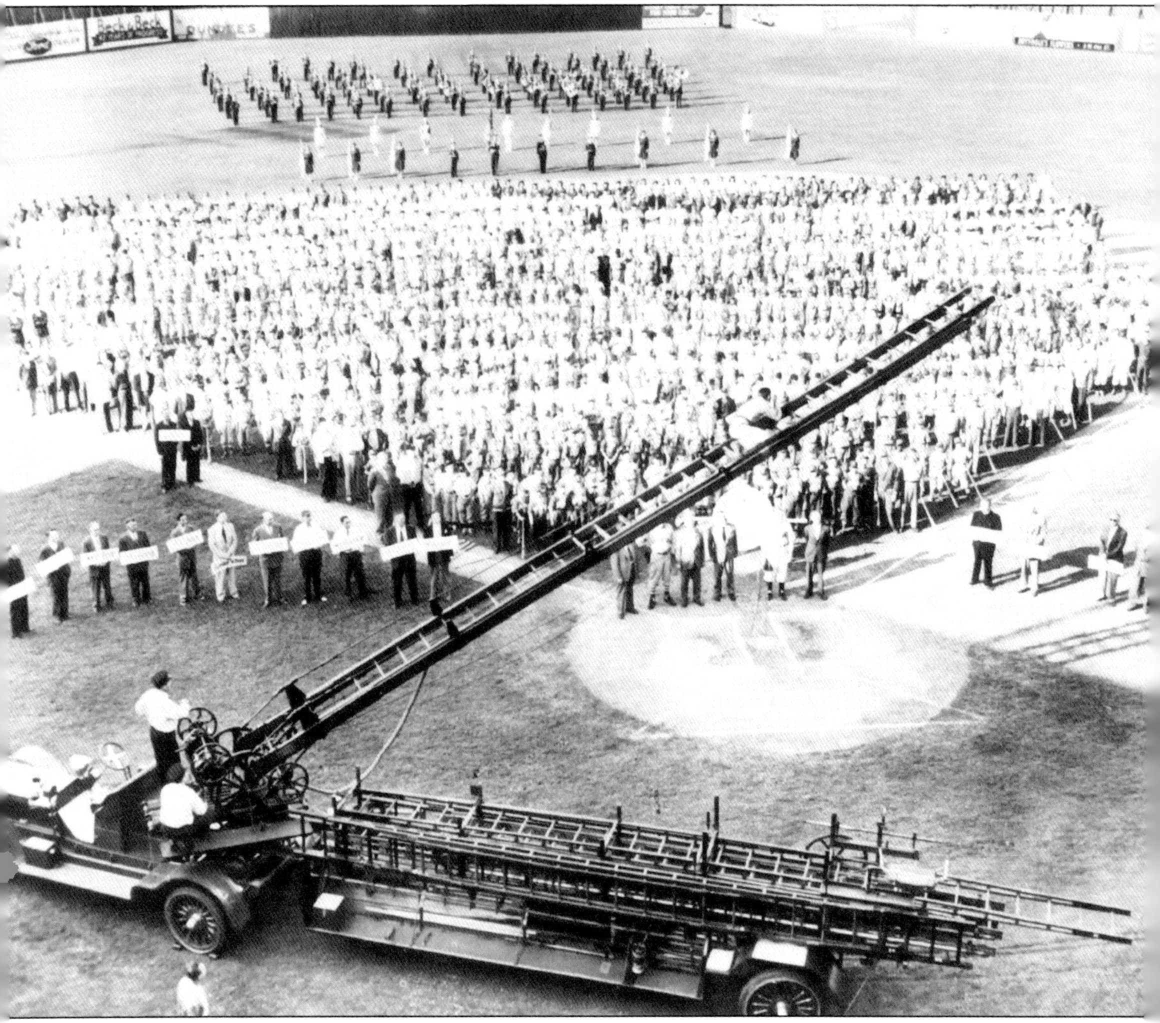

Baseball Town U.S.A. (1947). In 1947, *Life Magazine* dispatched a photographer to Williamsport to feature the town's love affair with baseball. As the birthplace of Little League Baseball and heir to a rich minor-league tradition, the city opted to celebrate in grand style. Replete with a marching band (in center field), all the city's youth baseball teams and members of the Williamsport Tigers (players and front office personnel) assembled in the infield area for this overhead group shot. In the foreground the *Life* staff photographer can be seen perched on the aerial ladder with his camera. The image was subsequently published in the magazine and cemented Williamsport's image as the foremost baseball town in America. (PV-LCHS.)

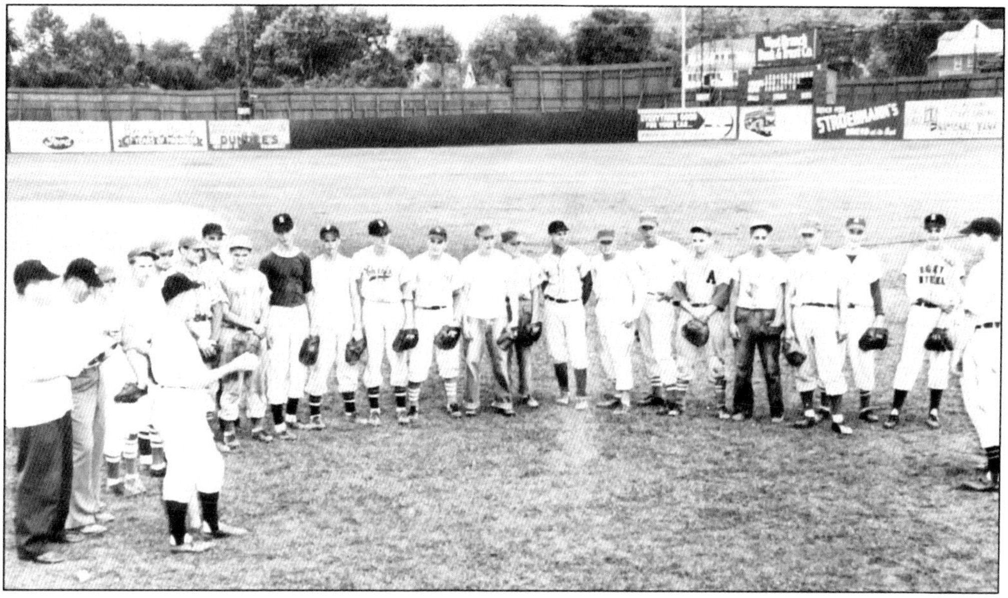

BASEBALL TRYOUT AND CLINIC, BOWMAN FIELD (1949). Over the decades many local sandlot players hoped to capture the attention of baseball scouts by showcasing their talents at tryout camps sponsored by the host club, in this case the Tigers. Here, Williamsport Tigers' manager Gene Desaultels instructs young ballplayers in a session held at Bowman Field. (*GRIT*.)

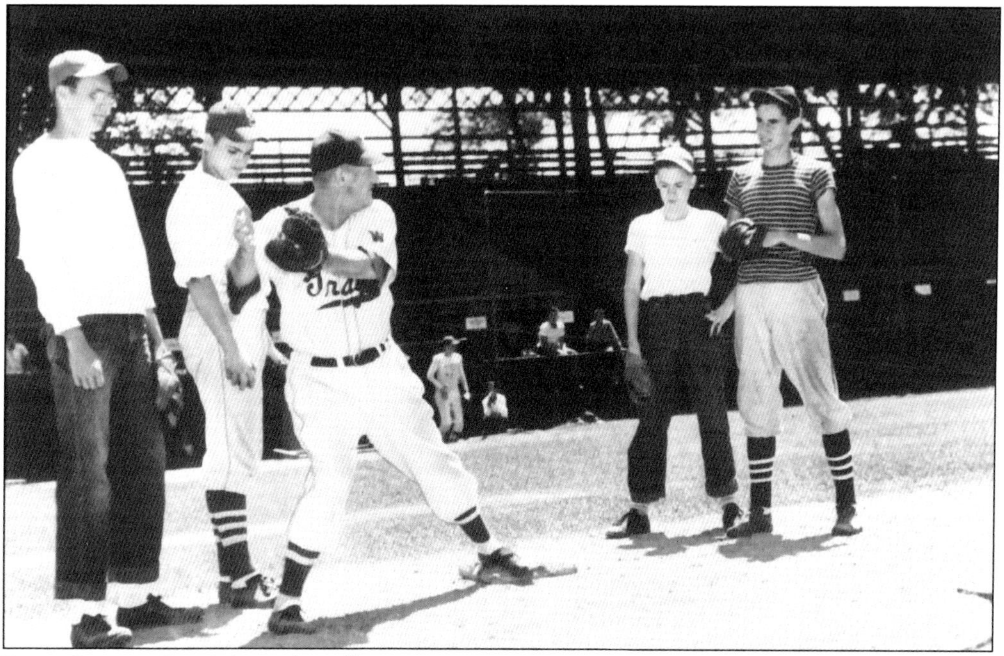

PUSH OFF THE BAG! (1945) Williamsport Grays' manager Ray Kolp instructs future prospects on the art of fielding first base. Down through the years Williamsport's minor-league clubs have always been active in promoting the game of baseball among local youths. The annual baseball clinic held at Bowman Field was a summer ritual. This author fondly recalls one he attended led by professional scouts Elmer Valo (Phillies) and Hank Madjeski (Astros). (*GRIT*.)

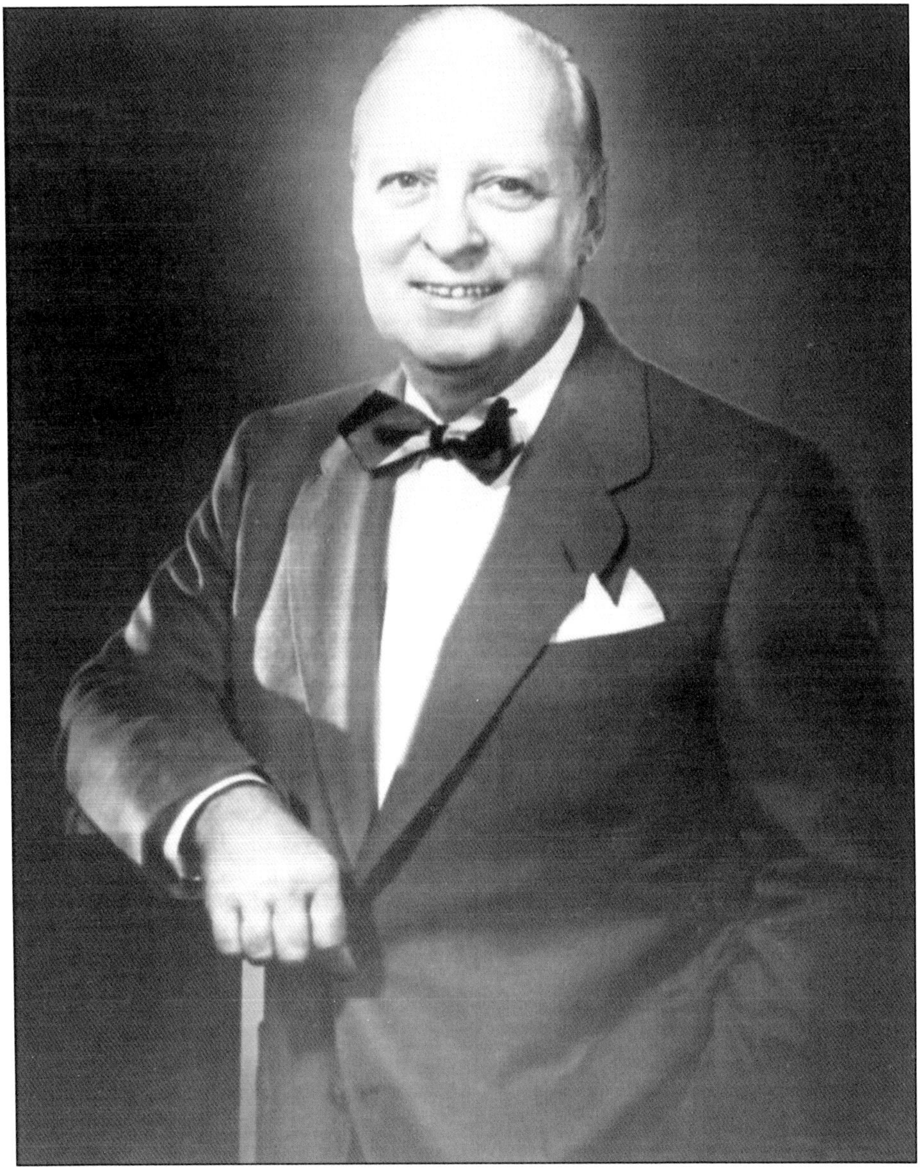

Tommy Richardson, Ambassador of Sunshine (early 1950s). This portrait captures Richardson in all his splendor and glory. Perhaps the most influential baseball booster, publicist, and administrator Williamsport ever had, Richard rose from his humble Second Street origins to the presidency of the Eastern League. He held this post for 27 years and even served as president of the International League from 1961 to 1965. A vaudevillian, professional toastmaster and raconteur, and successful car dealer, he truly was the "Man of a Thousand Stories." Richardson was one of the original directors of the Grays and had assumed a variety of administrative functions before his selection as president of the Eastern League. His close friendship with Connie Mack and the Philadelphia A's not only paved his own way in baseball circles, but also enabled Williamsport to sustain minor-league baseball during lean financial years. Richardson's accomplishments as an innovative baseball executive are recognized in an exhibit area devoted to minor-league baseball at the Baseball Hall of Fame in Cooperstown, New York. (*GRIT.*)

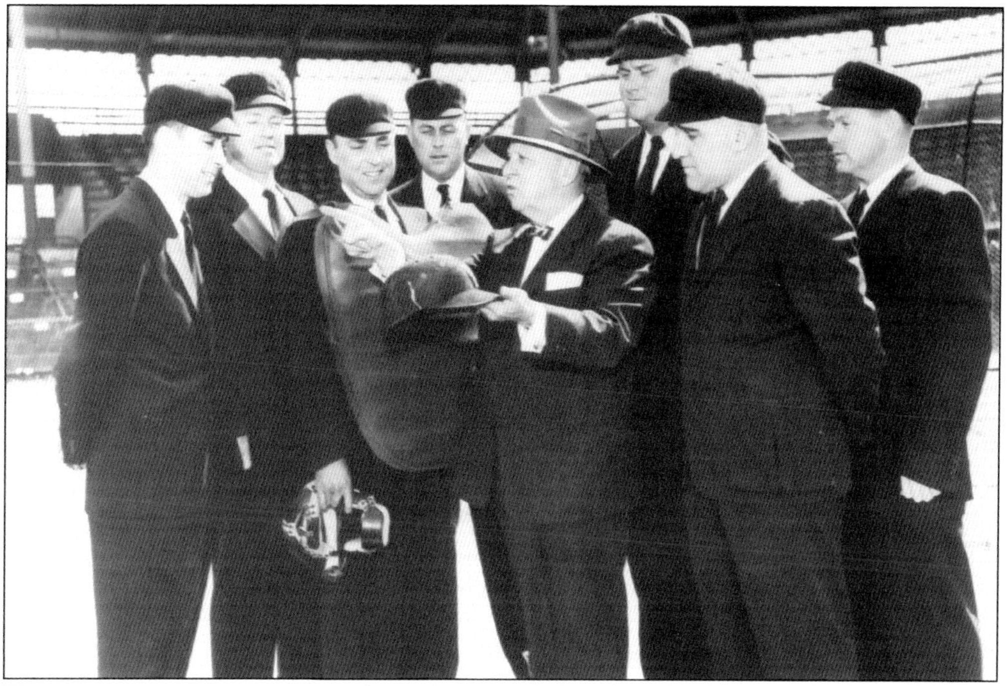

TOMMY WITH THE MEN IN BLUE (1949). Eastern League president Tommy Richardson goes over the ground rules with league umpires in a publicity photo taken at Bowman Field prior to the start of the 1949 baseball season. The umpires convened in Williamsport to receive their crew assignments and one last briefing by the chief. (*GRIT*.)

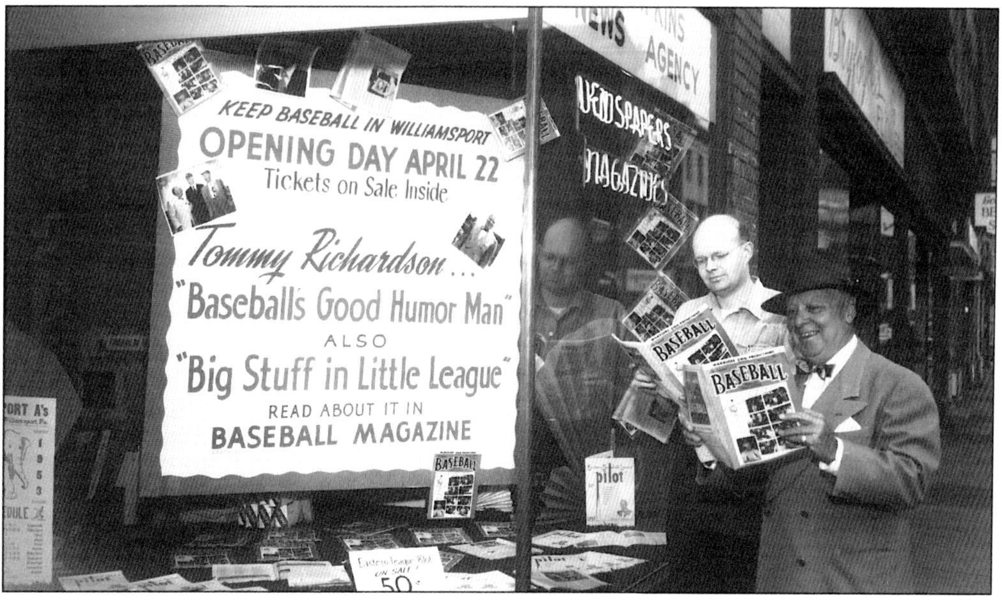

HOT STOVE LEAGUE HEADQUARTERS (EARLY 1950S). Tompkins' News Agency in downtown Williamsport served as the unofficial center of the winter hot stove league. Baseball fans gathered there to chat about the upcoming season, swap baseball stories, and purchase baseball publications. In this photograph Tommy Richardson and proprietor Fred Tompkins try to drum up business for the new season. (*GRIT*.)

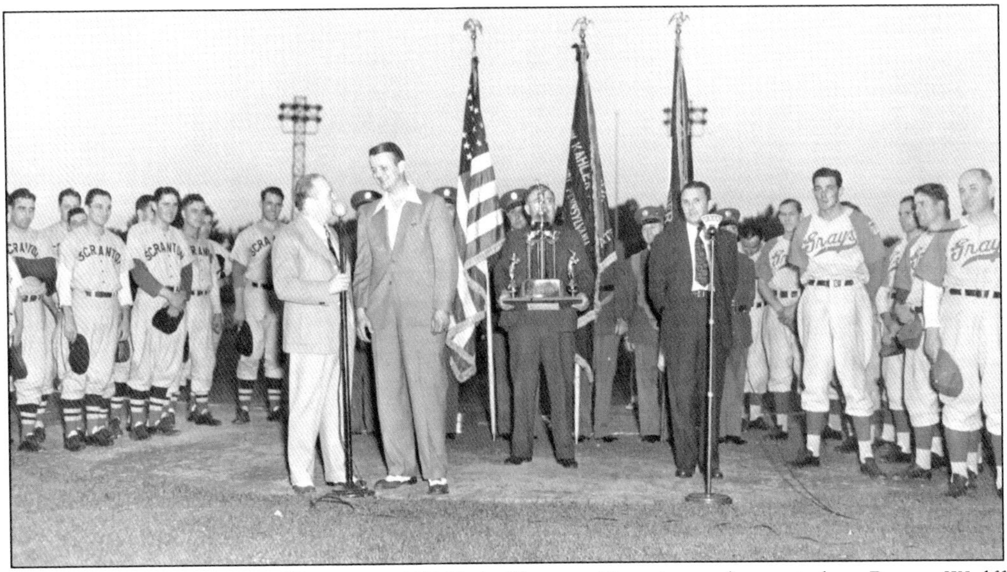

Pitcher Roger Wolff Honored (1940s). Former Grays' standout pitcher Roger Wolff receives special honors at Bowman Field prior to the start of the Williamsport-Scranton game. Wolff, a knuckleball pitcher with the Washington Senators, had been a key member of the 1941–1942 Grays' team. (TR.)

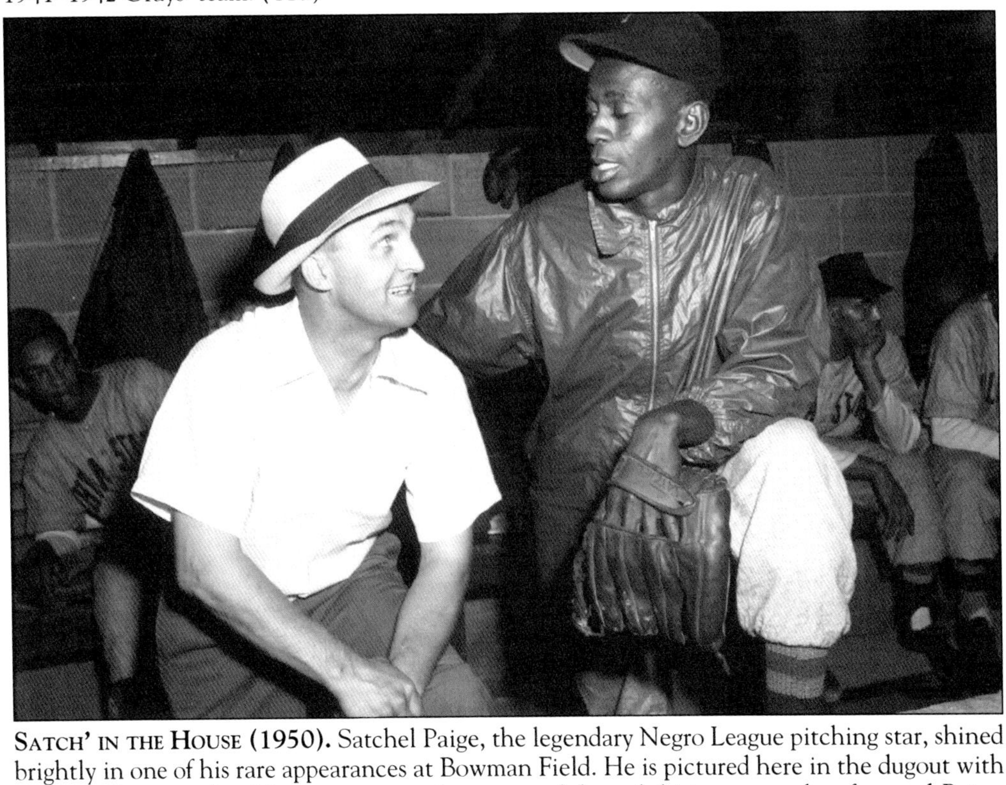

Satch' in the House (1950). Satchel Paige, the legendary Negro League pitching star, shined brightly in one of his rare appearances at Bowman Field. He is pictured here in the dugout with Frank Delycure, a local businessman and sponsor of the exhibition game that featured Paige. Paige led his Philadelphia Stars against the Baltimore Elite Giants in an exhibition game that thrilled Williamsport baseball fans. (PV-LCHS.)

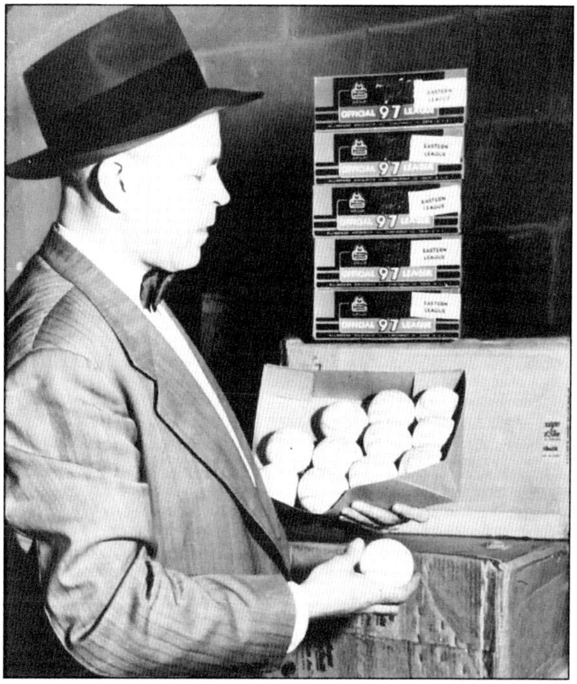

EVERYTHING IN ORDER (APRIL 20, 1952). Williamsport Tigers' business manager Bob Steinhilper checks the club's stock of new baseballs in anticipation of the new season. Steinhilper was one of the most talented business managers to run the local franchise. Formerly city editor of the *Williamsport Gazette and Bulletin*, he became a successful baseball executive. Steinhilper later worked as assistant director of public relations for the parent Detroit Tigers. (*GRIT*.)

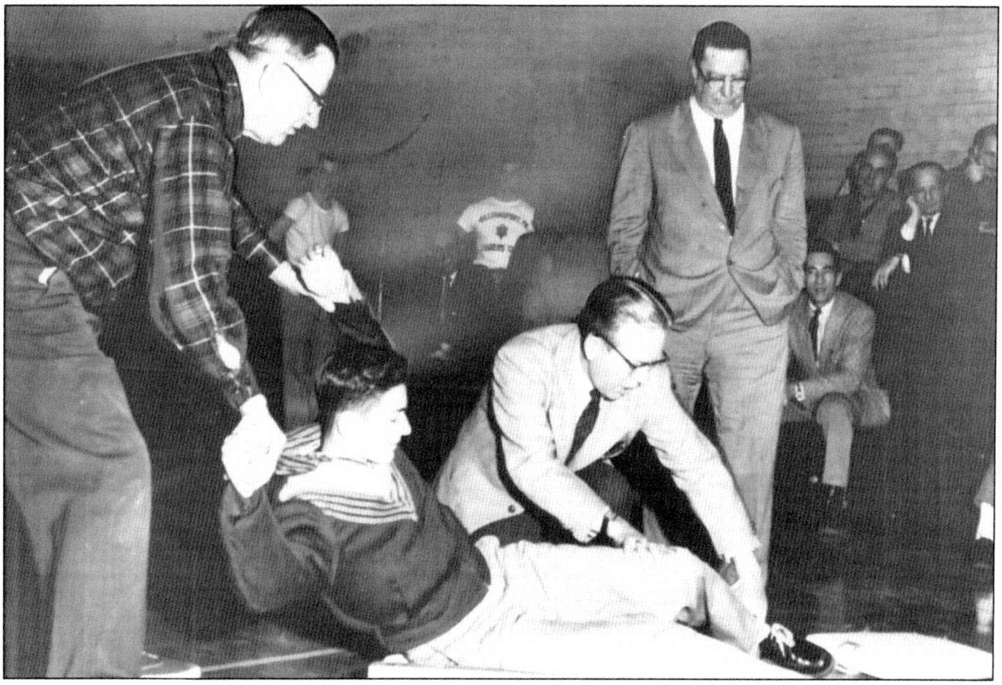

HOOK SLIDE CLINIC (FEBRUARY 17, 1957). A lucky youth gets first-hand sliding instructions from some of the best minds in the game at the Williamsport YMCA. Looking on are baseball executives Art Dede of the Brooklyn Dodgers front office; Mickey McConnell, Little League Baseball; and Branch Rickey Sr. of the Pittsburgh Pirates. Over the years Williamsport's baseball boosters have sponsored and hosted many luminaries associated with the national pastime. (*GRIT*.)

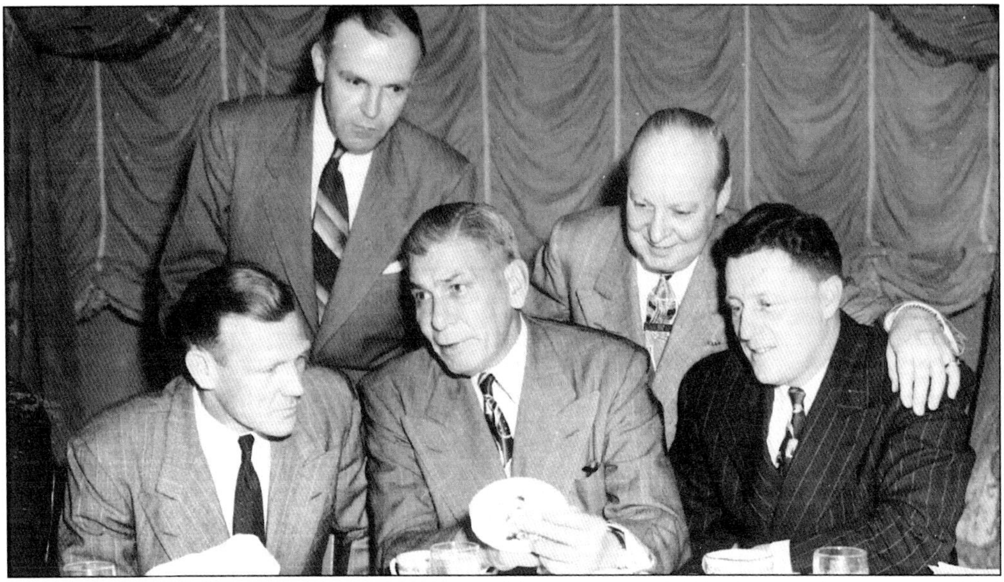

WINTER BASEBALL BANQUET, LYCOMING HOTEL (FEBRUARY 8, 1948). Among the stars assembled at Williamsport's 1948 gala baseball banquet are the following, from left to right: (front row) Yankee pitching great "Red" Rolfe, Hall of Famer "Chief" Bender of the Philadelphia A's, and Williamsport Tigers' manager Gene Desaultels; (back row) Bob Steinhilper and Tommy Richardson. The winter banquets were usually linked to pre-season ticket sale promotions for the local team. (*GRIT*.)

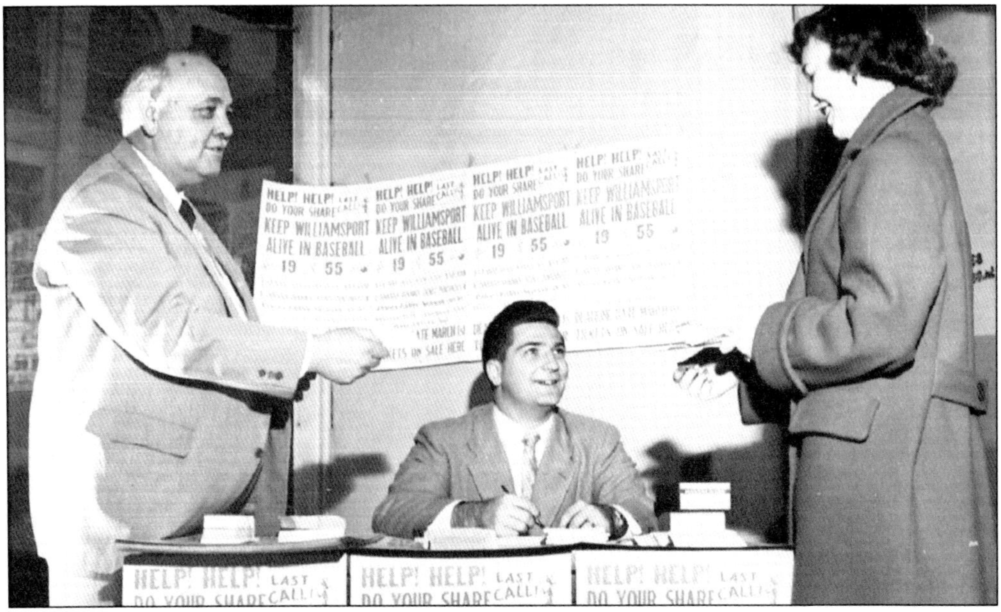

KEEP BALL ALIVE IN 1955. Financial losses in 1954 nearly cost Williamsport its baseball franchise. In response, the Grays' club directors launched a pre-season ticket sales goal of $50,000 to keep the team in the city. The campaign centered around the slogan, "Keep Baseball Alive in '55." Mary Mitsdarfer prepares to purchase a ticket from Paul Bailey (standing) and Charles Lucas (seated) at the baseball campaign headquarters, PP&L office in downtown Williamsport. (*GRIT*.)

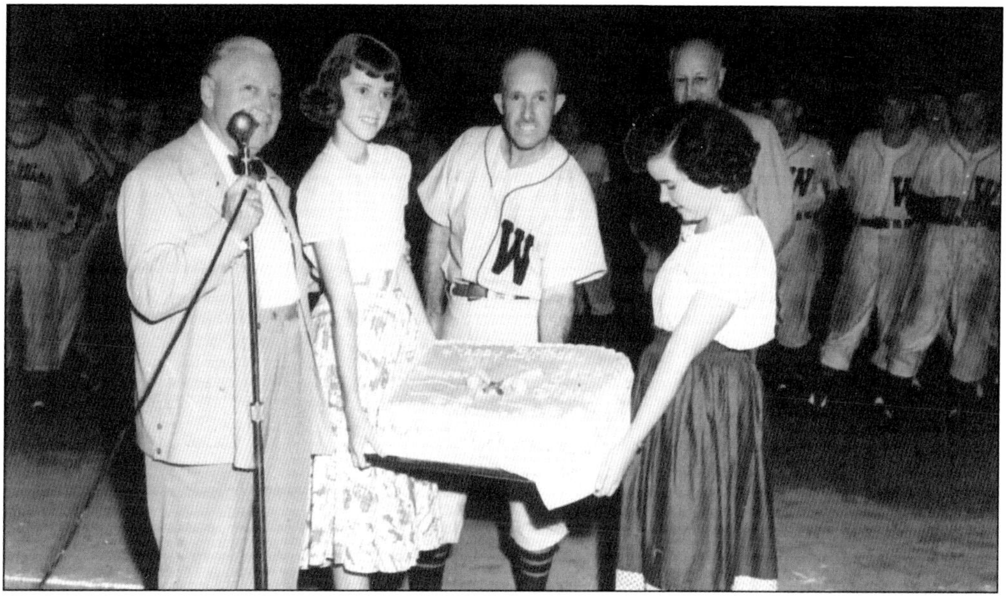

Happy Birthday Jack (September 3, 1950). Williamsport Tigers' manager Jack Tighe (in uniform) receives a large birthday cake from Tigers' fans Lynn Copestick and Mary Steinhilper (the daughter of Bob Steinhilper, the Grays' business manager), while Tommy Richardson (MC) leads the hometown crowd in a rousing happy birthday song for the skipper. Birthday celebrations at the ballpark for popular players and managers solidified the bond between local fans and their adopted team. (*GRIT*.)

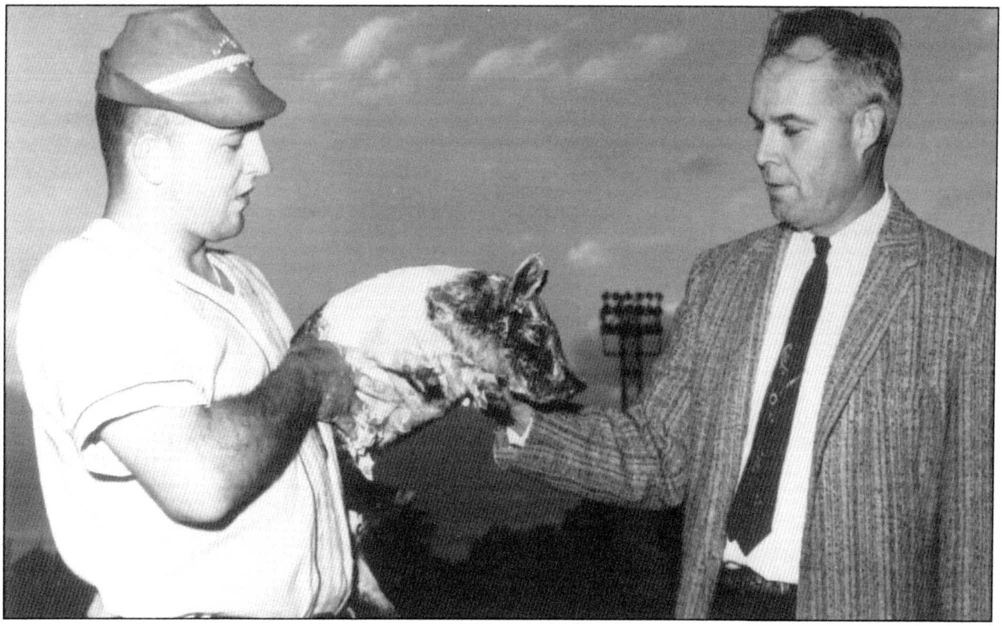

Hamming It up for the Camera (1959). An unidentified Grays' player holds the special guest star for the evening as business manager Rankin Johnson Jr. looks on. This photograph was taken prior to a "greased pig contest" involving members of the Grays and the opposing team. The objective was to chase and ultimately capture the slippery pig. Such promotions were popular with fans and helped to increase attendance at Bowman Field. (*GRIT*.)

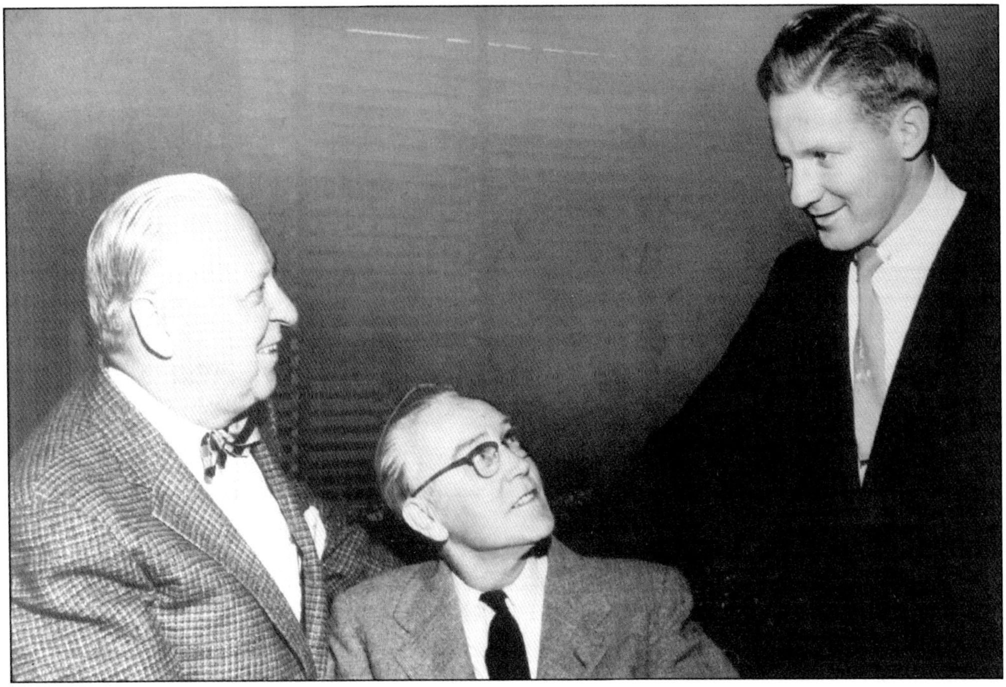

"WHITEY" FORD IN BILLTOWN (1955). During the off-season the Grays' directors often sponsored special baseball banquets, winter caravans, and booster meetings featuring famous baseball stars and personalities. Here, Tommy Richardson (left) and Robert Lilly (seated) meet with Yankee pitching great Whitey Ford (right) at one of the baseball dinners held in Williamsport during the 1950s and 1960s. These baseball affairs helped generate interest in the local club during the winter months. (*GRIT*.)

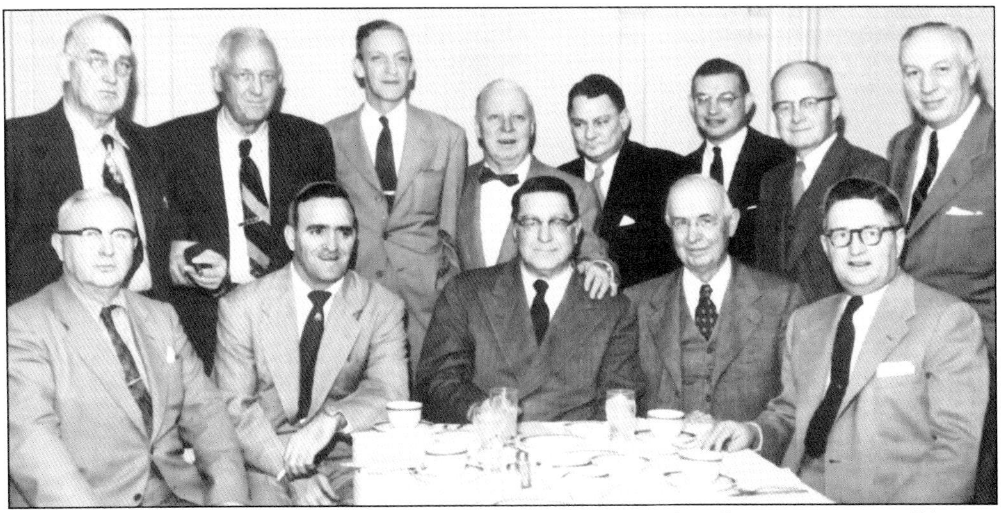

WINTER MEETING (JANUARY 10, 1954). The announcement of Williamsport's new affiliation agreement with the Pittsburgh Pirates was cause for celebration at this winter meeting held in 1954 at the Lycoming Hotel. Among the attendees, from left to right, were the following: (sitting) Joseph C. Meyers, Danny Murtaugh (Grays' new manager), Branch Rickey Sr., Harry Kiessling, and Floyd Bird; (standing) J. Roy Clunk, Joseph H. Mosser, Kenneth Blackburn, Tommy Richardson, Branch Rickey Jr., Ferris J. Edwards, and Richard H. Lundy. (*GRIT*.)

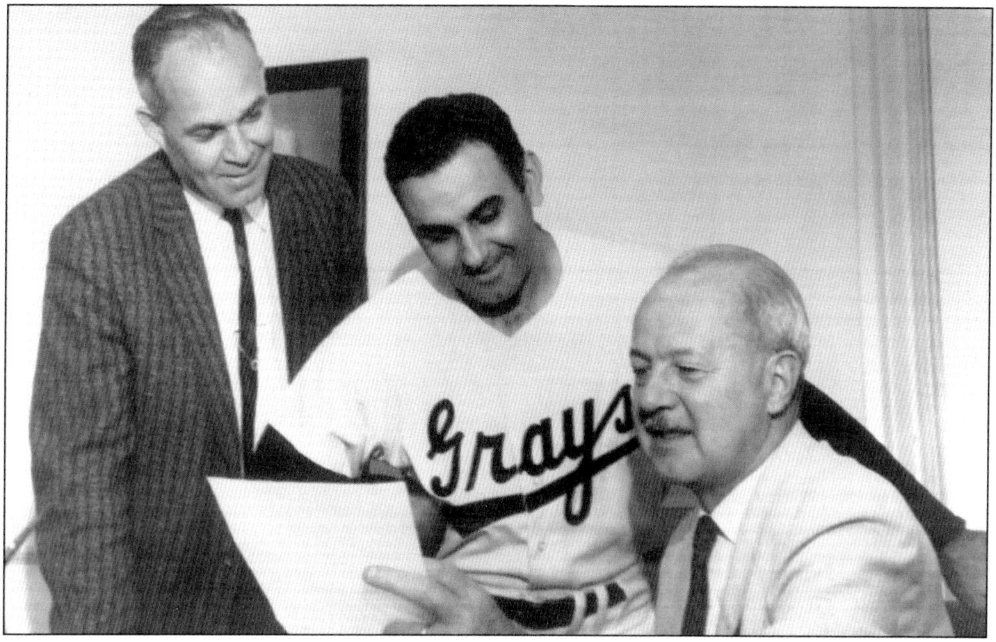

It's Official (1959). Grays' business manager Rankin Johnson Jr. and skipper Frank Lucchesi look over the proclamation signed by Mayor Thomas Levering (seated) declaring "Williamsport Grays' Day" in the city. The relationship between the city government and the operators of the local franchise has always been crucial to the success of minor-league baseball in Williamsport. Historically, Williamsport's mayors and the city council have done their utmost to support and sustain the game of baseball. (*GRIT*.)

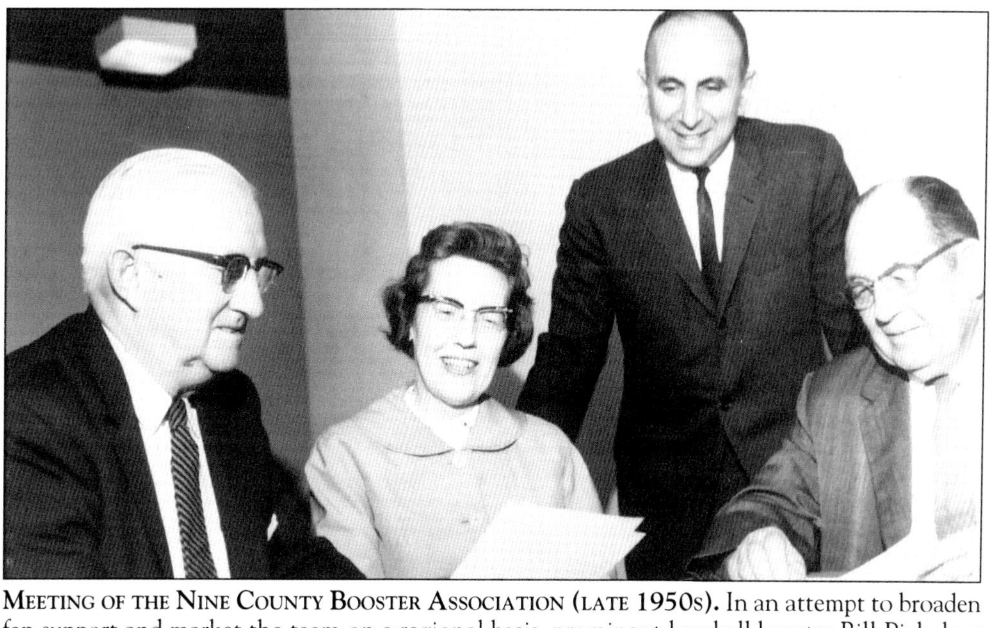

Meeting of the Nine County Booster Association (late 1950s). In an attempt to broaden fan support and market the team on a regional basis, prominent baseball booster Bill Pickelner took the lead in forming the Nine County Booster Association. In this photograph key members of the association, from left to right, Otto Stradley, Dorothy Parsons, Bill Pickelner, and Clair Bishop, discuss marketing strategy for the upcoming season. (*GRIT*.)

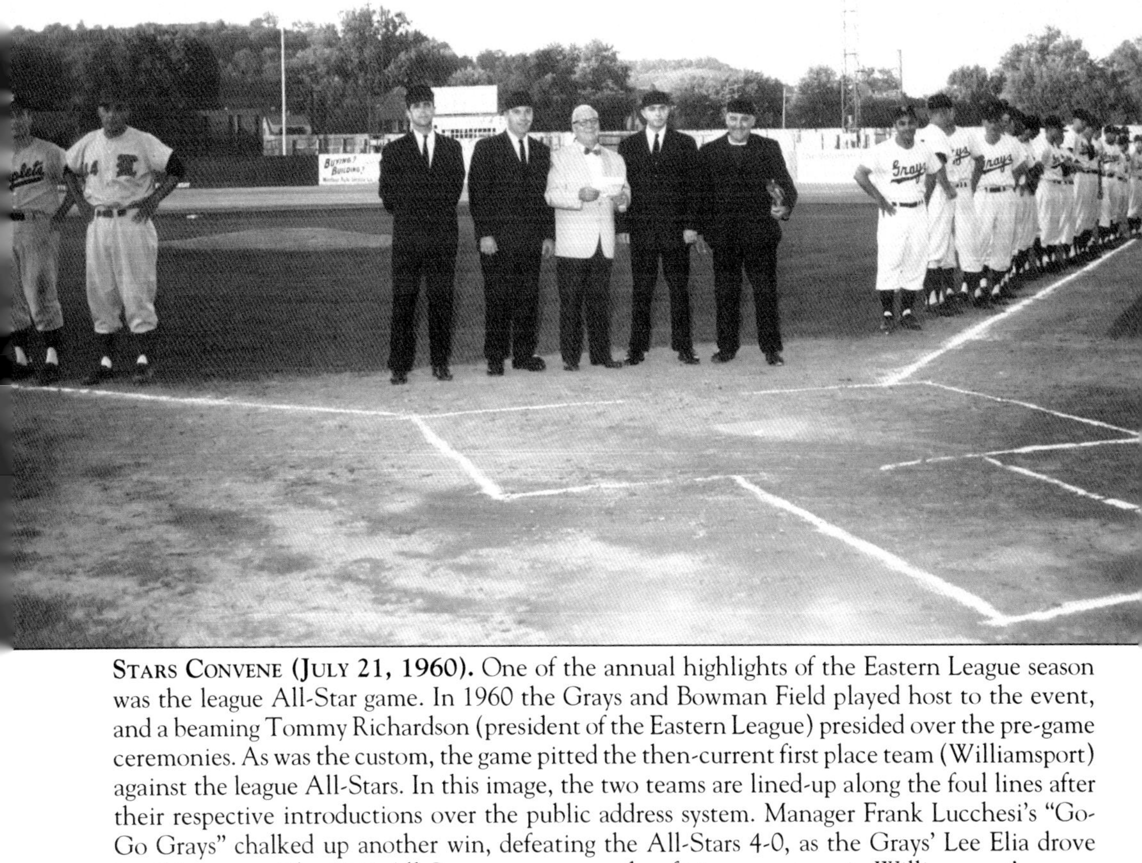

Stars Convene (July 21, 1960). One of the annual highlights of the Eastern League season was the league All-Star game. In 1960 the Grays and Bowman Field played host to the event, and a beaming Tommy Richardson (president of the Eastern League) presided over the pre-game ceremonies. As was the custom, the game pitted the then-current first place team (Williamsport) against the league All-Stars. In this image, the two teams are lined-up along the foul lines after their respective introductions over the public address system. Manager Frank Lucchesi's "Go-Go Grays" chalked up another win, defeating the All-Stars 4-0, as the Grays' Lee Elia drove in all four runs. The 1960 All-Star game was another fitting gemstone in Williamsport's crown jewel season. Many city fans consider the early 1960s to be the golden era of Williamsport minor-league baseball. (TR.)

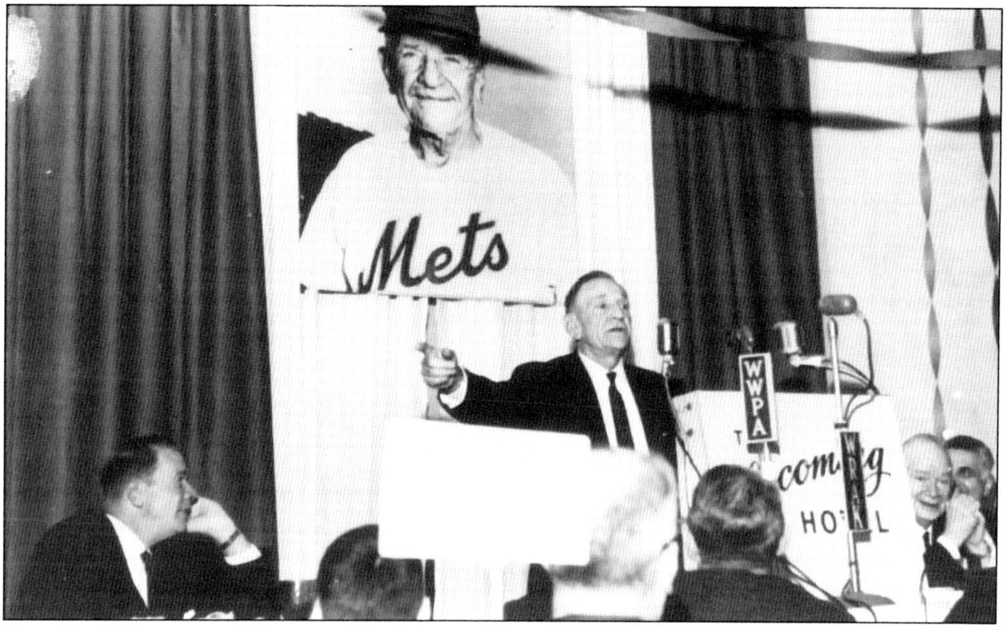

THE OLE' PROFESSOR WEAVING HIS MAGIC (FEBRUARY 9, 1964). New York Mets' manager Casey Stengel rolls the "Amazin' Mets" caravan into town in 1964. As the featured speaker at the boosters' winter baseball banquet to promote the Williamsport Mets, Stengel enthralled local fans with his humorous stories and animated gestures, as shown here in this photograph. Stengel's appearance at the Lycoming Hotel was broadcast by the radio station WWPA. (*GRIT.*)

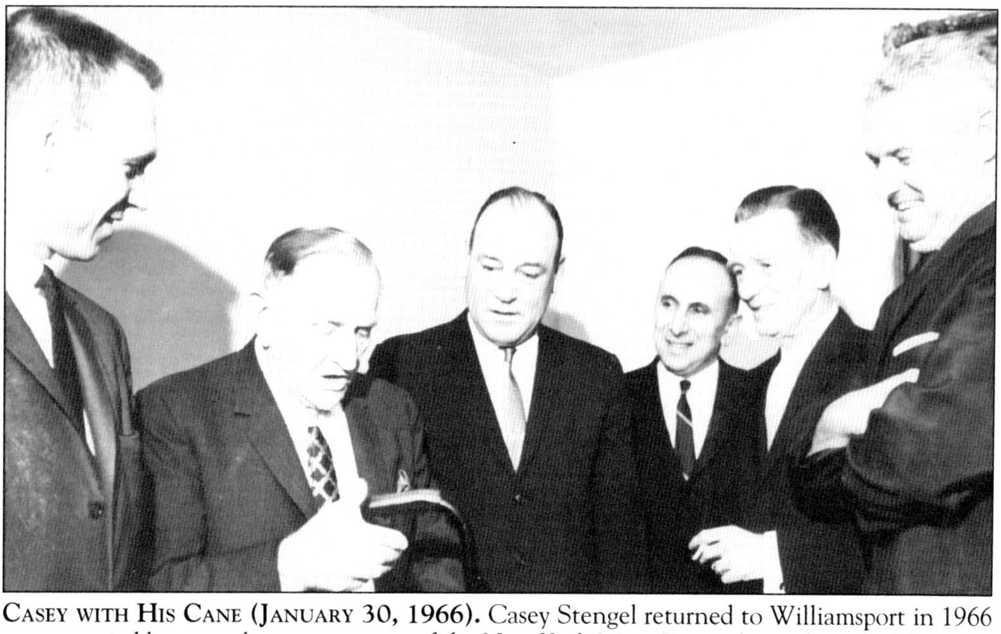

CASEY WITH HIS CANE (JANUARY 30, 1966). Casey Stengel returned to Williamsport in 1966 accompanied by several top executives of the New York Mets. Recently on the mend from hip and leg surgery, Stengel displayed his new walking cane to an admiring crowd. Among those attending the event, from left to right, were Bill Virdon (Williamsport Mets' manager), Stengel, Wes Westrum (New York Mets' manager), Bill Pickelner, Aaron Lanier (New York Mets' comptroller), and Bob Scheffing (New York Mets' director for player development). (*GRIT.*)

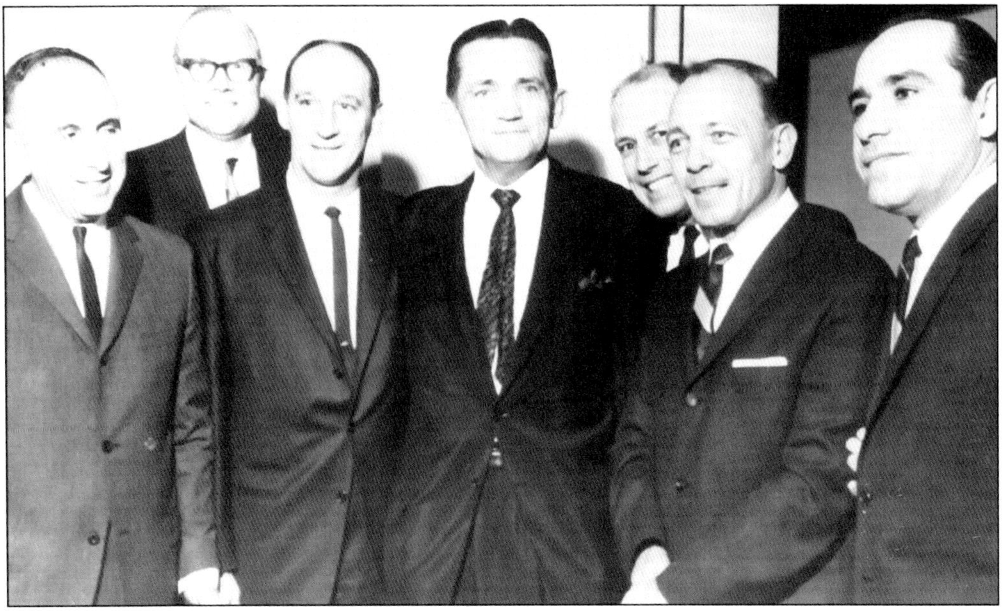

Mets' Baseball Banquet Draws Top Crowd (February 7, 1965). The 1965 Mets' pre-season baseball banquet attracted many well-known baseball stars to Williamsport. The attendees included Hall of Fame pitcher Warren Spahn (third from left), Kirby Ferrell (manager of the Williamsport Mets), Eddie Stanky (second from right), and Yogi Berra (first person on right). Bill Pickelner (first person, left) was instrumental in arranging another outstanding banquet program. (*GRIT*.)

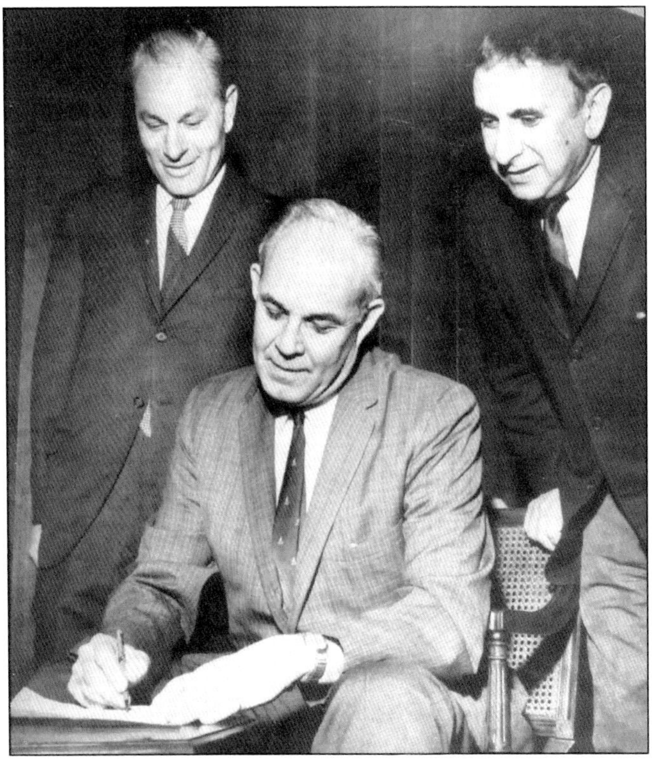

A New Williamsport Team (1968). Williamsport business manager Rankin Johnson Jr. puts his signature on the agreement that shifted the New York-Penn League's Erie franchise to the city for the 1968 season. Owner Joe Romano (left) and club booster Bill Pickelner (right) are anxious to conclude the deal. The new agreement marked Williamsport's entry into the short-season Class A New York-Penn League. (*GRIT*.)

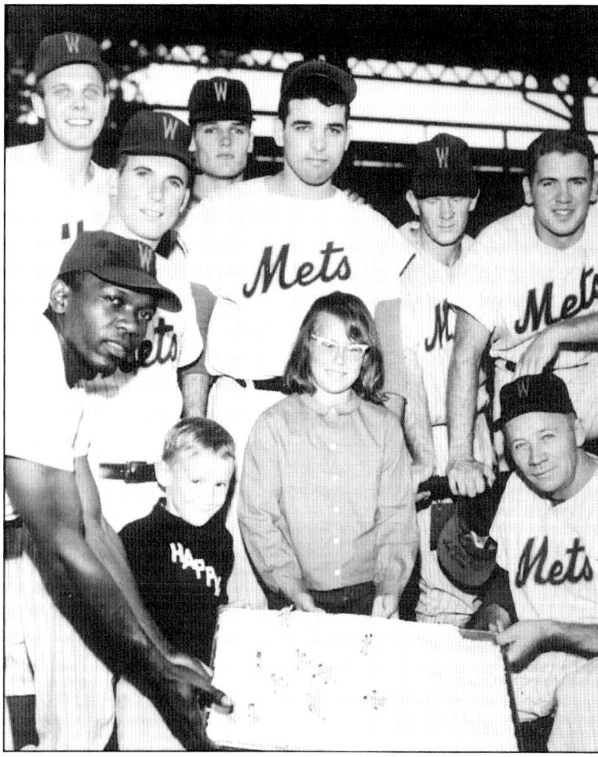

Birthday Greetings For Ernie White (1964). Williamsport Mets' manager Ernie White (kneeling, right) was the recipient of a birthday cake baked by Mrs. Raymond Knaur and presented by her children, Marcella (wearing glasses) and Mowry. Helping White to celebrate are several Williamsport Mets' players, including outfielder Bobby Sanders (left, holding cake). (*GRIT.*)

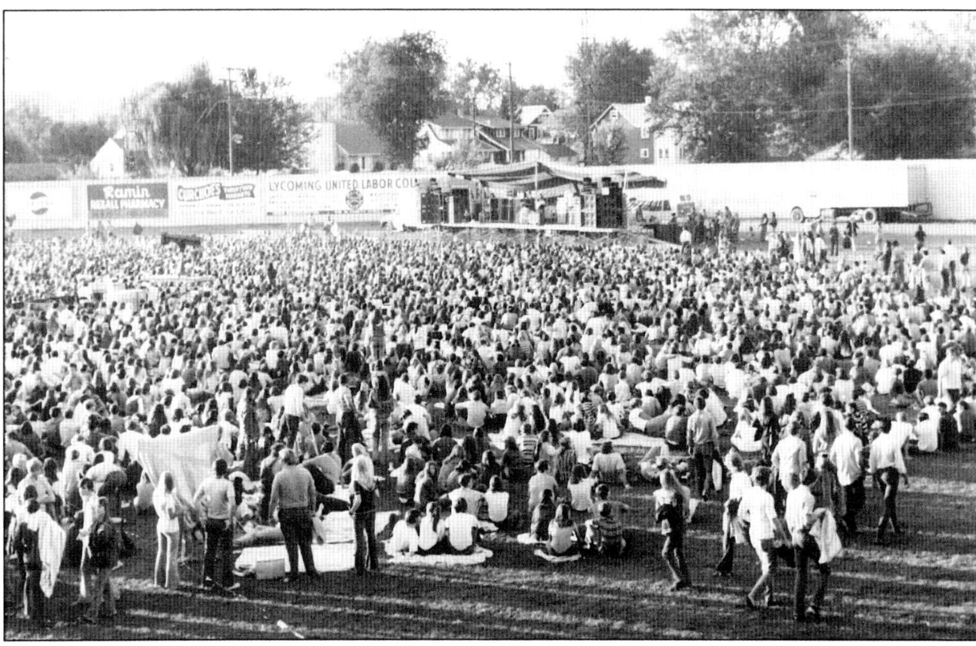

Three Dog Night Concert, Bowman Field (August 5, 1971). Local baby boomers will fondly recall this performance by the rock band Three Dog Night on a sweltering August evening at Bowman Field. The ballpark served as a venue for several rock concerts during the counterculture era, including the popular "Battle of the Bands" series that showcased local rock talent. (*GRIT.*)

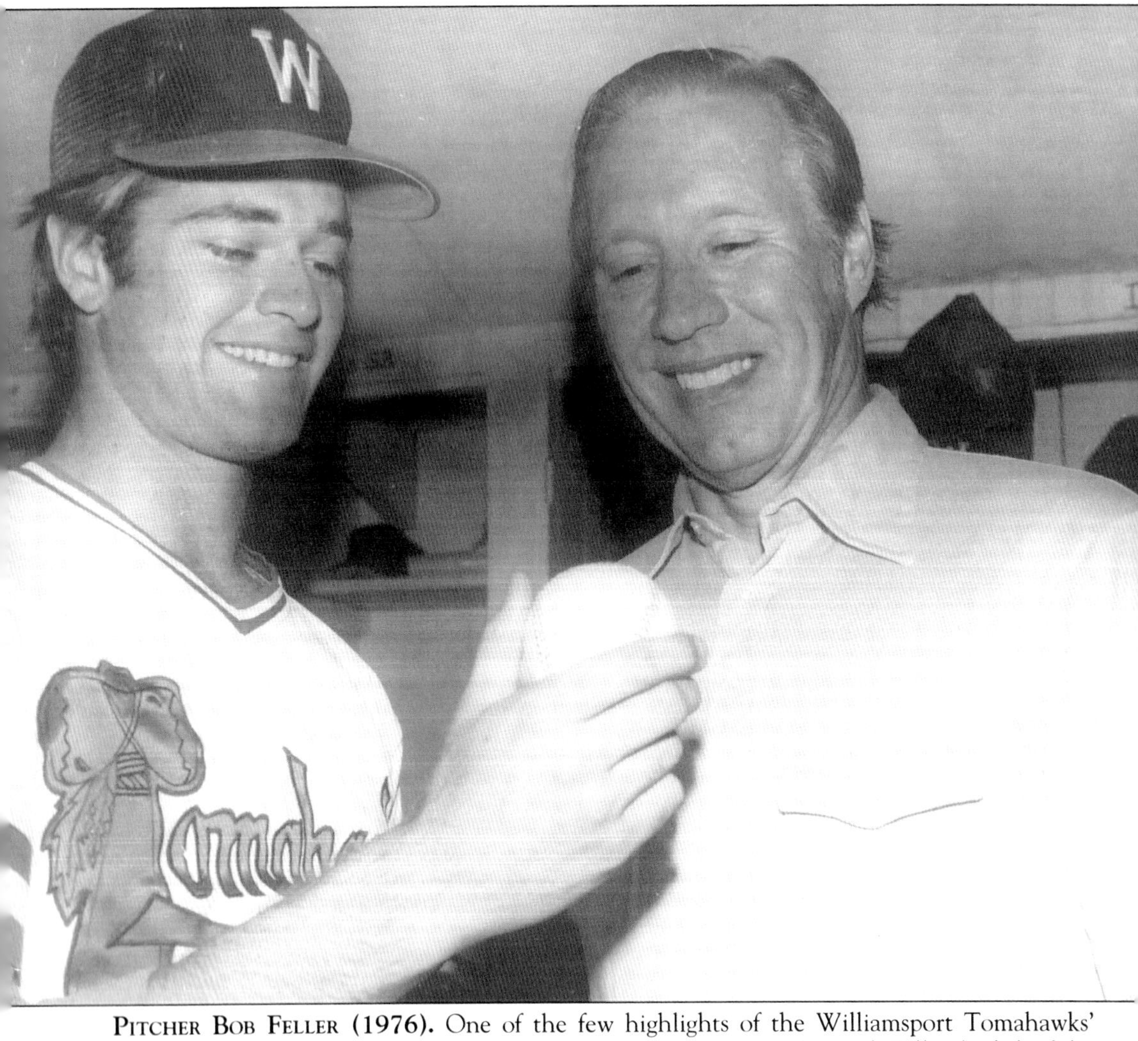

Pitcher Bob Feller (1976). One of the few highlights of the Williamsport Tomahawks' dismal season was a promotional appearance by Hall of Fame pitcher Bob Feller (right) of the Cleveland Indians. The Tomahawks, a farm club of the Indians, were one of several teams in the Indians' organization that hosted Feller for a special evening during the 1976 season. Tomahawks' pitcher Tom Brennan (left) met with Feller before the game to discuss pitching and get an autograph. (TR.)